Hellenic Studies 97

Imagined Geographies in the Mediterranean, Middle East, and Beyond

Recent Titles in the Hellenic Studies Series

Imagined Geographies in the Mediterranean, Middle East, and Beyond

Edited by
Dimitri Kastritsis
Anna Stavrakopoulou
Angus Stewart

CENTER FOR HELLENIC STUDIES
Trustees for Harvard University
Washington, DC
Distributed by Harvard University Press
Cambridge, Massachusetts, and London, England
2023

Imagined Geographies in the Mediterranean, Middle East, and Beyond, edited by
   Dimitri Kastritsis, Anna Stavrakopoulou, and Angus Stewart
Copyright © 2023 Center for Hellenic Studies, Trustees for Harvard University
All Rights Reserved.
Published by Center for Hellenic Studies, Trustees for Harvard University,
   Washington, DC
Distributed by Harvard University Press, Cambridge, Massachusetts and London,
   England
Printed by Gasch Printing, Odenton, MD
Cover Design: Joni Godlove
Production: Kerri Cox Sullivan

ISBN: 978-0-674-27846-2
Library of Congress Control Number: 2023933701

Contents

Contents

Acknowledgments

This book began as a workshop held in St Andrews in May 2018. We would like to thank the School of History and the Centre for Anatolian and East Mediterranean Studies at the University of St Andrews for their essential material and administrative support. Special thanks are due to Paul Churchill, whose commitment and attention to detail played an essential role in making the event such a success. We are also grateful for the financial support we received from Dumbarton Oaks, for which we would like to thank the Director at the time, Jan Ziolkowski, and especially Yota Batsaki, whose help was pivotal in our application for funding. Moreover, we would like to acknowledge the contribution of esteemed colleagues who presented papers at the workshop, even though they did not end up publishing their work here: Sahar Bazzaz, Koray Durak, Çiğdem Kafescioğlu, and Michael Puett.

We are indebted to Greg Nagy, the former Director of the Harvard Center for Hellenic Studies, for inspiring, supporting, and empowering us over the years. We would also like to thank Mark Schiefsky, during whose directorship of the CHS the volume is being published. Our editor at CHS was Jill Curry Robbins, who deserves special thanks for seeing the volume through. The peer review process was handled by Casey Dué Hackney, whom we would like to thank along with the anonymous reviewer. Both provided essential feedback for which we are most grateful. We would also like to thank Zoie Lafis at CHS-DC and Christos Giannopoulos at CHS-Greece for their support at various stages.

The volume's main editor, Dimitri Kastritsis, wrote the introduction and carried out much of the editing as a Member of the Institute for Advanced Study in Princeton, NJ, while also holding a fellowship from the British Academy (2020–2021). Thanks are due to both organizations for their generous support. Finally, Anna Stavrakopoulou and Angus Stewart would like to thank Dimitri Kastritsis for shouldering the main burden of editorial work on the volume, and for his unparalleled orchestration at every step of the process. In turn, he would like to thank them for their substantial editorial contribution and for always being there to provide collegiality and essential insights. This book is very much a collective effort, for which all editors and contributors deserve credit.

About the Contributors

DIMITER ANGELOV is Dumbarton Oaks Professor of Byzantine History at Harvard University.

YOTA BATSAKI is Executive Director of Dumbarton Oaks, Harvard University, where she directs the Plant Humanities Initiative.

DIMITRI KASTRITSIS is Senior Lecturer in Ottoman and Middle Eastern History at the University of St Andrews.

ILHAM KHURI-MAKDISI is Associate Professor of Middle Eastern History at Northeastern University.

KEELAN OVERTON is an independent scholar and historian of Islamic Art and Architecture.

ANDREW PEACOCK is Bishop Wardlaw Professor of Islamic History at the University of St Andrews.

ANNA STAVRAKOPOULOU is Associate Professor of Theater Studies at Aristotle University of Thessaloniki.

ANGUS STEWART is Lecturer in Medieval and Middle Eastern History at the University of St Andrews.

YANNIS STOURAITIS is Senior Lecturer in Byzantine History at the University of Edinburgh.

Introduction

Studying Imagined Geographies
across Time and Space

Dimitri Kastritsis

THE CONCEPT OF IMAGINED (OR "IMAGINATIVE") GEOGRAPHY is inextricably tied to the work of Edward Said, who introduced the term in his seminal study *Orientalism*.[1] Influenced by the work of Michel Foucault, who emphasized the fundamental role of knowledge in creating and perpetuating the structures of power,[2] Said's book focused on the period of modern European imperial expansion and colonialism, in which geographically and ethnically based concepts of self and other played a fundamental role. Like Benedict Anderson's *Imagined Communities*,[3] a similarly influential study focusing on nationalism published just five years later, what Said meant by imagination was social construction. Contrary to a purely scientific or empiricist view of physical space, Said argued that even (or especially) in cases where the representation of human geography was presented as a scientific enterprise, this should not be taken at face value. When dealing with non-Western parts of the world, especially the Middle East and other parts of Asia, scientifically minded Western scholars and creative writers (the people he called "Orientalists") made value judgments about the nature of these places and their inhabitants, which were part and parcel of various modern European imperialist and colonialist projects.

Egypt played a key role in Said's study. When Napoleon invaded the country in 1798, he famously left behind a committee of scholars to make a detailed description of the country and its people. The resulting publication, whose "imperial" first edition was only completed thirty years later in twenty-three enormous volumes, involved approximately 160 "savants" as well as a great many artists and artisans. It covers a wide variety of fields including topography,

---

[1] Said 1978.
[2] Foucault 1969; Foucault 1975.
[3] Anderson 1983.

antiquities, natural history, and the modern state of the country in the imme-diate aftermath of Napoleon's expedition.[4] Grounded in Enlightenment ideas of science and objectivity, this project and others that followed it were more than a disinterested academic endeavor. Instead, such scholarly projects played an essential role in defining how the West viewed Egypt and other non-Western lands, with implications that still resonate today. Viewed in this light, it is no accident that the term "Middle East" has a history rooted in the British Empire's history and geopolitical vision. From a purely spatial point of view, such a term makes little sense.[5] Geographical terms of this kind can only be understood with reference to Western social and political attitudes toward non-Western regions and political entities, whether past or present. The same is true for terminology of a more strictly political nature, such as "Byzantium," "the Ottoman Empire," and the once common equivalent "Turkey," in the sense of the former empire rather than the modern state.

The relationship between power, knowledge, and space is at the heart of the present collaborative volume. At first glance, the studies collected here may seem disparate and unconnected. What could medieval Byzantine, Ottoman, and European ideas of space have to do with networks connecting the early modern and later Middle East, India, and Indonesia, or with modern Greek liter-ature and the reception of European theater in contemporary Greece? But, in fact, all of the essays collected here share common themes and concerns, which give the volume the integrity of a coherent intellectual project. Moreover, the ubiquity of the so-called "spatial turn" in the humanities and social sciences makes this volume part of a wider ongoing discussion about ideas of space and geography in different cultures, periods, and regions of the world.[6] In addition to the questions raised by Said and those following in his footsteps, which have transformed the academic study of the Middle East and other non-Western cultures, space has become a key aspect of the growing field of digital humani-ties, notably through technical advances and new organizational frameworks (e.g. GIS).[7] Even for those practicing more traditional historical and literary analysis, problematizing space has resulted in interdisciplinary perspectives that challenge the boundaries of accepted academic fields.

The present volume is therefore highly interdisciplinary, both in concep-tualization and in content. It is a sequel to an earlier one, *Imperial Geographies in Byzantine and Ottoman Space*, published in the same series with many of the

---

[4] France, Commission des sciences et des arts d'Égypte, 1809–1828; Said 1978:83–87.
[5] Davison 1960; Bonine, Amanat, and Gasper 2012; Danforth 2016.
[6] E.g. Warf and Arias 2009; Oakes and Price 2008; Crang and Thrift 2000.
[7] Bodenhamer, Corrigan, and Harris 2010.

same contributors.[8] Both volumes share a strong focus on the Byzantine and Ottoman Empires, as well as on the role of empire and ideas of space viewed in inter-regional and interdisciplinary terms. As with the earlier volume, the focus of the present one is also broadly on the Greco-Roman and Islamicate cultural spheres, with a timeframe stretching from the high point of Byzantium (tenth–eleventh century CE) down to the present day. Both volumes bring together specialists in history, art history, literature, and theater studies. However, the present volume covers an even wider geography. For, in addition to the core provinces of Byzantium and the Ottoman Empire in the Eastern Mediterranean and Middle East, it also includes connections between these regions and others further east, notably Iran, Inner Asia, and the Indian Ocean. A recurring theme is the legacy of Alexander the Great, whose conquests brought together East and West, and whose largely legendary adventures (the so-called *Alexander Romance*) conveyed ideas of geography, eschatology, and universal empire that persisted throughout the Middle Ages.[9] Another major theme is the cultural influence of Rome and Iran, imperial traditions *par excellence*, which were transformed by the advent of Islam and other medieval reconfigurations, but whose legacy continued to assert itself in later empires and societies into the modern era.

As we have seen, key to Said's argument about imagined geography is the idea that conceptions of space are inextricably linked to relationships of power. In the case of the West and its domination of the Middle East in modern times, which is Said's primary subject of interest, his work has been widely accepted, and with good reason. However, at the same time, the extent of its scope has been debated and questioned, as the discussion continues about the extent to which these observations can be applied to other periods, relationships, and regions of the world.[10] Nonetheless, it is fair to say that by and large, Said's observations remain as relevant as ever in a world increasingly aware of divisions along such lines as East and West, North and South, rich and poor. Even within the boundaries of nation-states and larger unions and federations such as the EU, the US, and the UK, discourses of power and superiority are increasingly visible in the relationship between urban and rural areas, or more or less prosperous member states. There are many ways to explore these relationships, from classic Marxian critiques to more recent studies based on "big data." Yet, as pointed out even by Said's direct heirs in postcolonial studies, an exclusive focus on the phenomenon of Western domination—or more broadly, dominant voices rather than those of subalterns and other groups—may often blind us to the full dimensions of the

---

[8] Bazzaz, Batsaki, and Angelov 2013.
[9] Stoneman 2008.
[10] E.g. Phillips 2013; Kalmar and Penslar 2005; Todorova 1997.

connection between power dynamics and ideas of space.[11] People in the South and East have been speaking back to those in the North and West all along, at least within the timeframe investigated by Said. In so doing, they have sometimes appropriated the discourses of modernity for their own ends or reinterpreted them in light of their own experiences and cultural knowledge.[12]

A key question raised by *Orientalism* is the extent to which the study's observations apply outside the modern period, or can be extended to power relationships apart from European colonialism and empire in the "long" nineteenth and twentieth centuries. Given that even western European study of the Islamic Middle East has older roots dating to the medieval period, were the attitudes Said describes also present at times when it is too early to speak of European colonialism and empire, at least in the modern sense? Moreover, if Western ideas about other regions of the world have their roots in Greco-Roman antiquity, as Said suggests, how did this ancient heritage inform non-Western authors indebted to the same ancient traditions? For, as is still not always recognized in the West at least outside academic circles, in the medieval and early modern eras, Western civilization was not the only, or even the main heir to the civilization of ancient Greece and Rome. In the medieval period and beyond, Greek-speaking Byzantium and the Islamic Middle East, which benefited from extensive translations of ancient works into Arabic, had at least as great a claim to this ancient heritage as the West.[13] On the other hand, it is also a mistake to accept uncritically the still common narrative according to which the West "rediscovered" ancient knowledge during the Renaissance and Enlightenment, which had been lost to Europe during the so-called "Dark Ages," but was fortunately "preserved" and passed on dutifully (albeit passively) by the "Byzantines" and Muslim "Arabs." We still have much to learn about the ancient texts being read in different parts of the world in the medieval and early modern period, whether in the original or in translation, and the process of transmission and elaboration of this ancient knowledge, which often crossed the boundaries of language, culture, and religion.[14]

Such caveats notwithstanding, even if we accept that it is probably best to limit Said's specific observations about Western Orientalism to the modern period, it is still possible to say that his wider focus on power dynamics inherent in imagined geographies and other epistemological categories provides a

[11] For a broader view of the forces at work, defined largely in spatial terms, see Bhabha 1994.
[12] E.g. Jamal al-Din al-Afghani's response to Ernest Renan's critique of Arab-Islamic civilization, first published in the French *Journal des débats* in 1883 (Keddie 1968:181–187). See also the chapter by Ilham Khuri-Makdisi in the present volume.
[13] Gutas 1998.
[14] E.g. Mavroudi 2015; Melvin-Koushki 2017.

useful set of questions worth asking also about other times and places. As already suggested, the critical study of power relations and the underlying discourses through which they are created and perpetuated may also be traced to Foucault and other structuralist and poststructuralist thinkers, all the way back to Marx and Nietzsche. The theoretical focus on language, often referred to as "the linguistic turn"—a term with different meanings for different fields— has had a wide impact on the humanities and social sciences, extending beyond the study of colonialism and post-colonialist literature to such traditional fields as history, medieval studies, and the classics.[15] Although the relevance of such critiques of power is perhaps most obvious when we study recent history and current events, in order to appreciate their full extent and applicability to other times and places, it is necessary also to consider a far wider range of cultures, geographies, and historical periods. The present volume aims to do just that, by bringing together essays on topics as diverse as medieval ideas of cultural geography in Byzantium, western Europe, and the Islamic world; mutual perceptions and networks connecting the Eastern Mediterranean with Central and Inner Asia and the Indian Ocean; as well as the reception of modern Western cultural categories and creations (the novel, the encyclopedia, the Theater of the Absurd) in the local context of the late Ottoman Empire and modern Greece.

Description of Contents

As suggested above, this sequel to the previously published *Imperial Geographies in Byzantine and Ottoman Space* shares many of the same preoccupations. Many of the contributors show a similar concern with empire in general, and more specifically the Byzantine and Ottoman Empires and their legacy in Greece, the Eastern Mediterranean, and the Middle East. However, the present volume widens the discussion by focusing on less obviously imperial periods of Byzantine and Ottoman history, as well as on geographical regions and relationships that transcend the boundaries of these empires and the modern states to which they eventually gave rise. In the spirit of Foucault and Said, the essays collected here suggest that the phenomenon of imagined geographies is essentially discursive in nature, since Self and Other may only be defined relative to one another.

In all of the volume's chapters, power is an essential component of the equation, albeit not always in the same way. In Byzantium and the Ottoman Empire, as in other cultures, the science of geography, with its ancient foundations and modern advances and elaborations, was an intrinsic part of political discourse

---

[15]   Spiegel 2005; Brown 1992; Cameron 1992.

and culture. In the chapters by Dimiter Angelov and Ilham Khuri-Makdisi, it becomes clear that in both twelfth-century Byzantine Constantinople and late nineteenth-century Ottoman Beirut, the ability to present an authoritative analysis of different aspects of physical and cultural geography, no matter how different the terms, was intrinsic to participation in the elite classes of these two societies, however differently defined. Angelov's chapter "Repurposing Ancient Knowledge: Eustathios of Thessaloniki and His Geographical Anthology" makes clear that the work it describes is a detailed, systematic study of geography affirming common Byzantine cultural assumptions, such as the unity of Greco-Roman culture and the fundamental role of the ancient Greek tradition. At the same time, Angelov shows that its author aimed also to educate his readers in a more critical way, by presenting some questions as unresolved and discussing debates among ancient authorities. In so doing, he foreshadowed later humanist projects involving the management and repurposing of existing knowledge. Precisely such a project, albeit from a much later era, is described in Ilham Khuri-Makdisi's chapter "Worlds in Motion: Al-Bustani's Arabic Encyclopedia (*Da'irat al-Ma'arif*) and the Global Production of Knowledge in the Late Ottoman Levant and Egypt (1870s–1900s)." As Khuri-Makdisi shows, for the nineteenth-century Arab intellectual Butrus al-Bustani and the heirs who continued his intellectual project, the aim was not only to curate and classify existing knowledge, but also to propel Arabic readers onto a global stage. Using the format of the dictionary, which like the modern internet connects entries by means of links ("see under ..."), the work became a "dream machine" (to use Roland Barthes's term) for travel and exploration of a vast, globalized new world.

Needless to say, though, during the long timespan covered in this volume, not all perceptions of space were framed explicitly in terms of classically inspired geographical anthologies and Enlightenment-influenced dictionaries and encyclopedias. Comparable discourses about space may also be found in other written works belonging to very different genres, which were similarly steeped in influential literary traditions of their own. For example, Angus Stewart's chapter "Imagination and Experience in Thirteenth-Century Latin Encounters with the 'Orient': John of Plano Carpini, the Mongols, and Monsters" centers on the Latin account of the Mongols by John of Plano Carpini (d. 1252). This work is generally thought of as belonging to the genre of medieval travel literature—understandably so, since the Franciscan friar who wrote it was indeed describing an actual embassy from the Pope in France to the Great Khan in Mongolia. However, as in the case of the Muslim author Rashiduddin (d. 1318), who wrote a history of the Mongols and Turks in Persian and whose lifetime briefly overlapped with that of Plano Carpini, in many ways it is also an ethnographic work based on his own observations of the Mongols.[16] As Stewart explains, regardless of the eyewitness character of the account or the question of whether Plano Carpini shared biases about "the Other" similar to those studied by modern anthropologists, parts of his account can only be explained by the literary environment of medieval Latin Europe with which the author was familiar. These included preconceptions about the physical world and its inhabitants rooted in the medieval *Alexander Romance*, a vast body of legends in many languages concerning the ancient conqueror Alexander the Great and his conquests.[17] In the Islamic world, this same *Alexander Romance* tradition may be found in parts of the Qur'an, as well as in the Persian national epic, the *Shahnameh* ('Book of Kings'), a work by the poet Ferdowsi completed in the year 1010 CE.[18]

The *Alexander Romance*, *Shahnameh*, and wider Perso-Islamicate epic traditions are also essential for understanding the two early Ottoman panegyric poems forming the subject of the chapter by Dimitri Kastritsis, entitled "Ottoman Imagined Geography in the Verses of the Court Poets Ahmedi and Abdülvasi (ca. 1402–1414)." Although both works discussed are historical in nature, and are indeed the oldest firmly datable historical texts produced in Ottoman courts, as in the previous case examined by Stewart, their presentation of geography is based partly on historical experience and partly on literary tradition. Knowledge of the literary context is essential for understanding their political messages, which include criticizing the excessive ambition of Ottoman princes foolish enough to venture outside the former Roman (i.e. Byzantine) lands. As in the case of the Byzantine geography discussed by Angelov, literary context is also essential for understanding views of space in Byzantine historical works, alongside political events that may play an equally crucial role. Several such works, notably the history by Niketas Choniates, form the subject of the essay by Yannis Stouraitis, entitled "The Lands of the *Rhomaîoi*: Imagined Geographies in Byzantium before and after 1204." As the author makes clear, works written in the aftermath of the Fourth Crusade (1204) deploy existing discourses from the ancient and Byzantine traditions, in order to represent the changing realities of Byzantine space following the 1204 Latin sack of Constantinople and its Byzantine recapture in 1261. Depending on the author and time of writing, this could be done in different and indeed contrasting ways.

A key element connecting several contributions to the present volume involves the many meanings of the term Rome and its derivatives (*Rum*,

---

[16] Thackston 1998–1999.
[17] Stoneman 2008.
[18] Davis 2007.

Romanía, Rumeli) when used with reference to the core regions of the Byzantine and Ottoman Empires. As Anthony Kaldellis has demonstrated in a recent study, ideas of a clearly defined, Greek-speaking Roman homeland corresponding to core territories of Byzantium have a long history stretching from late antiquity into the Ottoman period.[19] On the other hand, more common terms used today, such as "medieval Hellenism" and "Byzantium," represent early modern European impositions onto a space which as far as its medieval inhabitants were concerned was simply "Romanland" (*Romanía*). For the Ottomans and the wider Islamic world, the equivalent term was Rum (*bilād al-Rūm, diyār-ı Rūm*) and its derivatives, such as the later Rumeli (almost certainly derived from *Romanía*, regardless of its Turkish etymology *Rūm-eli*, 'land of Rum'). Over the centuries, Rum came to have several different meanings, including but not limited to the ethnic one discussed by Kaldellis. The Ottomans used the term continually with reference to the eastern Roman legacy of Byzantium, calling their Greek-speaking Christian Orthodox subjects Romans (Rum) until the end of the empire in 1923. Indeed, Orthodox Christian Turkish citizens are still called that today. However, when used geographically the term may also refer to Muslims. In his chapter "Pan-Islamic Plot or Colonial Paranoia? Ottoman Policies towards Southeast Asia, 1824–1916" Andrew Peacock shows that as late as the First World War, the Indonesian Muslims of Aceh were calling the Ottoman sultan "Raja Rum." The idea of a Muslim ruling over eastern Roman lands dates back to the Seljuks of Rum, an offshoot of the Great Seljuk Empire of the Middle East; and Aceh's relationship with the Ottomans to the sixteenth century. As Peacock explains, its hopes of an anti-Christian alliance—originally against the Portuguese, now against the British and other modern colonial powers—had been fed by expectations created by the 1890 voyage through Southeast Asia of the Ottoman frigate *Ertuğrul*, on a diplomatic mission to Japan.[20] At a local level, the threat of pan-Islamism feared by the British in the First World War can only be understood in light of a much older history, itself connected to the place of Rum in wider Islamicate culture and literature.

On the level of material culture, similarly extensive trans-regional connections may be found in the cultural spaces connecting the Islamic Middle East, Central Asia, and India. Some of these are explored by Keelan Overton in her chapter on the so-called St Andrews Qur'an, entitled "Mapping the Safavid/

---

[19] Kaldellis 2019, esp. pp. 81–94.

[20] It is worth noting that the ship was named after the father of the Ottoman dynasty's founder Osman, the subject of written legends dating back to the fifteenth century. The ship's naming reflects late Ottoman interest in the dynasty's early, largely legendary history (see the chapter by Kastritsis in the present volume).

Bijapur/Mughal/Savanur/Mysore/St Andrews Qur'an: A Diachronic Life History." The Qur'an discussed by Overton is a complete luxury manuscript of Islam's holy scripture, taken by the East India Company from the possessions of Tipu Sultan of Mysore, following his elimination by the British (1799). Long considered to have been made for a fifteenth-century Timurid prince in Iran, this provenance turns out to be more imagined than real. In fact, most of the manuscript was made in sixteenth-century Iran under the Safavids, where the cultural legacy of the Timurid dynasty was still strong. The manuscript continued to evolve as it made its way around the Deccan region of India in the hands of its various owners. The many faces of the St Andrews Qur'an demonstrate that physical objects in circulation can also have political meaning connected to their real or purported geographical associations. In the case of a manuscript such as this, these go well beyond the text itself—largely set since it is holy scripture—and are mostly embodied in material and artistic elements.

In other words, when considered carefully and in context, just as tales about Ottoman princes campaigning in the Balkans could evoke Persian epic heroes, and a late Ottoman frigate sailing to Japan could remind Indonesians of early modern links to the "Raja Rum," a luxury Qur'an in India could be made to represent real or imagined cultural connections between the Timurid dynasty, Iran, and various Muslim rulers of the Deccan. Of course, the Qur'an's travels do not end there. Now it is at St Andrews, Scotland's oldest university, having become part of the British Empire's colonization and cultural appropriation of the East, the very process that forms the subject of Said's *Orientalism*. As a corrective or addendum to Said, however, it is clear that the Western appropriation and attempt to classify this quintessentially "oriental" object represents but the final stage in a long history of projection onto it of various imagined geographies. From its very creation, the St Andrews Qur'an shows a desire among the early modern Safavids of Iran to connect with the influential artistic legacy of the Timurids who came before. By the sixteenth century, Timurid patronage had produced works that were remarkably influential in Iran and beyond, a cultural influence and prestige that spread as far as the Deccan, where the Qur'an assumed its current form.

However great the role of educated elites and princely patrons in shaping ideas of imagined geography in premodern times, or the global influence of later European empires and Enlightenment ideas of science and progress, not all imagined geographies should be conceived in top–down terms. Thanks to the rise of literacy and the proliferation of available sources in the modern period, it becomes possible to access and consider a far wider range of ideas about the relationship between imagined space, society, and the experience of power (or the lack thereof). Sources for such analysis include such popular forms as the modern novel and theater, which may be considered in their own right using the tools of literary criticism, but also in light of their reception, which may be studied through media reports and even direct participation. For premodern times, the question of reception is a difficult one, which can only be tackled by such means as studying the number of extant manuscripts or more or less oblique references in various literary and archival sources. By the nineteenth century, however, it is much easier, as demonstrated by Khuri-Makdisi's essay on the first modern Arabic encyclopedia, to which reference has already been made. It is even clearer in Yota Batsaki's study of topophilia in Alexandros Papadiamantis's 1903 novel *The Murderess*, and Anna Stavrakopoulou's essay on the reception of Samuel Beckett's *Endgame* in contemporary Greece.

As Batsaki demonstrates in her chapter entitled "Island Topophilia: Alexandros Papadiamantis' *The Murderess* (1903)," the author's native island of Skiathos plays an essential role that goes well beyond that of a mere backdrop for the novel's plot and action. An author whose very style (to say nothing of his choice of subjects) challenged received categories and boundaries separating learned and vernacular versions of Greek, Papadiamantis uses the landscape of an Aegean island, normally associated with nostalgic ideas of the nation and Mediterranean cultural purity, as an essential character in a gothic drama. Apart from the island itself, the main protagonist is a local woman struggling with the realities of gender in a traditional society, who becomes a criminal in an effort to rid families of the burden of raising daughters. As Batsaki explains, Papadiamantis's imagined geography is a form of topophilia—a term intro-duced by the humanist geographer Yi-Fu Tuan around the same time as Said's *Orientalism*.[21] Despite Papadiamantis's strong attachment to his native Skiathos, visible also in other novels, in *The Murderess* his knowledge of the landscape allows him to explore ideas of crime and justice in largely spatial terms. In many ways, this is a dark island more reminiscent of Scotland or Ireland than of most people's idyllic view of the Greek Isles. Of course, as Batsaki explains, the island has been a topos in Greek and European literature since Homeric times. Indeed, it plays an essential role also in the *Alexander Romance*, a body of litera-ture, which, as we have seen, connects many of the contributions to this volume.

However important the connection between Papadiamantis and his native land, he was writing in a Western form, and his work must therefore be consid-ered also in terms of the reception of modern European culture in other parts of the world. A similar process is at work in Anna Stavrakopoulou's chapter entitled "'Ten Feet by Ten Feet by Ten Feet': *Endgame*'s Confinement and Devastation on

---

[21] Tuan 1974.

the Greek Stage (2009–2017)." The connection between Ireland and Greece has been noted for a long time, and goes both ways.[22] In this case, it involves the work of a playwright whose uses of space pushed the boundaries of how this was normally thought of in theater. It may seem paradoxical to include in a volume about imagined geographies a piece about the reception of the so-called Theater of the Absurd in today's Greece. After all, Beckett's play *Endgame* (as it is known in English) lacks a clearly defined setting, since like its predecessor *Waiting for Godot*, it aims to convey the tragicomedy of human existence through the sparse use of props and characters. As Stavrakopoulou explains, the play's imagined landscape is one of devastation, only partly conveyed by the emptiness of the stage, which is of course subject to the staging of each specific production. The dialogue plays an equally essential role in creating the play's sense of desolation and dislocation, which can be traced at least in part to Beckett's experience as an Irish Protestant living in post-Second World War France, writing in both French and English.

How does this explain *Endgame*'s enduring popularity in Greece, particularly following the extensive financial, political, and social crisis of 2009? The answer lies partly in these very landscapes of devastation, and partly in the fact that the play is also fundamentally about the vanity of power and the nature of the relationship of master and servant. This power relationship, which is central to the play, has allowed directors to evoke for contemporary Greek audiences echoes of the relationship of Greece to the European Union following 2009, and on a broader level the powerlessness of ordinary citizens facing the state, political establishment, and economic interests. Once again, we see the interconnectedness of space and relationships of power, albeit in a landscape whose most striking characteristic is a bleak emptiness and absence of hope. Perhaps it is not too far-fetched to draw a connection here to representations of Hades and the ends of the earth as conceived in antiquity and the Middle Ages. Beckett's empty landscape in *Endgame* is not unlike the Land of Darkness explored by Alexander in his fabulous adventures to the ends of the earth, an essential part of the *Alexander Romance* in its medieval Greek, Latin, and Islamicate versions. From antiquity to our own time, such empty, apocalyptic landscapes have been used by a wide variety of authors representing many languages and traditions to make statements about the vanity of power. One wonders to what extent Beckett may have been influenced, either consciously or unconsciously, by the *Alexander Romance* and the many traces it left on subsequent world literature and culture.

---

[22] E.g. Kruczkowska 2017.

Works Cited

Anderson, B. 1983. *Imagined Communities: Reflections on the Origin and Spread of Nationalism.* London.

Bazzaz, S., Y. Batsaki, and D. Angelov, eds. 2013. *Imperial Geographies in Byzantine and Ottoman Space.* Hellenic Studies 56. Washington, DC.

Bhabha, H. K. 1994. *The Location of Culture.* London.

Bodenhamer, D. J., J. Corrigan, and T. M. Harris. 2010. *The Spatial Humanities: GIS and the Future of Humanities Scholarship.* Bloomington.

Bonine, M. E., A. Amanat, and M. E Gasper. 2012. *Is There a Middle East? The Evolution of a Geopolitical Concept.* Stanford.

Brown, P. 1992. *Power and Persuasion in Late Antiquity.* Madison.

Cameron, A. 1992. *Christianity and the Rhetoric of Empire: The Development of Christian Discourse.* Berkeley.

Crang, M., and N. Thrift. 2000. *Thinking Space.* London.

Danforth, N. 2016. "How the Middle East Was Invented." *Washington Post*, May 19.

Davis, D., trans. 2007. *Shahnameh: The Persian Book of Kings. Abolqasem Ferdowsi.* New York.

Davison, R. H. 1960. "Where Is the Middle East?" *Foreign Affairs* 38:665–675.

Foucault, M. 1969. *L'archéologie du savoir.* Paris. [English trans. A. Sheridan. 1972. *The Archaeology of Knowledge.* New York.]

———. 1975. *Surveiller et punir.* Paris. [English trans. A. Sheridan. 1977. *Discipline and Punish.* New York.]

France, Commission des sciences et des arts d'Égypte. 1809–1828. *Description de l'Égypte; ou, Recueil des observations et des recherches qui ont été faites en Égypte pendant l'expédition de l'armée française.* Paris.

Gutas, D. 1998. *Greek Thought, Arabic Culture: The Graeco-Arabic Translation Movement in Baghdad and Early 'Abbasid Society (Second–Fourth/Fifth–Tenth c.).* London.

Kaldellis, A. 2019. *Romanland: Ethnicity and Empire in Byzantium.* Cambridge, MA.

Kalmar, I. D., and D. J. Penslar. 2005. *Orientalism and the Jews.* Waltham, MA.

Keddie, N. R. 1968. *An Islamic Response to Imperialism: Political and Religious Writings of Sayyid Jamāl ad-Dīn "al-Afghānī."* Berkeley.

Kruczkowska, J. 2017. *Irish Poets and Modern Greece: Heaney, Mahon, Cavafy, Seferis.* Cham, Switzerland.

Mavroudi, M. 2015. "Translations from Greek into Arabic and Latin during the Middle Ages: Searching for the Classical Tradition." *Speculum* 90:28–59.

Melvin-Koushki, M. 2017. "Introduction: De-orienting the Study of Islamicate Occultism." In Melvin-Koushki and Gardiner 2017:287–295.

Melvin-Koushki, M., and N. Gardiner. 2017. *Islamicate Occultism: New Perspectives.* Special double issue of *Arabica* 64.

Oakes, T. S., and P. L. Price. 2008. *The Cultural Geography Reader*. Oxford.

Phillips, K. M. 2013. *Before Orientalism: Asian Peoples and Cultures in European Travel Writing, 1245-1510*. Philadelphia.

Said, E. W. 1978. *Orientalism*. New York.

Spiegel, G. M., ed. 2005. *Practicing History: New Directions in Historical Writing after the Linguistic Turn*. New York.

Stoneman, R. 2008. *Alexander the Great: A Life in Legend*. New Haven.

Thackston, W. M., trans. 1998–1999. *Rashiduddin Fazlullah's Jami'u't-tawarikh*. Cambridge, MA.

Todorova, M. N. 1997. *Imagining the Balkans*. New York.

Tuan, Y. 1974. *Topophilia: A Study of Environmental Perceptions, Attitudes, and Values*. Englewood Cliffs.

Warf, B., and S. Arias. 2009. *The Spatial Turn: Interdisciplinary Perspectives*. London.

1

Repurposing Ancient Knowledge

Eustathios of Thessaloniki and His Geographical Anthology

DIMITER ANGELOV

IN THE SECOND HALF OF THE TWELFTH CENTURY, Eustathios of Thessaloniki made the following description of the Caspian Sea in an ambitious work that laid out detailed geographical information about the entire known world. Claudius Ptolemy (second century CE), he noted, had considered the Caspian to be an enclosed sea and Herodotus had been in full agreement. But Dionysius Periegetes (second century CE), an Alexandrian geographer of the Roman imperial period, held the opinion that the Caspian Sea was connected with the Northern ("Cronian") Ocean, a view originating from Strabo, the famous Greek geographer of the Augustan era. The "ancients" (hoi palaioi)—Eustathios continued—had contrived to reconcile these different views by suggesting that perhaps the northern ocean flows "through unknown places" into the Hyrcanian Gulf (that is, the Caspian Sea). Eustathios concluded the matter in a sobering fashion by saying that it should be treated as unresolved for the foreseeable future. "So both the argument stating that the Caspian Sea can be walked around and the argument stating that it is generated by the northern ("Cronian") sea should be retained."[1]

The entry on the Caspian Sea is typical of a singular and superbly researched work of scholarship, whose audience and features are of interest to us here. Its author, Eustathios (ca. 1115–1195/96), was a prominent Constantinopolitan teacher of rhetoric and a prolific author who became the archbishop of Thessaloniki in the later part of his life.[2] Eustathios is well known for his

---

[1] The text by Eustathios can be found in Müller 1861:227.4–18. Elsewhere Eustathios summarizes the same debate among the ancient authorities: Müller 1861:344.8–30.

[2] The life of Eustathios has been difficult to reconstruct. For a fuller discussion, see Kazhdan and Franklin 1984:115–140; Merianos 2008:27–61. For a summary of events in Eustathios' career, see Kolovou 2006:3*–5*.

commentary on the *Iliad* and the *Odyssey*, imperial orations, and sermons, but he is somewhat less familiar to us as the author of one of the most substantial medieval Greek geographical works: his meticulously compiled commentary (*parekbolai*) on the poetic *Description of the World* (*oikoumenês periêgêsis*) by the Roman author Dionysius Periegetes.[3] The work immerses us into the imagined geographies of the Byzantines as a leading example of what I have elsewhere termed "academic geography," a method of geographical ordering of space based on ancient texts read and emulated in Byzantine schools.[4] Eustathios keeps nearly full silence about contemporary political geography and is similarly uninformative about living geography shaped by religious and popular imagination. His work is also disconnected from the tradition of "apostolic geography" oriented toward Christian holy sites and Jerusalem.[5] The peculiarity of his ivory-tower approach is conspicuous in the section on the Levant, where he presents ancient testimonies on Syria, Palestine, and cities such as Tyre, Sidon, Laodicea, Apamea, and Antioch without ever mentioning the Christian Holy Land or Jerusalem itself.[6] An armchair geographer, Eustathios assiduously collected information from ancient authors available in abundance in his library: geographers, poets, historians, playwrights, philosophers, and others.

His compilation was not randomly produced, however, and its epistemic principles are yet to be investigated. Philologists have long mined Eustathios' *parekbolai* on Dionysius Periegetes for precious citations from ancient authors, yet the study of the text as a twelfth-century work of Byzantine scholarship and education is still in its infancy. Aubrey Diller laid the foundations in 1975, in a survey of the substantial manuscript tradition consisting of over fifty Byzantine and post-Byzantine manuscripts, in which he identified two textual families.[7] His lead has not been followed.[8] Our understanding of the text is still hampered by reliance on the old and antiquated editions by Gottfried Bernhardy (1828) and Georg Müller (1861). Textual questions that remain open include the extent of the role of the scholia on Dionysius Periegetes in the genesis of Eustathios' work, the relationship of his work with the prose

---

[3]   All references to the text of Dionysius Periegetes as well as the English translations are based on Lightfoot 2014. For a discussion on the date of the work, see Lightfoot 2014:4n6.

[4]   Angelov 2013.

[5]   Johnson 2010.

[6]   Müller 1861:373–381.

[7]   Diller 1975:181–207. For another count of the manuscripts, see Tsavari 1990:61. Herbert Hunger (1978 I:534–536) devoted two paragraphs to Eustathios' work in his *Geschichte der byzantinischen Literatur*.

[8]   One significant exception is Pérez Martín 2022.

paraphrase of the poem, and the reception of the work by readers and schools in the later Byzantine period.[9]

The absence of a critical edition and textual studies should not, however, hold us back from scrutinizing Eustathios' overall approach and setting his work within the context of a twelfth-century Constantinopolitan school milieu. Eustathios constantly made choices on the inclusion of excerpts, highlighted variations and disputes among the ancient authors, and offered his own interpretations, whether subtly or more directly. His selectivity itself favored certain interpretations. An example is his treatment of the "ancients" (*hoi palaioi*) in his description of the Caspian Sea. The "ancients" represent here scholia, namely explanatory comments, on Dionysius Periegetes found in Byzantine manuscripts. Eustathios copied one part of the relevant scholion regarding the northern sea perhaps flowing into the Caspian "through unknown places," but preferred to ignore the other part about the Caspian Sea being supplied with water by rivers.[10] His agenda here clearly was to leave this geographical quandary open and unanswered.

The discussion begins with an investigation of the vexed question of the aristocratic commissioner of Eustathios' work, a question that sheds illuminating light on the circumstances of its genesis. The discussion then continues with an examination of key principles followed by Eustathios in selecting and repurposing the large amount of geographical, ethnographical, and historical information. The career of the patron, his commission to Eustathios, and Eustathios' management and arrangement of the rich source material unveil a range of motivations and interests of the community of pupils and scholars pursuing geographical studies in the empire of the Komnenoi.

John Doukas (John Doukas Kamateros), a Twelfth-Century Patron of Geography

The lengthy proem of Eustathios' work consists of two parts. The first is a long and informative dedicatory letter to his patron. The second is a preface dealing with Dionysius Periegetes as an author, the characteristics of his descriptive guide (*periêgêsis*) of the world, and the purpose of geography as a discipline in contrast to chorography and *periêgêsis*—the last component of the preface being inspired by the introduction to Ptolemy's *Geography*. The heading of the letter

---

[9] On the scholia, see Tsavari (1990:37–41), who attributes them to late antiquity and shows that at least some of them were known by the ninth century. One of the scholia, nonetheless, dates to or after the seventh century. See below p. 35 n. 88. On the paraphrase, see Tsavari (1990:58–59), who tentatively dates it to the tenth or the eleventh century.
[10] On the scholion, see Müller 1861:433.

explicitly mentions the patron, but his identification is more complicated than it appears at first sight. A text editorial issue, as well as the large number of individuals bearing the same name, has sown confusion and led to disagreements among scholars. The edition by Bernhardy (1828) features the addressee's name as John Doukas (Δούκαν κῦρ Ἰωάννην),[11] whereas the edition by Müller (1861) renders the name as the *doux* John (δούκα κῦρ Ἰωάννην).[12] Thanks to Diller's critical edition of the heading, as it is found in the oldest and most reliable codices, the textual problem can safely be put aside. The patron was undoubtedly called John Doukas. He was the son of Andronikos Doukas Kamateros and bore at a certain stage of his career the title of *epi tôn deêsôn* ("Master of Petitions"). The Greek text of the epistolary heading is given below with an accompanying English translation. The angular brackets indicate a bifurcation of the manuscript tradition, which Diller suspected may have started from two separate autograph manuscripts that do not survive. The brackets refer to words found in the first manuscript family (designated by Diller as R) and missing from the other (designated by Diller as β):[13]

Πρὸς τὸν πανσέβαστον <σεβαστὸν> Δούκαν κῦρ Ἰωάννην <τὸν μετὰ ταῦτα ἐπὶ τῶν δεήσεων> τὸν υἱὸν τοῦ πανσεβάστου σεβαστοῦ καὶ μεγάλου δρουγγαρίου κῦρ Ἀνδρονίκου τοῦ Καματηροῦ, Εὐσταθίου διακόνου ἐπὶ τῶν δεήσεων καὶ μαΐστωρος τῶν ῥητόρων τοῦ καὶ <ὕστερον γεγονότος ἀρχιεπισκόπου> Θεσσαλονίκης ἐπιστολὴ ἐπὶ ταῖς Διονυσίου τοῦ περιηγητοῦ παρεκβολαῖς, <μεθ' ἣν προοίμιον εἰς τὸ πρᾶγμα καὶ μετὰ τὸ προοίμιον αὗται αἱ παρεκβολαί>.

Letter by Eustathios, deacon, *epi tôn deêseôn*,[14] and master of the rhetors, <who later became> also Archbishop of Thessaloniki, addressed to the *pansebastos <sebastos>* Lord John Doukas, <who afterwards was *epi tôn deêseôn*>, the son of the *pansebastos sebastos* and *megas droungarios* Lord Andronikos Kamateros, concerning the commentary on Dionysius Periegetes, <a letter after which comes the preface to the work, and after the preface comes the commentary itself>.

---

[11] Bernhardy 1828:67. This reading has been adopted as correct by most scholars.

[12] Müller 1861:201. Jean Darrouzès (1970:45–46) preferred this reading.

[13] Diller 1975:181–183 (edition of the heading), 184–186, 193–195 (notes on the most important manuscripts). I have verified the heading, with the reading Δούκαν, in two early manuscripts representing family β—Par. gr. 2723, f. 98r (dated to 1282) and the fourteenth-century Par. gr. 2855, f. 1r—as well as in a fourteenth-century representative of R: Par. gr. 2852, f. 48v. The folio with the heading has been lost in the thirteenth-century Vaticanus gr. 1910, an early and important representative of R.

[14] As suggested by Kazhdan and Franklin (1984:120), this office refers to the *epi tôn deêseôn* ("Master of Petitions") in the patriarchal hierarchy, not the imperial civil service.

According to the dedicatory letter, Eustathios had promised to John Doukas at a certain time in the past to compose a work on Dionysius Periegetes, but had been delayed. John Doukas is said to have repeatedly made the request, even after he progressed in his education and learning, and Eustathios was now finally fulfilling his old vow and repaying with interest what had long been due.[15] The letter alludes to a teacher–student relationship. Eustathios notes rhetorically that he was ridding Dionysius' text of "ossified poetic roughness" through his commentary in a way comparable, and superior, to the centaur Chiron who had brought up Achilles by feeding him with the marrow of wild beasts.[16] The most likely reconstruction of the sequence of events is that Eustathios had promised to compose a commentary on Dionysius Periegetes when he was John Doukas' teacher. Years later, he composed the work and dedicated it to his powerful pupil. The letter makes clear that Eustathios had taught John Doukas the poetic geography of Dionysius and implies that the work resulted from, and was aimed at, school instruction. The work often reads like a series of lecture notes on language and content, which enforces the impression of its gestation within an educational context.

The heading of the letter indicates the *termini* of composition. It postdates Eustathios' appointment in about 1168 as "master of the rhetors" (teacher of rhetoric with the accompanying duty of delivering annual panegyrics of the emperor) and predates his elevation to the archbishopric of Thessaloniki in around 1178.[17] Eustathios, thus, produced the work in Constantinople at a time when he was also preparing the first redaction of his Homeric commentaries. The many cross-references bear witness to the interrelationship between the two projects.[18] John's studies with Eustathios, as we have seen, predated the composition of the work on Dionysius. A sense of chronological orientation about John's *floruit* emerges from the career of his brother, Basil Doukas Kamateros, who is attested serving as *prôtonotarios* (that is, head secretary under the logothete of the drome) in 1166.[19] It is not known whether John was

---

[15] Müller 1861:202.4–203.29.

[16] Müller 1861:204.20–33.

[17] On Eustathios' appointment as "master of the rhetors," see Browning 1962:192 (between 1166 and 1168); Kazhdan and Franklin 1984:122 (between 1166 and 1170). According to Kuhn (1889:254–256), the commentary on Dionysius was composed between 1170 and 1175, with 1161 being a firm *terminus post quem*. On Eustathios' departure for Thessaloniki as its archbishop, see Schönauer 2004.

[18] Van der Valk 1971:CXXXVIII–CXXXIX; Kuhn 1889:251–252; Hunger 1978 I:534–536; Cassella 2003:27–29. Traditionally, the composition of the *parekbolai* on Dionysius has been seen as preceding the Homeric commentaries. See most recently Cullhed 2016:*6–*9.

[19] See the attendees of the council of March 1166 in PG, vol. 140, col. 253C; Magdalino 1993:507. On his genealogy and career, see the references below in nn. 33 and 40.

Basil's older or younger brother, but it is reasonable to suppose that he received instruction from Eustathios in the 1160s at the latest.

A number of individuals of high status named "Ioannes Doukas" and "Ioannes Kamateros" lived in the twelfth century. In 1968 Demetrios Polemis identified Eustathios' student with what are in fact several different men of the same name, including the *megas hetaireiarchês* John Doukas, a prominent general and a diplomat active in Italy, Hungary, and the Levant from the 1150s until the 1170s. The multiple identifications, especially the identification with the *megas hetaireiarchês* John Doukas, have been convincingly disproved.[20] The student of Eustathios should also be distinguished from three prominent individuals of the second half of the twelfth century named John Kamateros. Two of them can be mentioned here and the third one will follow shortly. The *epi tou kanikleiou* ("keeper of the imperial inkstand") John Kamateros held this position during the reign of Manuel I Komnenos (1143–1180).[21] According to Niketas Choniates, he was among the officials who had the sad duty of arranging for the burial at sea of the beheaded body of the child emperor Alexios II (1180–1183) after the usurpation of Andronikos I Komnenos (1183–1185) and was later appointed as Archbishop of Ohrid.[22] This man is different from our John, because the latter, also a supporter of the usurper emperor, appears at a different point and with a different title in Choniates' account of Andronikos I's violent accession. The *chartophylax* and later patriarch John X Kamateros (1198–1206), who has been identified as the rhetor and *hypertimos* John Kamateros, the author of an Epiphany oration delivered before an emperor from the Angelos family, is also different from Eustathios' student, who is not known to have pursued an ecclesiastical career.[23]

---

[20] The conflation by Polemis (1968:127–130) of at least four different individuals as the same Ioannes Doukas was critiqued by Kazhdan 1969; Karlin-Hayter 1972; Stone 1999. Kazhdan and Franklin (1984:139) identified the *megas hetaireiarchês* with our John Doukas, the son of Andronikos Kamateros, even though Kazhdan was less certain in 1969. As Archbishop of Thessaloniki, Eustathios addressed an oration (dated to 1179 and translated by Stone 2013:131–145) to the *megas hetaireiarchês* packed with references to the latter's career. Kazhdan (1969) and Karlin-Hayter (1972) conveniently provide a list of the twelfth-century individuals named John Doukas.

[21] He was listed among the attendees of the council of March 1166: PG, vol. 140, col. 253C; Magdalino 1993:507. He has sometimes been identified as the author of versified astrological works dedicated to the emperor. See Darrouzès 1970:46. Magdalino (1993:269, 367) leans toward identification with the logothete of the drome John Kamateros in the 1150s and 1160s. Laurent (1931:266–267) identified the *epi tou kanikleiou* with the astrologer as well as the rhetor and *hypertimos* John Kamateros. The conundrum has been pointed out by Kazhdan 1991b.

[22] Niketas Choniates, *History*, in Van Dieten 1975:274.21–29.

[23] See Nikephoros Kallistos Xanthopoulos, PG, vol. 157, col. 464D. On the tense relations between Niketas Choniates and the *chartophylax* John Kamateros, see Van Dieten 1971:106–115; Simpson 2013:28–29. For the identification of the *chartophylax* with the rhetor and *hypertimos*, see Darrouzès 1970:46–47.

Who, then, was our John Doukas? His father Andronikos Doukas Kamateros is known for his trailblazing career during the reign of Manuel I. He is attested as holder of the positions of *epi tôn deêsôn* (master of petitions) in 1155, as eparch (mayor) of Constantinople in 1157–1161, and as *megas droungarios tês viglas* (high Constantinopolitan judge) in 1166.[24] Andronikos was born of the marriage of Irene Doukaine and Gregory Kamateros, also a high imperial official, who was recruited by the emperor Alexios I Komnenos (1081–1118) and held the financial and ministerial offices of *logaristês*, *prôtoasêkrêtis*, and logothete of the *sekreta*, among others.[25] Another son of Gregory Kamateros and Irene Doukaine, besides Andronikos, was John Kamateros—the third prominent individual bearing this name. He was logothete of the drome in the 1150s until his death in around 1165 and is to be distinguished from his nephew, Eustathios' student.[26] Our John Doukas thus belonged to a politically influential Constantinopolitan family. His father Andronikos, his uncle John, and his grandfather Gregory were all high ministers, and both he and his brother Basil (already a *prôtonotarios* in 1166) followed careers in the civil service. It is with good reason that the Kamateroi have been called "the most powerful bureaucratic dynasty of the late twelfth century."[27] The branch of the Kamateroi to which our John belonged was blood-related to the imperial family through his grandmother Irene Doukaine, which explains why Eustathios calls him "a royal man by family origin" in the dedicatory letter.[28]

Epi tôn deêsôn ("Master of Petitions"), ca. 1178

Traces of the *epi tôn deêsôn* John Doukas have already been detected in Eustathios' correspondence.[29] A letter composed in Thessaloniki, dated by its most recent editor to about 1178, addresses an anonymous *pansebastos sebastos* and *epi tôn deêsôn*. The titles are the same as those borne by John Doukas in the dedicatory epistle. This circumstance, together with the chronology and content of the letter, demonstrates that Eustathios was writing to his former student, now a high-positioned civil official in Constantinople. Eustathios mentions having

---

[24] On the *cursus honorum* of Andronikos Doukas Kamateros, see Bucossi 2009:114–115.

[25] On Gregory Kamateros, see Darrouzès 1970:44; Guilland 1971:82–83. Irene Doukaine, his wife, has been identified with a niece of Alexios I's wife Irene Doukaine, which would make Andronikos Kamateros second cousin of Manuel I. See Polemis 1968:78–79; Bucossi 2009:115–116.

[26] Niketas Choniates, *History*, in Van Dieten 1975:111–115; Darrouzès 1970:45; Guilland 1971:59–61; Magdalino 1993:255–256; Polemis (1968:130n2) equated the logothete of the drome John Kamateros, a correspondent of George Tornikes the Elder, with Eustathios' student John Doukas.

[27] Magdalino 1993:255.

[28] Müller 1861:204.28–30 (ἀνδρὶ … βασιλικῷ τὴν τοῦ γένους φύην).

[29] See Angold (1995:188–189) for a commentary and analysis of Ep. 35, which has since been reedited and dated by Kolovou 2006:150*–152*, 103.

petitioned his correspondent in the past and inquires whether the emperor plans to travel to the western provinces, expressing a wish to pay his respects, even though a month-long illness has prevented him from journeying all the way to the capital. If, however, the emperor was outside Constantinople, Eustathios declares his willingness to see him even if he has to be carried on a litter. The letter confirms 1178 as a firm *terminus ante quem* for the composition of the commentary on Dionysius Periegetes, for the heading of the dedicatory epistle in the proem refers to the appointment of John Doukas to the office of *epi tôn deêseôn* as a future event.

Eparch of Constantinople, 1181

The next stage of John Doukas' career emerges from reports about the power struggle following Manuel I's death. In 1181, the regency government led by the *prôtosebastos* Alexios, Manuel's nephew, faced mounting opposition. A faction in the city supported the claims of Manuel's cousin Andronikos—the future emperor Andronikos I Komnenos (1183–1185). The arrested ring leaders included the eparch of Constantinople, whom different sources identify as "John Doukas" (Eustathios in his account of the Norman capture of Thessaloniki), "John Kamateros" (Niketas Choniates in his *History*), and "John Doukas Kamateros" (the thirteenth-century *Synopsis Chronikê* traditionally attributed to Theodore Skoutariotes).[30] The variance can be explained through the circumstance that the eparch John belonged to the Doukas Kamateros branch of the Kamateroi. The individual must be identical with the former *epi tôn deêseôn* John Doukas for several reasons. First, both his father Andronikos and his brother Basil are attested with the double-barrel name "Doukas Kamateros" in literary sources and seals.[31] Second, Eustathios hints at his fondness for the eparch John Doukas in his account of the Norman capture of Thessaloniki. "His very appearance," Eustathios writes, "gave evidence that he would be found to be among good men." Last but not least, the promotion of John from *epi tôn deêseôn* to eparch of Constantinople mirrors exactly the career of his father Andronikos, who occupied the two positions in the same order.[32]

---

[30] Eustathios, *The Capture of Thessaloniki*, 14–15 in Melville Jones 1988:20–23; Niketas Choniates, *History*, in Van Dieten 1975:231; *Synopsis chronikê* in Sathas 1894:311.5–6.

[31] For the poetic preface to Andronikos Kamateros' *Sacred Arsenal*, which presents the author as "Doukas Kamateros," see Bucossi 2009:115. For the seal of the *prôtonatarios* "Basil Doukas Kamateros," see Laurent 1931; Polemis 1968:131.

[32] Bucossi 2009:114–115.

Logothete of the Drome (?), 1188–1190

No source tells us what happened with the eparch John Doukas (John Doukas Kamateros) after he was arrested for his support of Andronikos I. He and his brother Basil took different sides during the violent accession of Andronikos I. Basil Doukas Kamateros was logothete of the drome in 1182—he was probably appointed to this post already under Manuel I—and firmly opposed Andronikos' regime, for which he was punished with blinding and was exiled among the Rus. He reemerged as a powerful figure at the court of the Angeloi and later at the exiled Laskarid court in Anatolia after 1204. His position of influence for over twenty years is explainable with the marriage of the powerful Euphrosyne Kamatere, his and John's sister, to the emperor Alexios III Angelos (1195–1203).[33]

John Doukas (Kamateros), Eustathios' student, appears to have occupied for some time the position of logothete of the drome formerly held by his brother Basil. In late 1188, Isaac II Angelos (1185–1195) sent a certain logothete of the drome John Doukas to Nuremberg to arrange for an agreement with the crusader emperor Frederick I Barbarossa on the provisioning of his army during its impending passage through Byzantine territories. The imperial letter of December 1188 introduces him as the *pansebastos sebastos, oikeios*, and logothete of the drome John Doukas, and a chronicle of the Third Crusade speaks of him as John, the emperor's "secretary" (*cancellarius*).[34] Choniates adds that a year later, in 1189, the emperor dispatched the logothete of the drome John Doukas to welcome Frederick in the Balkans during his ill-fated journey to the Holy Land.[35] The same individual is also known to have supervised a fiscal survey in the Balkans.[36] There are good reasons to adopt, in this case, Polemis' identification of the logothete of the drome active in 1188–1190 with Eustathios' student John Doukas.[37] Eustathios' student, whose preferred surname was apparently "Doukas," pursued a career solely in the civil administration (the family pattern among the Kamateroi) in contrast to the general and *megas hetaireiarchês* "John Doukas."

---

[33] For the blinding of the logothete of the drome Basil Doukas Kamateros in 1182, see Niketas Choniates, *History*, in Van Dieten 1975:266.24–267.41. See also the oration of Michael Choniates addressed to Basil Kamateros (cited below in n. 40), which gives some valuable information on his life. On his genealogy and career, see Guilland 1971:62–63; Polemis 1968:130–131.

[34] Miklosich and Müller 1865:2.11–14. Ansbert in Chroust 1928:15.17–18.

[35] Niketas Choniates, *History*, in Van Dieten 1975:402.29–39; *Synopsis chronikê* (Sathas 1894:311.5–6) also calls him the logothete of the drome John Doukas.

[36] See Michael Choniates' petition to Alexios III Angelos in Lampros 1879–1880, I:310.

[37] Polemis 1968:129. Karlin-Hayter (1972:264–265) favored identification with the *megas hetaireiarchês* John Doukas. Darrouzès (1971:63–65) preferred to leave the question open.

The family origins and career of Eustathios' student and patron allow us to approach from a different angle his introduction at a young age to the tradition of ancient geography and his subsequent request for an exegetical work. Members of the Kamateros family, his relatives, specialized in foreign diplomacy and served as ambassadors. His father Andronikos Kamateros took part in the delegation to the crusader principality of Antioch in 1161 that received Manuel I's new bride Mary, the daughter of Constance of Antioch and Raymond of Poitiers, and accompanied her on her journey to Constantinople.[38] Charged with formulating the official position in negotiations with the papacy and the Armenian church, Andronikos composed between 1172 and 1174 his influential polemical work, the *Sacred Arsenal*.[39] Andronikos' son and John's brother, Basil, was active in foreign affairs, even after his blinding. In around 1200 he went on an embassy to the German imperial court in Sicily. When he stopped in Athens, its archbishop Michael Choniates, Eustathios' student, welcomed him with an oration praising Basil's versatile abilities to negotiate with different foreign powers: Georgian, "Persian" (that is, Seljuk), "Islamic" (distinguished from the "Persians"), and German.[40] Basil was still active after the fall of Constantinople and was sent in around 1213 on an embassy to Cilician Armenia by the Nicaean emperor Theodore I Laskaris.[41] His brother John Doukas, if he was identical with the logothete of the drome of 1188–1190, was himself active in diplomatic dealings with the West. We may be reminded that one of the traditional duties of the logothete of the drome was to serve as a foreign minister, although in the twelfth century his functions pertained mainly to the imperial chancery.[42] Most strikingly, Eustathios himself appears to have been selected toward the end of his life to participate in an embassy to the Holy Land. According to a later Latin source, the bishop of Thessaloniki (namely, Eustathios) met with the English king Richard the Lionheart in Acre in 1191.[43]

Studies of world geography, thus, emerge as a welcome qualification for ambassadorial service in Byzantium in the late twelfth century. It is relevant to

---

[38] John Kinnamos in Meineke 1836:210. The historian John Kinnamos mentions here also an embassy by another Kamateros, the *akolouthos* Basil, during the negotiations leading to Manuel's marriage alliance. This Basil has been identified as the future patriarch Basil II Kamateros (1183–1186) by Loukaki 1996:29–36.

[39] Bucossi 2009:130.

[40] The oration is published by Lampros 1879–1880 I:312–323. The heading calls the addressee "the brother of the emperor's wife and logothete Basil Kamateros." The embassy is mentioned in Lampros 1879–1880 I:313, 323, and is discussed in Lampros 1879–1880 II:522. Lampros (1879–1880 II:520) dates the oration to about 1200, while Brand (1968:152) to around 1199.

[41] Van Dieten 1971:49, 181–186; Simpson 2013:29–30.

[42] Guilland 1971:31–38; Oikonomides 1976:131.

[43] Alberic of Trois Fontaines in Scheffer-Boichorst 1874:867.17–18; Lilie 1993:242n76; Angold 1995: 190 and n. 66.

add—and it is highly worth noting—that diplomatic missions by members of the educated Komnenian elite led in one case to the composition of a geographical travel account. A description of the Holy Land variously dated to the late 1170s and the 1180s, and traditionally ascribed to one John Phokas, has recently been reattributed to John Doukas. The coincidence with the name of the student of Eustathios is remarkable, but the author is likely to have been the *megas hetaireiarchês* John Doukas.[44] The account of Christian sites begins with a visit to Antioch and proceeds southwards with the description of port cities and the holy sites. It makes political statements, casting the emperor Manuel I as the Christian protector of the Holy Land, and displays marked literary features, such as ekphrastic passages (its very title is *ekphrasis*) and a reference to Achilles Tatius' novel *Leucippe and Clitophon* in the description of the port of Sidon.[45] This connection between geography and rhetoric is worth keeping in mind as we approach Eustathios' work.

Ancient Geography for a Constantinopolitan Audience

An anthology of Strabo, Herodotus, Homer, and others

Eustathios' choice of Dionysius Periegetes as a teaching text was in many ways natural. A pre-modern bestseller, the poem was the most copied ancient geographical text in the Greek Middle Ages and has come down to us in at least one hundred and thirty-four Byzantine and post-Byzantine manuscripts.[46] Two features made the poem suitable for classroom instruction. The first is its brevity: a dizzying account of lands, seas, and peoples, which is squeezed into 1186 hexameter verses. Dionysius opens the poem with a description of the oceans and their gulfs, moves to the continent of Libya (Africa), continues with Europe (starting with western Europe followed by Greece and islands of the Mediterranean, the Aegean, and the Black Sea) and the Oceanic islands, and ends with Asia, shifting rapidly the lens from the Scythians to Asia Minor, the Middle East, and eventually India. The second feature that made the poem welcome by pupils is its poetic form, which served as a mnemonic device and

---

[44] The Greek can be found in PG, vol. 133, cols. 927–961; for an English translation, see Wilkinson 1988:315–336. See Messis 2011 for the reattribution the work to John Doukas and the well-argued hypothesis (Messis 2011:148) that the *megas hetaireiarchês* composed the description after a diplomatic visit to Phoenicia, Palestine, and "Libya" in 1177 mentioned in Eustathios' panegyric of the *megas hetaireiarchês*. See the relevant passage in the English translation by Stone 2013:140–141.

[45] PG, vol. 133, col. 932D.

[46] The count is by Tsavari 1990:80–207. No less than eleven printed editions were made of Dionysius Periegetes in the sixteenth century. See Tsavari 1990:425–433.

made it a sequel to the study of Homer. The twelfth century marked a peak in the popularity of Dionysius Periegetes' poem. Quotations have been detected in a number of works.[47] Geographical terminology and toponyms derived from Dionysius Periegetes influenced twelfth-century authors. For example, they refer to the pillars of Dionysus as the eastern extreme of Asia, a notion deriving from the geographical poem—"a point in the far East where Dionysus, son of Thebes, has left his pillars by the utmost Ocean's stream"—and matching the mythical western pillars of Heracles (Gibraltar or Cádiz).[48] Another example is Aornis ("the birdless land"), an invention by Dionysius Periegetes, which allegedly was a tall mountain at the extremity of Indian Peninsula near the ocean. In his *History*, Niketas Choniates compares the citadel of Kerkyra with "the celebrated Aornis" and in the middle of the thirteenth century the Nicaean emperor Theodore II Laskaris considered Aornis to mark a faraway place lying on the exact opposite side of Britain in the inhibited world.[49]

While the choice of Dionysius as the basis for a commentary is hardly surprising, what Eustathios did is most unusual. The term "commentary" does little justice to his achievement. The word *parekbolai* contained in the title has a broader meaning than a commentary, referring to extracts from scholia as well as a compilation consisting of excerpts and annotations.[50] In the dedicatory letter to John Doukas, Eustathios explicitly notes that he was engaged in the double project of commenting and collecting. He designates his work as *hupomnêma*[51] and *hupomnêmantismos*,[52] words that signify "commentary" or "notes," but also describes it as a "collection of recorded saying" (*sôreia apomnêmôneumatôn*), namely, citations and testimonies that he gathered.[53] In this way Eustathios signals the resemblance of his work to the anthological tradition of textual assembly, for *apomnêmôneumata* is the title of the popular middle Byzantine florilegium of Pseudo-Maximos the Confessor traditionally known

---

[47]   Tsavari (1990:65–68), with reference to the *Etymologicum Magnum*, John Tzetzes's *Chiliads*, the *Lexikon* of Pseudo-Zonaras, the scholia on Lykophron's *Alexandra,* and an anonymous epitome of rhetoric.

[48]   Dionysius Periegetes, vv. 623–625. See Anna Komnene, *Alexiad* 6.11.3 (Reinsch and Kambylis 2001:193). On the usage of the term by John Tzetzes, Michael Italikos, and Niketas Choniates, see Lightfoot 2014:404. On the pillars of Heracles, see Lightfoot 2014:279.

[49]   Dionysius Periegetes, vv. 1141–1151; Niketas Choniates, *History*, in Van Dieten 1975:78.45–46: τὴν ᾀδομένην Ἄορνιν; Theodore Laskaris in Krikonis 1988: Laskaris, *Second Oration against the Latins*, in Krikonis 1988:139.85–140.92. See Lightfoot 2014:500.

[50]   See Kolovou (2011) on the *parekbolai* on the *Iliad*; LSJ s.v., παρεκβολή (p. 1334): "compilation of a set of critical remarks."

[51]   Müller 1861:205.33, 206.41, 207.26.

[52]   Müller 1861:205.26.

[53]   Müller 1861:207.26–27: φιλοίη ἂν καὶ τὸ παρὸν ὑπόμνημα καὶ τὴν τῶν ἐν αὐτῷ ἀπομνημονευμά-των σωρείαν.

as the *Loci Communes*.[54] Moreover, Eustathios created what is essentially a new work, one that is seven times longer than Dionysius' poem. His vision is truly authorial and authoritative. He selected verses from the poem, glossed upon the names of places and peoples by quoting verbatim or summarizing his sources, used his sources to make substantial digressions and additions, and inserted his own opinions. His interests lay in the mythological and historical origin of various terms, in etymology and spelling, in conflicts of opinion among ancient authors, and in curiosities of various kinds.

The outcome of these interests was a chain of informative entries and discussions that vary in length between a paragraph and few pages of the modern edition. Put into the language of literary theory, the entries function as extensive and elaborated paratexts in prose loosely linked with the verse hypotext of Dionysius. The entire work is best understood as an anthology, a term that Eric Cullhed has proposed for the *parekbolai* on the *Odyssey*, as well as a collection, whose entries are organized neither thematically nor alphabetically, but by following the structure of Dionysius' poem.[55] The methodology derives from the school tradition of scholia, but the end result comes close to the spirit of the Macedonian era of 'encyclopedism.' In this regard, it is significant that Eustathios copied and edited the tenth-century *Souda* lexicon in Cod. Marcianus gr. 448, a project that links him directly to an earlier and highly productive period of the creation of anthologies and collections.[56]

In the proem, Eustathios constructs an elaborate justification of the need for a detailed work. He invokes the regrettable brevity of Dionysius' poem, which has led him to unfold, fatten, and enlarge the ancient text, even if moderately and only on the basis of related sources.[57] The author stresses that he keeps close to Dionysius, who emerges as a consequence in a better light: Dionysius becomes "two-tongued" (*diglôssos*) and can now speak in verse as well as in prose.[58] Given the ambitious scope of the work, one discerns defensiveness on the part of Eustathios, something that can also be inferred from his readiness to attribute the initiative to his readers, including the insistent John Doukas. The curiosity of "eager listeners" and "lovers of learning" is said to have prompted the author to make additions to the poem.[59] Would not, Eustathios asks, the two brief verses devoted in the poem to the Boeotians, Locrians, Thessalians, and

---

[54] Ihm 2001:1. On the Byzantine florilegium tradition, including Pseudo-Maximos the Confessor, see Alexakis 2015.

[55] Cullhed 2016:4*.

[56] Maas 1935; Maas 1936:305–307; Wilson 1973:226–227; Gamillscheg 1981:385, 389–390.

[57] Müller 1861:205.9–16, 206.39–41: εἴ τι τούτοις ἑτέρωθέν ποθεν σύμφωνον ἢ κατὰ συγγένειαν σύντροφον.

[58] Müller 1861:205.5–9, 207.1–25.

[59] On the concept of the "eager reader" in Eustathios, see Pizzone 2016.

Macedonians arouse further interest? Would not the passing mention of the three continents (Africa, Europe, and Asia) kindle a desire for deeper inquiry about foreign lands and cities? [60]

The ambitious nature of Eustathios' collecting project is seen in the vast variety of his source material. He sometimes mentions the names of the authors excerpted. At other times he signals that he is conveying older views through the expressions "they say" and "according to the ancients." These two expressions are omnipresent—"they say" is used over three hundred times. It is the task of the future editor of the text to identify the sources behind these phrases, as well as the many occasions in which Eustathios cites his sources, including Strabo, without giving any indication that he is doing so. The explicitly mentioned sources include geographers (Strabo, called "the Geographer," Ptolemy cited far less than Strabo, and Eratosthenes), poets (Homer, called "the Poet," Lykophron, Pindar, Hesiod, Callimachus, and Oppian), historians (Herodotus, Arrian with his *Anabasis of Alexander* and other lost works, Xenophon, Dionysius of Halicarnassus, Cassius Dio, and Plutarch), Stephanus of Byzantium's geographical lexicon *Ethnika*, the philosophers Aristotle and Poseidonios, Athenaeus (called the "Deipnosophist"), the astronomer-poet Aratus, the grammarian Herodian, the lexicographer Pausanias, the playwright Aristophanes (called "the Comedian"), and the tragedians Aeschylus, Sophocles, and Euripides.

Eustathios derived material directly from manuscripts available in his large Constantinopolitan library, a veritable treasury of ancient texts. Philologists have shown that he had access to the full texts of Strabo's *Geography*, Homer, Herodotus' *Histories*, and Arrian's *Anabasis of Alexander*. A manuscript of Strabo heavily annotated by Eustathios, now lost, was the basis for the production of the so-called Vatican Epitome of Strabo.[61] On his desk Eustathios also had a number of manuscripts with Dionysius' poem, one of which contained a large-scale map (called *pinakographia tês periêgêseos* and *pinax tês kosmographias)*, for he complains that the map does not feature the Sporades islands in the Aegean in contrast to the inclusion of the Cyclades.[62] The scholia on Dionysius Periegetes served themselves as sources; they already contained explanations or additions drawn from ancient texts and gave Eustathios an impetus for further research in his library. His sources are almost all ancient, but there are exceptions. The seventh-century historian Theophylaktos Simokatta was used (as

---

[60] Müller 1861:205.32–33, 206.1–25.

[61] Groeger 1911:43–64. The Vatican Epitome of Strabo survives in Cod. Vaticanus gr. 482; it was copied in the circle of the thirteenth-century teacher and patriarch Gregory of Cyprus. See Diller 1975:61–62, 86–87; Leroy 2013:41–46.

[62] Tsavari 1990:61–65; Müller 1861:320.12–14, 320.37–39.

we will shortly see) for an ethnographic excursus on the Turks, who are never mentioned in Dionysius' text. When Eustathios comments on the location and name of Armenia, he quotes a legal text. This is the Novel 31 (*Basilika* 6.14.1) of the sixth-century emperor Justinian, which outlines the main cities of the newly created provinces of the First, Second, and Third Armenia.[63] Eustathios' sources are almost exclusively secular. Among the most rare exceptions is a quotation from the Psalms of "the wise king David."[64]

The ancient authors who are most invoked are Strabo ("the Geographer"), Homer ("the Poet"), and Herodotus. This distinguished trio has the effect of making Eustathios' anthology even more about cultural geography than Strabo—with plenty of entries on myth and history. Mentioned more than a hundred times as "the Geographer," Strabo is the author who exerted the strongest influence on Eustathios and was especially relied upon for the information about faraway places in Africa, India, and the Far East.[65] In the proem, Eustathios explains that Strabo is the true geographer, whereas Dionysius Periegetes came close to being a geographer, but was not one: his descriptive guide (*periêgêsis*) was related to geography as a genus to a species.[66] The dependence of Eustathios on Strabo is worth exploring in some detail, for it is central to the project of the Byzantine scholar. The dependence is often unstated. For example, when Eustathios mentions Alexander as a patron of geography who had amassed information about new places and peoples, he is silently referencing the second book of Strabo.[67] Strabo is sometimes introduced simply as the "ancients." When Eustathios remarks in the proem that the "ancients" had found geography useful to generals and rulers, he cites the first book of Strabo.[68] Eustathios derives material from scholia on Strabo in Byzantine manuscripts. According to Strabo, followed by Dionysius Periegetes, the Indian subcontinent had a rhomboid shape.[69] Eustathios felt the need to explicate the meaning of the geometrical shape and included a scholion on Strabo, which he presented as the words of the ancient geographer. He used the scholiastic tradition to draw a diagram illustrating the rhomboid shape of India. The diagram appears, with

---

[63] Müller 1861:341–342. The novel is wrongly attributed to Justinian I's uncle Justin I. The family relationship between Justin I and his nephew Justinian I, however, was well known to Eustathios. See Müller 1861:380.1–3.

[64] Müller 1861:338.18–19, with reference to Psalm 147.5.

[65] Pritchard 1934:64; Diller 1975:86–87. The total rises to over four hundred when the *parekbolai* on Homer are added.

[66] Müller 1861:212.

[67] Strabo, *Geography* 2.1.6; Müller 1861:211. Alexander is also said (Müller 1861:214) to have wished to describe the eastern ocean.

[68] Strabo, *Geography* 1.1.16; Müller 1861:214.30–38.

[69] Strabo, *Geography* 15.1.11; Dionysius, v. 1131.

different geometrical forms and legends, in Byzantine manuscripts of Strabo, in the ninth-century *Chrêstomathiai* (a selective paraphrase of all seventeen books of Strabo that has been attributed to the circle of Patriarch Photios), and in the Vatican epitome of Strabo[70] (figs. 1 and 2).

Eustathios approached Strabo with an ever-selective eye. Large sections of his anthological collection are a creative and critical synthesis between Strabo and other authors, with Eustathios putting their ideas into dialogue and advancing specific interpretations. A prominent example is his entry on the name and features of the European continent.[71] Eustathios begins by citing ancient authorities holding different opinions on the origin of the word "Europe": Lykophron, Arrian, Euripides, Hippias of Elis (a fragment known solely from this citation), and Herodotus. He remarks that, according to Lykophron, Europe bears the name of Europa, the daughter of Agenor of Tyre. Her son Sarpedon, Eustathios continues, is different from Sarpedon of Lycia, the hero who fought for the Trojans in the *Iliad*. He adds that the name Europe may derive, according to Hippias of Elis, from the sea nymphs Asia and Europa. Eustathios goes on to cite a well-known passage from Herodotus (*Histories* 4.45) about the three continents being named after mythical women: Libya (that is, Africa) was named after a local lady; Asia was the mother of Prometheus (his wife, according to Herodotus); and Europe was named after Europa from Tyre. Some people, Eustathios notes, did not like the derivation of "Europe" from a female character and attributed it to "some man called Europos." After commenting on matters of lexicography and morphology, Eustathios suddenly switches subjects and cites a view of the "ancients" lifted straight from the second book of Strabo (*Geography* 2.5.26), which extols Europe for its virtue and wealth, and glorifies the rise of Rome: "One should also know that the ancients say that Europe differs from Asia not only in the virtues of its men as well as in its wealth and agricultural products, but also in the rarity of wild animals." Eustathios' interest in the praise of Europe stands out in comparison with the ninth-century *Chrêstomathiai*, whose Byzantine author chose to paraphrase another passage from *Geography* 2.5.26 describing the shape of the continents: Europe is the continent "most diverse in form" (*poluskhêmonestatê*) and Libya (Africa) is the simplest, while Asia lies in the middle.[72] Eustathios paraphrased, too, this passage, but was also drawn to the ideologically charged statement of Europe as the continent cultivating virtue under Rome's domination. His selective lens here is worth keeping in mind, for we will soon see that it is closely

---

[70] Müller 1861:401.18–402.20. On the diagram and the scholion on Strabo, see Diller 1954:40–41.

[71] Müller 1861:264–265, commenting on Dionysius Periegetes, v. 270.

[72] For the relevant passage in the *Chrêstomathiai*, see Müller 1861:539; Radt 2010:252. On the question of its authorship, see Diller 1954:49–50.

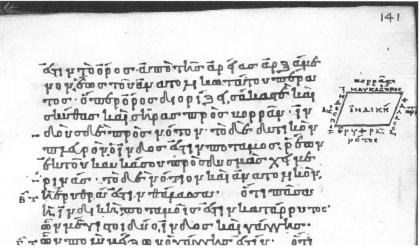

Fig. 1. Diagram of the shape of India drawn in the margin of the text of the *Chrêstomathiai* of Strabo, Universitätsbibliothek Heidelberg, Cod. Palat. gr. 398 (9th century), fol. 141r.
Source: https://doi.org/10.11588/diglit.303#0421

Fig. 2. Diagram of the shape of India embedded in Eustathios' geographical work, Cod. Vaticanus gr. 1910 (13th century), fol. 174v.

tied to his fascination with the past of Italy and Greece, and with his sense of the organic unity of the Greco-Roman world.

The entry on the Seres, that is, the Chinese, is another telling example of how Eustathios used information that he culled from Strabo, but this time in order to develop a point not found in the ancient geographer. Here Eustathios introduces Strabo—just as he does elsewhere—with the expression "they say," then quotes Strabo without an acknowledgment, and juxtaposes Strabo to other authors.[73] According to Dionysius (vv. 752–757), the Seres produced their fabric, one finer than a spider's web, by combing "the bright blooms of their lonely land." Eustathios was fascinated by this section. He notes that the Seres are Scythians and the textile called *sêrika* (the ancient and medieval Greek word for silk) has acquired its name from the Seres. After citing lines from Dionysius (vv. 754–756), he adds: "They say that flax (*bussos*) is collected from plants. But note that the Seres collect their fabrics from flowers." This statement is puzzling, not the least because Eustathios foregoes the fact well known by his times that silk was made from larvae of silkworms. His approach becomes more understandable, however, when we consider that here he is bringing Dionysius into dialogue with Strabo (*Geography* 15.1.20), who reports that the "Chinese fabric" (*sêrika*), namely silk, is scraped from the leaves of flax (*bussos*). Eustathios compares his sources and prefers the testimony of Dionysius on this occasion.

Curiously, he approaches the exotic Seres as an example of fair and honorable commercial practices. On the basis of a brief scholion on Dionysius dating back to an unknown time before the twelfth century, and without acknowledging the dependence, Eustathios switches the subject to describe a type of commerce known as silent trade.[74] The Seres are said (in the scholion and in Eustathios' work) to be "uncommunicative and unsociable people," which is reflected in their trading practices. They write down the sales price on bags with merchandise and withdraw from the location of the transaction, after which the foreign merchants come to inspect the goods, set the purchase price, and leave. The Seres either accept the deal upon returning or engage in bargaining in the same silent and polite manner until a deal is reached. Leaving this topic for a while, Eustathios digresses to quote verbatim a sentence filched from Strabo (*Geography* 15.1.37) about the reported longevity of the Seres: "They say that the Seres are very long-living, exceeding the age of two hundred years." Notably, here the phrase "they say" is already part of Strabo's text as an indicator of reported speech. Eustathios then returns to the subject of silent trade with faraway lands by adducing another example absent from the scholion. He notes that he has read in Herodotus about something similar happening "beyond the pillars of Hercules" and sums up the story about Carthaginian merchants sailing along the coast of Africa and conducting silent trade with the locals who paid them generously in gold (Herodotus, *Histories* 4.196). Eustathios offers a concluding thought: "Histories (*historiai*) tell that both the Carthaginians and the Seres are just (*dikaioi*) in commercial dealings."

---

[73] Müller 1861:348. For another example of a passage from Strabo being introduced with the expression "they say" without a reference to authorship, see the section on the pygmies (Müller 1861:226.2–5) based on Strabo, *Geography* 17.2.1.

[74] On the scholion, see Müller 1861:453.

The remark on fair trade had a special resonance in Constantinople in the 1170s. The Venetians, who had obtained the right to carry out duty-free commerce in the Byzantine Empire since the reign of Alexios I, were increasingly perceived as an alien minority that abused its privileges. In March 1171, when Eustathios already served as the "master of the rhetors," Manuel I broke relations with Venice and ordered its citizens to be arrested and their goods confiscated.[75] By focusing on the fair commercial practices of the Seres and the Carthaginians, Eustathios appears to have given his students an example useful for a rhetorical comparison and contrast with the Venetians. Eustathios' position as the chief teacher of rhetoric in Constantinople, as well as his special interest in the past of Venice analyzed in the next section, makes this interpretation particularly plausible.

Knowledge, rhetoric, and a twelfth-century vision of the Greco-Roman world

What principles did Eustathios follow in the selection of his sources and in the interpretations that he favored through the selection? What goals did he pursue when he composed his massive anthology? To begin to address these large and complex questions, we should start with Eustathios' own answers in the dedicatory epistle. He ascribes to his patron the following request:

> You know yourself that you have charged me with selecting the best parts from Dionysius' *Description*, as many as are capable of contributing to further knowledge, to an explanation needed, to the rhetorical eloquence of writing, and to the accumulation of experience, but it is necessary to expand and sometimes make additions to his work, because the text of Dionysius is very sketchy and thin in its descriptions.[76]

Whether John Doukas phrased his commission to Eustathios with these precise words is doubtful, but it is clear that Eustathios wished to project the goals of the *parekbolai* in this way and strove to legitimate them through the authoritative voice of his patron. Eustathios' understanding of his overall goals becomes clearer once we unpack what he means by the five mentioned agenda items: (1) "further knowledge," (2) "an explanation needed," (3) "the rhetorical eloquence

---

[75] Magdalino 1993:93–95.

[76] Müller 1861:204.4–11: Οἶδας οὖν καὶ αὐτὸς ὅπως ἐπιτάξας ἔσχες τὰ κάλλιστα τῆς τοῦ Διονυσίου περιηγήσεως ἀπανθίσαι σοι, ὅσα συντελεῖν ἔχει πρός τε ἄλλην γνῶσιν, καὶ πρὸς ἀνάπτυξιν δέουσαν, καὶ πρὸς ῥητορείαν γραφῆς, καὶ πρὸς ἐμπειρίας συναγωγήν, προσερανίσασθαι δὲ τοῖς ἐκείνου καὶ εἴ τι που ἄλλο προσεπιτεθῆναι χρεών, διὰ τὸ τοῦ Διονυσίου πάνυ ἐπελευστικὸν καὶ ἐν στενῷ περιηγήσεως κείμενον.

of writing," (4) "accumulation of experience," and (5) necessary "additions" to Dionysius' text.

The first two goals, "further knowledge" and "explanation needed," capture features of the *parekbolai* that we have already observed: a rich anthology that presents information unobtainable from the brief poem and that explicates its content. The cultivation of "rhetorical eloquence of writing" is hardly a surprising goal for the leading Constantinopolitan teacher of rhetoric, but it is one easy to miss. His massive collection of explanations and citations was a true godsend for Byzantine rhetoricians. The entries on ancient places and peoples could easily enter works of epideictic rhetoric (the rhetoric of display), such as Eustathios' own orations. The poem itself was useful for teaching rhetoric. In the proem, Eustathios calls attention to its commendable rhetorical features, such as use of fiction, figurative language, spontaneity, florid word choices, use of meter and dialect, and skillful insertion of "imperial encomia."[77] In the actual commentary, Eustathios highlights spontaneity and encomium, drawing attention, for example, to the use of a "brief imperial encomium" (*suntomon enkômion basilikon*) in a verse glorifying a Roman victory over the Parthians.[78] The targeting of contemporary rhetoricians as the audience is not unique to Eustathios' work on Dionysius. In his *parekbolai* on the *Iliad* he also recommended to rhetoricians specific ways of reusing Homeric verses and advertised himself in the proem as a master teacher of rhetoric.[79]

The goal described by Eustathios as "accumulation of experience" is most intriguing and raises further questions: Whose experience is the author collecting? How is empiricism in the way understood by Eustathios useful? At a basic level, this is the vast experience of the ancients summarized by Dionysius and reflected in the works of Strabo, Homer, Herodotus, and other authors. Eustathios distinguished between their time and his own, displaying a keen sense of historical awareness and sometimes engaging in historical source criticism. For example, when he comments on Dionysius' description of Rome as the "great homeland of my lords" (v. 355), he notes that the choice of the word for "lords" (*anaktes*) shows that the author lived under the emperors, for the consuls of the Roman republic were never called "lords."[80] He explains that Dionysius begins with the description of Africa, in contrast to Strabo, who starts with Europe, because he "preferred his own people over the rest."[81] Eustathios uses

---

[77] Müller 1861:213.26–214.17.

[78] The spontaneity of Dionysius' style: Müller 1861:331.33, 338.1–2, 346.22. The use of encomium: Müller 1861:254.21, 258.25, 259.5, 382.8–9. For the "brief imperial encomium," see Müller 1861:393.35–38, which comments on v. 1052 ("An Ausonian spear-tip chastened them").

[79] Nünlist 2012; Van den Berg 2017.

[80] Müller 1861:279.23–29.

[81] Müller 1861:219.1–7.

the temporal adverb "now" (*nun*) over twenty times in reference to new or still surviving ancient toponyms. Cape Karambis on the Black Sea is said to "preserve the antiquity of its name until today."[82] When Eustathios speaks of the Rhodope Mountains, he passingly mentions "the settlement now called Klokotnitza" lying in this area. This is one of the two earliest literary attestations, both in the twelfth century, of the place name in present-day Bulgaria.[83] Eustathios cares to explain a current term of administrative geography. "What now is called Thrakesion" (a reference to the Byzantine theme of Thrakesion in western Asia Minor) is said to derive its name from the Thracians who, according to Arrian's testimony cited by Eustathios, resided both in Europe and Asia.[84]

Sometimes Eustathios links—and historicizes in the process—contemporary ethnicities with peoples known from the ancient sources. One prominent example is the excursus on the people residing by the Caspian Sea who are called *Thunoi* by Dionysius (v. 730), an ethnonym, which, centuries later, Eustathios read as *Ounnoi* or *Thounoi*, that is, the Huns. Eustathios notes that the Huns are Scythians residing near the Caspian and proceeds to connect them with the Turks. He does so by summarizing a passage from the seventh-century historian Theophylaktos Simokatta, who reports that the Turks inhabited an area to the northeast of the Huns, acquired the name "Turks" from the Persians, and had a fabulous wealth allowing them to hammer out gold tables, thrones, and pedestals.[85] On another occasion, when he comments on the people north and south of the Danube River, Eustathios introduces several contemporary ethnonyms.[86] He inserts the Rus after the Tauri, the ancient population of the Crimea mentioned by Dionysius, and explains that the monstrous Hippopodes, or "Horse-Feet People" mentioned by Dionysius, are, "according to some," the same people as the Khazars. Eustathios' source is unclear and must have been an old one, for the Khazar confederation on the lower Volga was crushed in the tenth century, well before his time. We can be certain, however, that the scholion glossing the Pannonians as the Bulgars lay at the origin of Eustathios' note that "according to some the Pannonians are Bulgars."[87] This scholion must date back to the seventh century when a branch of the migrating Bulgars settled down in Pannonia.[88]

---

[82] Müller 1861:244.18–20.
[83] Müller 1861:269.12–13. The other earliest attestation of Klokotnitza is found in a letter by John Tzetzes (*Epistle* 19), Eustathios' fellow teacher and contemporary, addressed to its bishop. See Leone 1972:34–37. On the location, see Soustal 1991:310.
[84] Müller 1861:274.30–37.
[85] Müller 1861:345.15–27; Theophylaktos Simokatta, 3.6.9–11, in De Boor and Wirth 1972:121.11–23.
[86] Müller 1861:269.18–32, based on Dionysius Periegetes, vv. 302–329.
[87] Müller 1861:269.27–28, 444, based on Dionysius Periegetes, v. 322.
[88] Theophanes in De Boor 1883:357.24–25; Browning 1991. Interestingly, the Bulgars are mentioned alongside the Pannonians in the prose paraphrase of Dionysius, which indicates a *terminus post quem* for the latter text.

Some parts of Eustathios' work, then, served in the twelfth century as historical guides on contemporary ethnography. "Accumulation of experience" meant the gathering of knowledge from antiquity to explain the historical development of geographical and ethnographical vocabulary until his own day.

Eustathios wove together past and present also by refocusing the discussion on regions in which he and his readers were more interested. Thus, the necessary "additions" to Dionysius' poem, which Eustathios mentions in the dedicatory letter as part of his agenda, followed a logic dictated by the contemporary audience of students and scholars. Scrutinizing the proportion of text in Dionysius' poem and in Eustathios' anthology assigned to different parts of the world reveals an interesting pattern. Eustathios substantially expands the material on Greece, on the Greek, Mediterranean, and Black Sea Islands, and on Western Europe. Whereas Dionysius had allocated about one fourth of his poem to cover these areas, Eustathios devotes to them one third of his work.[89] The proportion of text on Asia Minor and the Pontos area remains roughly the same. The most marked reduction is the coverage of the Scythians, which seems to be the flipside of his increased focus on Europe and Greece. The figure of the barbarians, who rarely appear in Dionysius' poem, begins to feature more prominently in Eustathios.[90] Certain regions mentioned by Dionysius receive more detailed attention than others. Among them is the area around Constantinople, including the straits of the Bosporus and the Dardanelles.[91] As a Constantinopolitan, Eustathios was interested in the origin myths going back to Hesychios Illoustrios about Byzas, the eponymous founder of Byzantium, and about the renaming of the city to Antonina during the reign of Septimius Severus.[92] Particular attention is paid to the Hellenic past of the city, with the theory of the *translatio imperii* from Rome to Constantinople being conspicuously absent. We find legends about the Athenians depositing their wealth in Byzantium, the renaming of the city to Anthousa by Constantine (a curious confusion with the *tyche* of Constantinople by the same name), and the alcoholic addiction of the citizens of ancient Byzantium (a story borrowed from the comedian Menander and Philarchus through the intermediacy of Athenaeus).[93]

---

[89] The statistic is based on the following breakdown of the texts: Dionysius, vv. 270–398 (Western Europe and Italy), 399–446 (Greece), vv. 447–553 (Mediterranean, Greek and Black Sea islands); Eustathios in Müller 1861:264–290 (Western Europe and Italy), 290–302 (Greece), 302–325 (Mediterranean, Greek, and Black Sea islands).

[90] Lightfoot (2014:159–160) notes one sole occurrence of the word "barbarian" applied to the Seres in the poem.

[91] Müller 1861:240–242, 356–358.

[92] *Patria Constantinopolitana*, I, 1–7 and I, 36, in Berger 2013:2–6, 22.

[93] Müller 1861:357.2–25.

If the collection of material on the ancient history of the city of Byzantium is understandable, Eustathios' extensive focus on Western Europe, Italy in particular, is more puzzling. Eustathios displays interest in the Latin language and had access to a Latin lexicon. When he discusses the location and name of the Liburnian Islands in the Adriatic, he digresses to say that "it should be known that one can find in a Latin lexicon that the Liburnian ships are the long ones."[94] "Up until now," Eustathios points out, the Latins use *palation* (a Greek word of Latin origin) to refer to residences befitting kings.[95] Interestingly, the myth of the foundation of Rome preferred by Eustathios is that of an ancient Greek migration and settlement—a myth favored by Greek authors of the Roman era, such as Dionysius of Halicarnassus. Eustathios equates the Etruscans with the Pelasgians, the autochthonous people of Greece, and reports the story of an Arcadian migration headed by Evander who founded Pallantium on the future site of Rome. If Strabo's *Geography* is among Eustathios' sources here, it is notable that the Byzantine author keeps silent about the rival story of Aeneas which Strabo gives alongside that of the Arcadian migration.[96] Longer than the section on the ancient history of Rome is that on Venice occasioned by the passing mention of Aquileia in Dionysius' poem. Eustathios refers to Venice by its contemporary name. Under the influence of Strabo (*Geography* 5.1.4–5) and Arrian, he speculates about the origins of the Enetoi, the ancient ancestors of the Venetians, who were either Paphlagonian migrants after the Trojan War or a Celtic tribe, and cites verbatim a passage from Strabo on the canal projects similar to those in lower Egypt.[97] The section on Venice is hardly incidental, given the empire's current relations with the Italian maritime republic and Eustathios' own interest in Venice stimulated by firsthand observations of Venetians resident in Constantinople. Thus, in a sermon to the Thessalonians, Eustathios presented the Venetian constitution as a mixture between a monarchy, aristocracy, and democracy.[98]

Eustathios leaves the distinct impression of advocating a culturally interconnected and integrated Greco-Roman world, in which the older culture, Greece, played the foundational role. This mental outlook explains the decision to expand the sections of his geographical anthology devoted to Greece and the European continent, as well as his choice to include Strabo's praise on the virtue and wealth of Europe (*Geography* 2.5.26) and to give prominence to the concept of the barbarians. His vision of the Greco-Roman world is notable for

---

[94] Müller 1861:289.8–10.
[95] Müller 1861:278.19–21.
[96] Müller 1861:278.9–19; Strabo, *Geography* 5.3.2–3.
[97] Müller 1861:286.31–288.12.
[98] PG, vol. 136, col. 717. For an analysis, see Magdalino 1983:334–335.

its Hellenism and the role assigned to the Greeks in the foundation of Rome. Constantinople is compared not to Rome, but to Athens. "Constantinople today is the city (*polis*) is par excellence," remarks Eustathios at one point, "just as Athens once upon time was the city (*astu*) par excellence."[99] Elsewhere he comments, as we saw, on the Athenians having deposited their treasury in ancient Byzantium. The focus on Greece is explicable with the figure of the author as an erudite classical Hellenist and the general revival of Hellenism in the twelfth century, but also with the political realities of his time.[100] After the loss of most of Asia Minor to the Turks, the Byzantine state became more centered on the European provinces. Greece and the Balkans were the places where Eustathios and members of his circle (such as Michael Choniates) ended their careers as provincial bishops. And yet, in Eustathios' imagined cultural geography, the Latin world—both past and contemporary—formed an integral part of the common matrix of Greco-Roman culture. In the same vein, Eustathios' *parekbolai* on the *Odyssey* present the contemporary Latins as heirs to the clothing, hairstyle, and customs of the ancient Achaeans, no matter how alien these daily practices of the westerners looked in Byzantine eyes during the twelfth century.[101] An oppositional perspective was soon to take hold in the Greek-speaking eastern Mediterranean, according to which the militant Latins of the Fourth Crusade were the avenging Trojans. Eustathios' inclusive and nonconfrontational outlook was very different.

A monumental work of scholarship, Eustathios' *parekbolai* on Dionysius Periegetes defies genre classification. It is a creative compilation and an interpretative anthology devoted to physical and cultural geography, ethnography, history, and myth, with a focus on antiquity and with vignettes of Eustathios' own time. Eustathios wished school audiences to gain a profound knowledge of cities, islands, rivers, regions, and peoples known in and since antiquity, but also the erudition and skills to hone their oratorical eloquence. His project was as much scholarly as utilitarian—and not only because it served educational needs. The knowledge it provided was real and practical. Eustathios and his contemporaries were still surrounded by the rivers, seas, and islands well known and amply described in antiquity. Many place names were still the same. Ancient ethnography traditionally shaped the literary representation of foreign peoples in Byzantium, and was also the basis for understanding any subsequent change. The practical orientation of Eustathios' work emerges also from the figure of his addressee and student, the *epi tôn deêseôn* (ca. 1178), eparch of Constantinople (1181), and probably logothete of the drome

---

[99] Müller 1861:261.35–37.
[100] On the revival of Hellenism in the twelfth century, see Kaldellis 2007:225–316.
[101] See Cullhed 2017:293–294 for a translation of a long and fascinating passage.

(1188–1190), John Doukas. Eustathios' powerful patron came from a family of diplomats, who based and developed their knowledge of the contemporary, conflict-ridden world of the twelfth century on classical foundations. After all, the coexistence of ancient and current geographical and ethnographical vocabulary was a characteristic Byzantine phenomenon and a byproduct of the Byzantine educational system.

Eustathios' work lacks a single master plan and points in different directions. It can be called a work of systematization insofar as the Byzantine scholar adhered, whether consciously or unconsciously, to principles of selection and interpretation. Future research, it is hoped, can make additions to those few Eustathian epistemic methods that we have detected. The following three deserve to be restated by way of conclusion. First, Eustathios selected and presented evidence that reaffirmed the idea of a coherent Greco-Roman culture and redirected the attention of readers to the fundamental role played by ancient Greece. Second, he laid out and interpreted the material in ways that taught his audience morally didactic and rhetorically useful lessons. Third, he focused on open-ended debates among the ancient authorities and thus stimulated further interest in geography and in exploration. In this regard, Eustathios' discussion of disagreements regarding the sources of the Caspian Sea, with which we started, was integral to his agenda. The sense of critical distance and humility is truly remarkable for a work of this magnitude. Eustathios was guided by the enlightened idea that the rearrangement and re-systematization of old texts furthered the advancement of new knowledge. Embedded in Byzantine intellectual culture, his work is oddly forward-looking and beckons to early modern humanist projects of the management and repurposing of large bodies of received knowledge.

Works Cited

Abbreviations

LSJ = H. G. Liddell and R. Scott, *A Greek–English Lexicon*. Revised by H. S. Jones. With the assistance of R. McKenzie. 9th edition. Oxford, 1996.

PG = J. P. Migne, *Patrologiae cursus completus, series graeca*. 161 vols. Paris, 1857–1866.

Primary Sources

Berger, A. 2013. *Accounts of Medieval Constantinople: The Patria*. Cambridge, MA.

Bernhardy, G. 1828. *Dionysius Periegetes Graece et Latine cum vetustis commentariis et interpretationibus ex recensione et cum annotatione*. Leipzig.

Chroust, A. 1928. *Quellen zur Geschichte des Kreuzzuges Kaiser Friedrichs I.* Monumenta Germaniae Historica. Scriptores rerum Germanicarum. Nova series, 5. Berlin.

Cullhed, E. 2016. *Eustathios of Thessalonike. Commentary on Homer's Odyssey, I. On Rhapsodies A–B.* Uppsala.

Darrouzès, J. 1970. *Georges et Dèmètrios Tornikès. Lettres et discours.* Paris.

De Boor, C. 1883. *Theophanis chronographia*, vol. 1. Leipzig.

De Boor, C., and P. Wirth. 1972. *Theophylacti Simocattae historiae.* Leipzig.

Ihm, S. 2001. *Ps.-Maximus Confessor: Erste kritische Edition einer Redaktion des sacro-profanen Florilegiums Loci communes, nebst einer vollständigen Kollation einer zweiten Redaktion und weiterem Material.* Stuttgart.

Krikonis, C. 1988. *Θεοδώρου Β´ Λασκάρεως περὶ χριστιανικῆς θεολογίας λόγοι.* Thessaloniki.

Kolovou, F. 2006. *Die Briefe des Eustathios von Thessalonike.* Munich and Leipzig.

Lampros, Sp. 1879–1880. *Μιχαὴλ Ἀκομινάτου τοῦ Χωνιάτου τὰ σωζόμενα.* 2 vols. Athens.

Leone, P. 1972. *Ioannes Tzetzes. Epistulae.* Leipzig.

Lightfoot, J. L. 2014. *Dionysius Periegetes,* Description of the Known World, *with Introduction, Text, Translation, and Commentary.* Oxford.

Loukaki, M. 1996. *Grégoire Antiochos. Éloge du patriarche Basile II Kamatèros.* Paris.

Meineke, A. 1836. *Ioannis Cinnami epitome rerum ab Ioanne et Alexio Comnenis gestarum.* Bonn.

Melville Jones, J. 1988. *Eustathios of Thessaloniki. The Capture of Thessaloniki.* Canberra.

Miklosich, F., and J. Müller. 1865. *Acta et diplomata graeca medii aevi sacra et profana,* vol. 3. Vienna.

Müller, G. 1861. *Geographi graeci minores*, vol. 2. Paris.

Radt, S. L. 2010. *Strabons Geographika: Mit Übersetzung und Kommentar*, vol. 9: *Epitome und Chrestomathie.* Göttingen.

Reinsch, D., and A. Kambylis. 2001. *Annae Comnenae Alexias.* 2 vols. Berlin.

Sathas, K. 1894. *Μεσαιωνικὴ Βιβλιοθήκη*, vol. 7. Venice.

Scheffer-Boichorst, P. 1874. *Chronica Albrici monachi Trium Fontium.* Monumenta Germaniae Historica, SS. vol. 23. Hannover. 631–950.

Stone, A. 2013. *Eustathios of Thessaloniki: Secular Orations 1167/8 to 1179.* Leiden.

Wilkinson, J. 1988. *Jerusalem Pilgrimage, 1099–1185.* London.

Van der Valk, M. 1971. *Eustathii Archiepiscopi Thessalonicensis Commentarii ad Homeri Iliadem pertinentes ad fidem codici Laurntiani editi*, vol. 1. Leiden.

Van Dieten, J.-L. 1975. *Nicetae Choniatae Historia.* Berlin.

Secondary Sources

Alexakis, A. 2015. "Byzantine Florilegia." In Parry 2015:15–50.

Angelov, D. 2013. "'Asia and Europe Commonly Called East and West': Constantinople and Geographical Imagination in Byzantium." In Bazzaz, Batsaki, and Angelov 2013:43–68.

Angold, M. 1995. *Church and Society in Byzantium under the Comneni, 1081-1261.* Cambridge.

Bazzaz, P., Y. Batsaki, and D. Angelov, eds. 2013. *Imperial Geographies in Byzantine and Ottoman Space.* Hellenic Studies 56. Cambridge, MA.

Brand, C. 1968. *Byzantium Confronts the West, 1180-1204.* Cambridge, MA.

Browning, R. 1962. "The Patriarchal School at Constantinople in the Twelfth Century." *Byzantion* 32:167–202.

———. 1991. "Bulgars, Turkic." In Kazhdan 1991a, vol. 1:338.

Bucossi, A. 2009. "New Historical Evidence for the Dating of the *Sacred Arsenal* by Andronikos Kamateros." *Revue des études byzantines* 67:111–130.

Cacciatore, P. V., ed. 2003. *L'erudizione scolastico-grammaticale a Bisanzio.* Naples.

Cassella, P. 2003. "Sul commentario di Eustazio a Dionigi Periegeta." In Cacciatore 2003:27–36.

Cullhed, E. 2017. "Achaeans on Crusade." In Pontani, Katsaros, and Sarris 2017: 285–297.

Diller, A. 1954. "The Scholia on Strabo." *Traditio* 10:29–50.

———. 1975. *The Textual Tradition of Strabo's Geography.* Amsterdam.

Gamillscheg, E. 1981. "Autoren und Kopisten: Bemerkungen zu Autographen byzantinischer Autoren." *Jahrbuch der Österreichischen Byzantinistik* 31: 379–394.

Groeger, I. 1911. *Questiones Eustathianae. In codicibus Strabonis, Herodoti, Arriani ab Eustathio in commentario ad Dionysii periegesin usurpatis.* Trebnitz.

Guilland, R. 1971. "Les Logothètes: Études sur l'histoire administrative de l'Empire byzantin." *Revue des études byzantines* 29:5–115.

Hunger, H. 1978. *Die hochsprachliche profane Literatur der Byzantiner.* 2 vols. Munich.

Johnson, S. 2010. "Apostolic Geography: The Origins and Continuity of a Hagiographic Habit." *Dumbarton Oaks Papers* 64:5–25.

Kaldellis, A. 2007. *Hellenism in Byzantium: The Transformations of Greek Identity and the Reception of Classical Tradition.* Cambridge.

Karlin-Hayter, P. 1972. "Jean Doukas." *Byzantion* 42:259–265.

Kazhdan, A. 1969. "John Doukas: An Attempt of De-Identification." *Le parole e le idee* 11:242–247.

———, ed. 1991a. *Oxford Dictionary of Byzantium.* 3 vols. Oxford.

———. 1991b. "Kamateros, John." In Kazhdan 1991a, vol. 2:1098.

Kazhdan, A., and S. Franklin. 1984. *Studies on Byzantine Literature of the Eleventh and Twelfth Centuries.* Cambridge.

Kolovou G. 2011. "La réécriture des scholies homériques dans les *Parekbolai* sur l'*Iliade* d'Eustathe de Thessalonique." In Marjanović-Dušanić and Flusin 2011:149–162.

Kuhn, F. 1889. "Quo ordine et quibus temporibus Eustathius commentarios suos composuerit." In *Commentationes in honorem Guilelmi Studemund*, 249–257. Strasbourg.

Laurent, V. 1931. "Un sceau inédit du protonotaire Basile Kamatéros." *Byzantion* 6:253–272.

Leroy, P.-O. 2013. "Deux manuscrits vaticans de la *Géographie* de Strabon et leur place dans le *stemma codicum*." *Revue d'histoire des textes* 8:37–60.

Lilie, R.-J. 1993. *Byzantium and the Crusader States, 1096–1204.* Oxford.

Maas, P. 1935. "Eustathios als Konjekturalkritiker." *Byzantinische Zeitschrift* 35:299–307.

———. 1936. "Eustathios als Konjekturalkritiker." *Byzantinische Zeitschrift* 36:27–31.

Magdalino, P. 1983. "Aspects of Twelfth-Century Byzantine *Kaiserkritik*." *Speculum* 58:326–346.

———. 1993. *The Empire of Manuel I Komnenos, 1143–1180.* Cambridge.

Marjanović-Dušanić, S., and B. Flusin, eds. 2011. *Remanier, métaphraser: Fonctions et techniques de la réécriture dans le monde byzantin.* Belgrade.

Merianos, G. 2008. *Οικονομικές ιδέες στο Βυζάντιο τον 12ο αιώνα: Οι περί οικονομίας απόψεις του Ευσταθίου Θεσσαλονίκης.* Athens.

Messis, Ch. 2011. "Littérature, voyage et politique au XIIe siècle: l'*Ekphrasis des lieux saints* de Jean 'Phokas'." *Byzantinoslavica* 59:126–146.

Nünlist, R. 2012. "Homer as a Blueprint for Speechwriters: Eustathius' Commentaries and Rhetoric." *Greek, Roman, and Byzantine Studies* 52:493–509.

Oikonomides, N. 1976. "L'évolution de l'organisation administrative de l'empire byzantin au XIe siècle (1025–1118)." *Travaux et mémoires* 6:125–152.

Parry, K., ed. 2015. *The Wiley Blackwell Companion to Patristics.* Chichester.

Pérez Martín, I. 2022. "Geography at School: Eustathios of Thessalonike's *Parekbolai on Dionysius Periegetes*." In Van den Berg, Manolova, and Marciniak 2022:194–213.

Pizzone, A. 2016. "Audiences and Emotions in Eustathios of Thessalonike's Commentaries on Homer." *Dumbarton Oaks Papers* 70:225–244.

Polemis, D. 1968. *The Doukai: Contribution to Byzantine Prosopography.* London.

Pontani, F., V. Katsaros, and V. Sarris, eds. 2017. *Reading Eustathios of Thessalonike.* Berlin.

Pritchard, J. P. 1934. "Fragments of the Geography of Strabo in the Commentaries of Eustathius." *Classical Philology* 29:63–65.

Schönauer, S. 2004. "Eustathios von Thessalonike—ein 'fahrender Scholiast'?" *Byzantinische Zeitschrift* 97:143–151.

Simpson, A. 2013. *Niketas Choniates: A Historiographical Study*. Oxford.

Stone, A. 1999. "The 'Grand Hetaireiarch' John Doukas: The Career of a Twelfth-Century Soldier and Diplomat." *Byzantion* 69:145–164.

Soustal, P. 1991. *Thrakien*. Tabula Imperii Byzantini 6. Vienna.

Tsavari, I. 1990. *Histoire du text de la description de la terre de Denys le Périégète*. Ioannina.

Wilson, N. 1973. "Three Byzantine Scribes." *Greek, Roman, and Byzantine Studies* 14:223–228.

Van den Berg, B. 2017. "The Wise Homer and His Erudite Commentator: Eustathios' Imagery in the Proem of the *Parekbolai* on the *Iliad*." *Byzantine and Modern Greek Studies* 41:30–44.

Van den Berg, B., D. Manlova, and P. Marciniak, eds. 2022. *Byzantine Commentaries on Ancient Greek Texts, Twelfth–Fifteenth Centuries*. Cambridge.

Van Dieten, J.-L. 1971. *Niketas Choniates: Erläuterungen zu den Reden und Briefen nebst einer Biographie*. Berlin.

2

The Lands of the *Rhômaíoi*

Imagined Geographies in Byzantium before and after 1204

Yannis Stouraitis

MY MODEST AIM IN THIS CHAPTER, to show how the lands of the community we call Byzantine were imagined in the thought-world of the ruling elite, needs to start with a stereotypical 'decolonizing' statement. The so-called Byzantines were self-designated as *Rhômaíoi* (that is, Romans) and their empire was the Empire of the Romans, whose unbroken continuity from the times of Caesar and Augustus they professed.[1] This means that exploring 'Byzantine' imageries of the Roman lands is actually about exploring the evolution of Roman imagery of an imperial geopolitical and cultural space in the Middle Ages.

Based on this, my aim in what follows is twofold. In the first part of the chapter, I will attempt an overview of visions of territoriality before the late twelfth century in order to scrutinize the extent to which the Constantinopolitan ruling elite continued to adhere to the traditional Roman vision of a territorial empire in the High Middle Ages—an empire whose limits were constantly fluctuating and, therefore, remained indefinite in ideological terms. In the second part, I will focus on the transitional period from the late twelfth to the late thirteenth century, seeking to answer whether the centralized imperial order's disintegration in 1204 caused a major shift in the way the Roman lands were imagined.

Imagining the Roman Lands in the Early and High Middle Ages

Modern national communities and nation states are distinguished by the fact that they are imagined in a finite manner, both in political-cultural and

---

[1] On the Oriental aspects of the term Byzantine, see Cameron 2003; Angelov 2003; Marciniak 2018; Stouraitis 2022.

territorial terms. In the famous words of Benedict Anderson, no nation imagines itself as coterminous with mankind and, as a result of that, no national homeland can be imagined as infinite.[2] Contrary to this, in the Roman imperial worldview the notion of a finite homeland (*patria*) of the Romans was bound to the city-state of Rome and, after the empire's translation from the West to the East in the course of Late Antiquity, to Constantinople as the New Rome.[3] Beyond the walls of the Roman city-state lay the Roman lands, which were circumscribed by the—at any time—current limits of enforceable imperial authority and, therefore, could be imagined as infinite with regard to their potential extension. An insight into the Roman notion of a territorially fluctuating and infinite imperial political community in Late Antiquity is provided by the early fifth-century historical work of Eunapius:

> It was clear to all that if the Roman imperial power rejected luxury and embraced war, it would conquer and enslave all the world ... while they have all means with which to unite mankind and turn it into a single polity [*politeia*], our Emperors in their concern for the transient turn to pleasure without taking into account and showing interest in the immortality of glory.[4]

Irrespective of the utopian character of a such a statement in the context of the contemporary geopolitical status quo, its connotations with regard to geopolitical imagery are clear: the territory of the *politeia*, the political community under centralized imperial rule, could be imagined as encompassing the whole known world. *Rhômaíôn politeia* is one of the terms Greek-speaking authors used to denote the imperial order as a political-territorial entity. Other terms were *Rhômaíôn* or *rhômaikê archê*, *basileía*, or *hêgemonía*, *Rhômaíôn horia*, *hórois*, *gê*, or *Rhômanía*, and *Rhômaís*. As will become evident in what follows, these terms were used interchangeably to denote a territorial empire, that is, a geographical space whose Roman identity in present or past times was determined by its present or past status of subordination to the Roman imperial authority of Rome or Constantinople, respectively.

In order to better understand how the established late antique Roman notion of the Roman lands as the fluctuating territory of imperial authority was translated in medieval East Roman imaginary, one needs to consider the Constantinopolitan ruling elite's perception of the concept of *translatio imperii*

---

[2]   Anderson 2006:7.
[3]   Magdalino 2005:107–108; on the making of Constantinople into an imperial capital and New Rome, see Dagron 1974.
[4]   Eunapius, *Fragmenta*, 251.3–15.

from the old to the new Rome. A number of Byzantine texts written from the tenth century onwards, such as geopolitical treatises, world chronicles, and histories, propagated implicitly or explicitly the notion that the Roman *imperium* had ultimately crossed from Rome to Constantinople in the late fifth century.[5]

An explicit statement can be found in the late twelfth century history of John Kinnamos, a court official under emperor Manuel I Komnenos (1143–1180). The author claimed that the title of empire had disappeared in Rome a long time back, since the time of Augustulus. From that time onward, only barbarians had ruled over Rome with the exception of the short period of Justinian's reconquest. Therefore, a ruler of Rome in his own times could have no claim to the Roman imperial heritage despite being acclaimed as such by the pope. The only true Roman emperor was the emperor of Constantinople.[6]

In the mid-tenth century, Constantine VII (944–959) also alluded to the irreversible *translatio imperii* from Rome to Constantinople after the late fifth century, while emphasizing Constantinople's role as the reigning city of the whole world.[7] The notion that there could be only one Roman emperor in the world after late fifth century, whose seat was in Constantinople, was interrelated with the vision of the Roman lands in medieval East Roman imaginary. The exclusive claim to the Roman imperial heritage underpinned Constantinople's image as New Rome and the *patria* of the *Rhômaîoi*. This, in turn, made the city not simply the ruling center of the contemporary Roman Empire but of the whole world in the Middle Ages from a Byzantine viewpoint.[8] Thus, Constantinople could function as the main point of reference wherefrom the image of Roman lands could unfold, with regard to both current and past boundaries of imperial authority.[9]

A number of different kinds of sources testify to this. In the seventh-century text called *Doctrina Jacobi*, a product of a provincial author from North Africa, reference was made to the current territorial contraction of the Roman Empire (*Rhômanía*) whose old boundaries were still visible by the physical markers of imperial authority, namely the marble and bronze monuments of the Roman emperors.[10] The image of the *Rhômanía* as a space circumscribed by the emperor's enforceable authority is reaffirmed in the ninth-century collective

5   Cf. Stouraitis 2017:72.
6   John Kinnamos, *Epitome*, 218–219; trans. Brand 1976:165–166. Cf. the twelfth chronicle of Michael Glykas for a similar view, Glykas, *Annales*, 489–490.
7   Constantine Porphyrogenitus, *De thematibus*, 84; on the concept of *translatio imperii* in Constantine VII's treatises, see Stouraitis 2021:237–241.
8   Hunger 1965, esp. chapter 1; Magdalino 2005; Angelov 2013:52–64.
9   Koder 2002:18–19; Dagron 2005: Cf. the arguments on the notion of empire being bound to Constantinople in Gaul 2018:3–4.
10   *Doctrina Jacobi* III, 10 (169).

martyrion of the 42 Martyrs of Amorion, written in Constantinople, where the author stated that the current territorial extension of the Roman Empire (*Rhômanía*) was the result of the contraction of imperial rule during the seventh century, a development he attributed to the heretical beliefs of the emperors of that time.[11] This twofold image of present and past Roman lands is depicted in a full-blown manner in the treatises of emperor Constantine VII (944–959) and the eleventh-century provincial magnate Kekaumenos.

In the geographical treatise *De thematibus*, Constantine VII referred to past times when Julius Caesar, Augustus, Trajan, Constantine I, and Theodosius ruled by the force of arms over an empire that encompassed nearly the whole Oecumene (i.e. the civilized world).[12] He went on to remark that afterwards, the Roman Empire (*Rhômaîôn basileía*) had been contracted in East and West, and had been mutilated since the reign of Heraclius and those that succeeded him.[13] Kekaumenos testifies to the pervasiveness of this territorial perception of Roman lands in provincial elite society. His treatise contained advice to the emperor regarding how to best protect the interests of the Roman empire (*Rhômania*) at the current time. However, Kekaumenos makes also a reference to the lands that were subject to the Romans in the past, since the time of Constantine the Great, which included the entire Mediterranean and the Near East:

> The sovereigns and augusti of the Romans had entirely the same arrangement that I am telling you about—not only those who ruled in Rome, but also those in Byzantium: Constantine the great, and his son, Constantius, Julian, Jovian, and Theodosius. They spent their time sometimes in the East, sometimes in the West, but little of it in Byzantium. And, at that time, all the lands were peaceful; and all Europe, and Libya, and the loveliest part of Asia, as far as the Euphrates area, and the land of the Adiabeni, Armenia together with Syria, Phoenicia, Palestine, Egypt, and the great and far-famed Babylon itself, were subject to the Romans.[14]

The established view of a fluctuating imperial territory that had been much larger in the past provided the background against which Constantine VII could refer to the "changes that had taken place within the limits of the current imperial realm (*politeia*) and those that had occurred within the Roman Empire (*Rhômaîôn archê*) in different times" in his other political treatise, the *De*

---

[11] Evodius, *Vita martyrum* XLII Amoriensum, 63, 75.
[12] On Byzantine perceptions of the Oecumene, see Koder 2002.
[13] Constantine Porphyrogenitus, *De thematibus* 60.17–25.
[14] Kekaumenos, *Concilia et Narrationes* 104.8–19.

administrando imperio.[15] The terms *politeía* and *archê* seem to acquire a territorial dimension here, with the former alluding to current boundaries of imperial authority and the latter to their extension in past times.[16]

The nuanced notion of a present contracted Roman territory and of a past larger territorial empire provided the ideological point of departure for the medieval East Roman power elite to reimagine the potential territorial expansion of the empire in current times. Leo VI, the father and predecessor of Constantine VII, stated in his military treatise *Tactica* that the Saracens bordered on his state (*politeia*) and harmed his subjects (*to hypêkoon*).[17] This perception of current Roman territory ending in the East, where the emperor's enforceable authority stopped and the Caliph's enforceable authority began, was complemented by a historical image of lost Roman lands. In a sermon held at the imperial court, the bishop Arethas addressed the emperor's military policies on the eastern frontier and stated that the conquest of cities under Muslim rule there was justified on the grounds that the emperor did not claim what was not his own, but what had been under the Roman iron rod in the past.[18]

The notion that the contemporary Roman lands could be enlarged by expanding the current boundaries of imperial rule through means of war is presented in a full-blown manner in the mid-tenth-century historical account of Theophanes Continuatus. The author recounted the actions of the Roman general John Kourkouas in the reign of Romanos Lekapenos (920–944) and stated that the general had conquered numerous cities and regions, and places of the Hagarenes, thus doubling the *Rhômanía* which before this time was occupied by the deniers of Christ up to the castle of Charsianon, the Hyspsêlê, and the river Halys. The faithful and great *domestikos tôn scholôn* under emperor Romanos had expanded the Roman boundaries as far as the Euphrates and the Tigris, bringing gifts and a dowry to the Roman Empire (*Rhômanía*).[19] Such statements testify to the situational identity of territories in contemporary geopolitical East Roman imaginary; a situational character conditioned by the fluctuation of the borders of imperial authority, Roman or Muslim, respectively. What was viewed as Muslim (*Hagarene*) lands in the time before Kourkouas began his conquests, had become Roman lands (*Rhômanía*) by the time the author was recounting the achievements of a Roman general, that is, within roughly three decades.

---

[15] Constantine Porphyrogenitus, *De administrando imperio*, Proem 22–24.
[16] On different interpretations of this passage see Sode 1994:160–161; Magdalino 2013:39; cf. the relevant comments in Stouraitis 2017:73.
[17] Leonis VI, *Tactica* XVIII.135 (488, 690–692).
[18] Arethas, *Scripta Minora* II 62.33.14–15.
[19] Theophanes Continuatus, 426–427.

The situational identity of territories becomes further evident if we take a closer look at the fluctuating image of Roman lands in the Balkans as well. In the late sixth century, when the Balkan peninsula was still under Roman imperial authority, Roman subjects living in the city of Sirmion close to the Danube frontier could invoke God's help on behalf of the Roman Empire (*Rhômanía*) against the raids of Avars and Slavs.[20] Within half a century, these territories had lost their Roman identity due to the fact that they were now outside the boundaries of Constantinopolitan imperial authority. By the early tenth century, the established view of the largest part of the northern Balkan peninsula was that these were Bulgarian lands due to the large territorial expansion of Bulgarian rule under Tsar Symeon, whose state's boundary lay north of Thessalonike.

In the imaginary of members of the imperial court, however, what was currently viewed as the land of the Bulgarians could also be viewed as part of a historical Roman Empire. The court official Theodore Daphnopates was keen to remind Tsar Symeon of this in their diplomatic correspondence in the face of the latter's attacks on imperial soil. Speaking on behalf of the Roman imperial power, he stated that the Romans had not become accustomed to the fact that the Bulgarians occupied their own lands and that they blamed the emperors of the past for allowing them to settle on them.[21] The contrast between a contemporary situational and a historical essential view of what constituted Roman and Bulgarian lands, respectively, becomes evident in eleventh-century accounts as well. John Skylitzes reported that Basil II conducted yearly raids in the lands of the Bulgarians, based on the contemporary image of Roman and Bulgarian lands as circumscribed by current boundaries of political authority.[22] After the subjugation of the Bulgarian kingdom in 1018, however, the emperor could declare that, by subjugating the Bulgarian lands, he had brought back to the empire a part of it that had been recently separated.[23] The lands of the Bulgarians could be imagined now as a province of the Roman Empire, that is, as Roman territory again.

Within this framework, when the Roman bishop of Bulgaria Theophylact of Ohrid wrote the life of St Clemens of Ohrid in the late eleventh century, he could imagine the lands of the Bulgarians as part of the Roman Empire. Therefore, he was able to marginalize the geopolitical distinction between Bulgarian territory in the north and Roman territory in the south of the peninsula during the lifetime of the saint (early tenth century), opting to distinguish instead between the land of the *Boulgaroi* (Bulgarians) and the land of the *Graikoi* (Greeks) in his

---

[20] Noll 1989:145–148.
[21] Theodoros Daphnopates, *Letter* 65.121–124.
[22] Skylitzes, *Synopsis*, 348.
[23] Gelzer, *Bistumsverzeichnisse*, 44.

account.[24] Given that by Greeks he means Greek-speaking Romans in this case, the bishop's choice of identity discourse needs to be related to the viewpoint of his own times, according to which there was a region of Greek-speakers in the south and a region of Bulgarian-speakers in the north of the Balkans, who were both equally bearers of the status of Roman subjects, i.e. members of the Roman imperial community.

The adherence of the Byzantine ruling elite to the notion of an imperial political community, whose territorial image was both fluctuating and infinite, is best exemplified by a statement in the *Alexiad* of Anna Komnene, written in the 1140s. The author reported on the expansionary warfare of her father, Alexios I Komnenos (1081–1118), against the Turks in Asia Minor, and observed:

> The Emperor would take away the town [i.e. Nicaea] from the former [i.e. Seljuks] and make it his own, which at present was outside the orbit of the Roman Empire [*Rhômaiôn hêgemonia*]; after that he would gradually take another and yet another and thus enlarge the boundaries of the Roman Empire [*Rhômaiôn archê*] which had become very restricted; more especially since the sword of the Turks had grown so powerful. For there was a time when the limits of the Roman Empire [*Rhômaiôn hêgemonia*] were the two pillars which bound east and west respectively, those on the west being called the 'pillars of Heracles', those on the east the 'pillars of Dionysus' somewhere near the frontier of India. It is hardly possible to define the Roman Empire's [*Rhômaiôn basileias*] former width. Egypt, Meroë, all the Troglodyte country, and the region adjacent to the torrid zone; and in the other direction far famed Thule, and the races who dwell in the northern lands and over whose heads the North Pole stands. But in these later times the boundary of the Roman sceptre [*Rhômaiôn skêptrôn*] was the neighbouring Bosporus on the east and the city of Adrianople on the west. Now, however, the Emperor Alexius by striking with both hands, as it were, at the barbarians who beset him on either side and starting from Byzantium [Constantinople] as his center, enlarged the circle of the Empire [*basileias*], for on the west he made the Adriatic sea his frontier, and on the east the Euphrates and Tigris. And he would have restored the Empire [*basileias*] to its former prosperity, had not the successive wars and the recurrent dangers and difficulties hindered him in his purpose (for he was involved in great, as well as frequent, dangers).[25]

---

[24] *Vita Clementis Ochridensis* 68.1–4 (134).
[25] Anna Komnene, *Alexias* VI.11.2–3 (193).

That is an extraordinary statement insofar as it perfectly summarizes all the basic features of the Roman notion of a territorial empire in medieval East Roman geographical imagery. The extract begins with Alexios I Komnenos' effort to capture the city of Nicaea from the Turks and expand the current Roman territory in his immediate geopolitical sphere. The author justifies this effort as intended to enlarge the territory of an empire that had been radically contracted and confined almost to the hinterland of Constantinople in the East. Anna seems to have had in mind here different phases of territorial contraction, even though she stresses the latest and more damaging contraction caused by the Seljuks in the 1070s. This becomes evident in the subsequent statement in which she talks about the empire's former width. This recalls the aforementioned statements by Constantine VII and Kekaumenos, since Anna presents the limits of the Roman Empire as having included in the past the largest part of the ecumene, the inhabited world.[26]

Moreover, Anna makes use of the traditional image of the imperial city of Constantinople-New Rome as the center of the world and of an empire without limits. Beyond the walls of the imperial city-state extended the current Roman lands as the territory that was under the emperor's enforceable authority. Her father's expansionist endeavors that enlarged the Roman territory during his reign are presented as taking place in terms of an enlarging circle around the imperial center, Constantinople. The concluding statement leaves little doubt about the Komnenian power elite's adherence to the traditional Roman vision of an infinite empire: the territory of the Romans could have been expanded as far as to include almost the whole known world again, if only the military potential for such an achievement were not absent.

Anna's exaggerated and utopian statements regarding the potential of her father's policies of expansion in this case could be read as a reaction to current plans of expansion by her nephew and emperor at the time of the completion of her text, Manuel I Komnenos (1141–1180).[27] These mainly concerned the plan to restore Byzantine rule in parts of Italy, which materialized not very long after the completion of the *Alexiad*, albeit with very short-lived success.[28] Nonetheless, both Anna's imagining of a past Roman Empire encompassing the ecumene and Manuel's military-political aspirations of expansion in the West provide ample proof of how much the Roman notion of an empire *sine fine* in both chronological and territorial terms remained ingrained in the imaginary of the eastern Roman elite until well into the twelfth century.

[26] Cf. n. 13 above.
[27] On Anna's authorial agenda, see Magdalino 2000.
[28] On Manuel I Komnenos' imperial policies, see Magdalino 1993:41–108.

From Territorial Empire to Ethnic Homeland?

The evidence presented so far demonstrates that the medieval East Roman elite's perception of Roman lands was primarily conditioned by the existence of a centralized imperial state, the very heart of which was the imperial city-state of Constantinople–New Rome. Until the late twelfth century, even terms with distinct territorial connotations such as *Rhômanía* and *Rhômaís*, were not employed to refer to a finite Roman ethnic homeland, but to the territoriality of a state and a political community of Roman subjects, whose extension was determined both in historical and current terms by the extension of the imperial office's fiscal, military, and judicial authority.

Based on this, the events of 1204 can be said to represent a true watershed, since they caused the loss of the imperial city-state and the subsequent disintegration of a centuries-long centralized imperial order that informed the aforementioned dominant territorial vision of a united political community of Roman subjects.[29] In the aftermath of 1204, the image of the *Rhômaíoi* as an ethno-cultural group, which had been developing in the shadow of the dominant image of an imperial community of Roman subjects throughout the medieval period, came de facto to the fore after the loss of Constantinople's centralized imperial rule.[30] In this regard, the question that arises pertains to the extent to which this development contributed to a shift in the image of the Roman lands, from that of a fluctuating and infinite realm of Roman imperial rule to that of an abstract but nonetheless finite homeland of an ethnic group.

The most important source about this transitional period of East Roman history is the *Historia* of Niketas Choniates. This is an extraordinary historiographical text because the author started writing it in the 1190s in Constantinople only to finish his work in the first years after the loss of the city, when he had fled to Nicaea.[31] This means that Choniates is the only author of a Byzantine history who experienced both a united East Roman world under the centralized imperial rule of Constantinople and a world without the Roman empire of Constantinople. This makes his work not simply a history about a period of transition, but a history literally written during this transition. Therefore, it is particularly worth scrutinizing Choniates' projected image of Roman lands.

To begin with, it is interesting that terms bearing distinct territorial connotations, such as *Rhômanía* and *Rhômaís*, are conspicuously absent as designations

---

[29] On the Fourth Crusade, see Angold 2003, esp. 75–108.
[30] For various takes on medieval East Roman ethnicity, see Page 2008; Malatras 2011; Stouraitis 2017; Kaldellis 2017 and 2019.
[31] Simpson 2005:202–205.

of the Roman lands in the *Historia*. The author occasionally employed *Rhômaîôn archê* with some territorial connotation, but the main terms used to denote the current Roman territory in the text are *Rhômaîôn hória*, *Rhômaîôn hóroi*, *Rhômaîôn gê*, *rhômaikès chôres*, and *rhômaikê eparchía*.[32] This terminology seems hardly to deviate from the norm, which made the territorial image of the Roman community dependent upon the fluctuating limits of enforceable imperial authority. For instance, the term *rhômaikê eparchía* literally translates as "the area of Roman government or rule," whereas the terms *Rhômaîôn hória* and *Rhômaîôn hórois* were equally intended to refer to the current boundaries of imperial authority.

For the greater part of the period Choniates' account covers (1118–1204), these Roman lands still included territories in the northern Balkans that were designated as Bulgarian in former centuries.[33] In Asia Minor, they were demarcated by the boundaries of Roman and Turkish rule, respectively. For instance, in his account of Frederick Barbarossa's Crusade, the author refers to the German king crossing the land of the Romans (*Rhômaîon gê*) in Asia Minor and then leaving the Roman boundaries (*Rhômaîôn hória*) to pass to the land (*chôra*) of the Turks (*Ismaêlites*) in order to cross their boundaries (*hória*) and enter Armenia.[34] What was at that time the land of the Turks was designated as the land of the Romans two centuries earlier, as testified by the relevant references of Theophanes Continuatus presented above. This allowed Choniates to juxtapose on the current Roman lands of his own time the image of a larger space of imperial authority in the past that had now been lost. On more than one occasion, he refers to regions in Anatolia that were currently under Turkish rule as having previously been under the sway of the Romans. For instance, he states that the land of Chaldia was previously subordinate to the Romans, using the term *hypoforos,* which literally means "the one paying taxes."[35]

This kind of terminology tells a great deal about the conceptualization of the Roman identity of territories in Choniates' discourse. The author's report on emperor John II Komnenos' attack on a Christian community at Lake Pousgousê (modern Beyşehir Gölü) near Ikonion in Asia Minor sheds more light on this. According to Choniates, the local Christians shared common kinship and religion with the Romans—a clear allusion to a shared ethno-cultural identity.[36] Nonetheless, they declined the emperor's offer to return under his authority,

---

[32] For some characteristic examples, see Niketas Choniates, *Historia*, 116 (*Rhômaîôn hórois*), 171 (*rhômaikê eparchía*), 412 and 612 (*Rhômaîôn horia*), 476 (*Rhômaikas chôres*), 529 (*Rhômaîôn archê*).

[33] The former identity of those lands is reflected in their administrative label as part of the Roman Empire, namely *bulgarika themata* (Bulgar provinces), Niketas Choniates, *Historia*, 465.

[34] Niketas Choniates, *Historia*, 412, 415–416.

[35] Niketas Choniates, *Historia*, 226; cf. *Historia*, 116, for a similar discourse.

[36] Page 2008:83; Stouraitis 2014:201.

opting to remain loyal to the nearby Turks of Ikonion. As a result, the emperor claimed that the Christians of the lake had no right to hold the land, since this was an ancient possession of the Romans, and ordered his army to destroy them.[37]

The image of the Romans here is rather enlightening regarding the content of the ethnonym *Rhômaîôn* in phrases such as *Rhômaîôn horia*, *Rhômaîôn hórois*, *Rhômaîôn gê*, or *Rhômaîôn archê*, which Choniates employed to conceptualize the Roman lands. The choice of labels (Romans vs. Christians) was intended to emphasize that it was not common ethnicity demarcated by shared cultural markers, which made someone a Roman in the sense of a member of the Roman imperial-political community; it was loyalty and subordination to the central-ized rule of the Roman emperor in Constantinople. The Romans (*Rhômaîoi*) who claimed possession of the lake's land since ancient times were the emperors of Constantinople and by association all those currently subordinate and loyal to their authority.

Indeed, Choniates' discourse demonstrates that, from the viewpoint of the twelfth-century Constantinopolitan elite, the identity of current or past Roman territory was not determined by the notion of an ethnic group's homeland. It was rather related to those territories' historical status as lands currently or previously possessed by the Roman emperors of the imperial city of Constantinople. This interpretation is corroborated by a statement of the histo-rian John Kinnamos, a contemporary of Choniates writing roughly in the 1180s. In a passage of his history concerning the Second Crusade, Kinnamos employed interchangeably the terms *Rhômaîôn gê* (the land of the Romans) and *basiléôs gê* (the emperor's land) in order to designate contemporary Roman territory.[38]

Choniates' *Historia* not only bears witness to the persistence of the tradi-tional imperial image of Roman lands for as long as the centralized imperial rule of Constantinople stood firm in the twelfth century; it also demonstrates that in the immediate aftermath of the loss of the imperial city, the latter main-tained its traditional image as a geographical center, that is, the point that determined the distinction between East and West, in the imaginary of the medieval eastern Roman elite. In the part of the text recounting the events after the *halôsis* (capture) of Constantinople, Choniates distinguished between the Romans of the West (Balkans) and those of the East (Asia Minor) and talked about the eastern (*asianá*) and western (*hespéria*) Roman boundaries (*hória*).[39] This approach is confirmed by two sermons addressed by Choniates to the new

---

[37] Niketas Choniates, *Historia*, 612.
[38] John Kinnamos, *Epitome*, 68.
[39] Niketas Choniates, *Historia*, 612, 625.

ruler of Nicaea, Theodoros Laskaris, after 1206. In the title of the first sermon one reads: "Selection written to be read by Theodoros the ruler of the eastern Roman lands, since Constantinople had been captured by the Latins and was occupied by them together with the western Roman lands."[40] The second speech was titled: "A sermon to be read to Theodoros Laskaris ruler of the eastern Roman cities while Constantinople was occupied by the Latins and John of Mysia was raiding the western Roman regions."[41]

If both rubrics confirm that the author remained faithful to the typical division between East and West from the viewpoint of Constantinople, a different issue is raised by this kind of discourse in the new post-1204 geopolitical context. The main question that arises here is how the boundaries of what counted as Roman territory were now circumscribed. Given the disintegration of centralized imperial rule, Choniates could hardly be alluding to a historical image of a territorial empire here, like the one presented in the aforementioned statement of Anna Komnene, for instance. The author seems to depart from a more sober image of Roman lands in this case, as this had been configured by the contracted boundaries of imperial authority shortly before the events of 1204.[42] However, given the absence of centralized imperial authority over those territories at the time he was writing, it seems that the boundaries of the Roman lands at the current time followed new notional lines and were circumscribed by the boundaries of the Roman ethno-cultural identity of the populations inhabiting those lands. In other words, the Roman lands in East (Asia Minor) and West (Balkans) had now de facto acquired the abstract image of a homeland of the Romans as an ethno-cultural community.

This shift in the perception of Roman territory, as the effect of the lack of a centralized imperial state in the immediate aftermath of 1204, is corroborated by a letter of the brother of Niketas Choniates and bishop of Athens, Michael, to the ruler of Nicaea, Theodoros I Laskaris. There the bishop stated that Roman magnates under Latin rule in Greece looked upon Theodoros as the potential liberator of the Roman lands (*Rhômanía*).[43] In the socio-political context of the letter, the image of the *Rhômanía* seems again to be disassociated both from the image of an infinite territorial empire or from the image of an emperor's current realm of authority. The Roman lands that needed to be liberated in

---

[40] Niketas Choniates, *Sermons and Letters*, 120.

[41] Niketas Choniates, *Sermons and Letters*, 129.

[42] This is indicated by his report on the Latins occupying the eastern and western boundaries of the Roman lands, Niketas Choniates, *Historia*, 612.

[43] Michael Choniates, *Epistula* 138 (280). Interestingly, the term *Rhômanía* seems to have been absent from the vocabulary of the Lascarid emperors as testified by its absence from the surviving texts of John III Ducas Vatatzes and Theodoros II Ducas Laskaris.

this case seem to concern an abstract but nonetheless finite homeland of East Roman culture, namely, those territories in Asia Minor and the Balkans where Latins ruled over a population of predominately Greek-speaking Chalcedonian Christians.

This shift in the way the Roman lands were imagined shortly after 1204 was swiftly contrasted, however, by the revival of Roman imperial discourse in the so-called successor Byzantine states. The best-documented case study is, of course, the successor imperial state of Nicaea whose last ruler was able to take Constantinople from the Latins in 1261. The capture of Constantinople by Michael VIII Palaiologos (1261–1282) gave birth to a narrative of restoration of Roman imperial rule in the archetypical homeland of the Romans, a development that in turn enabled a retrospective legitimization of the Nicaean state and its rulers as the sole true continuators of the legacy of the Roman Empire of Constantinople during the period of Latin rule in the city.

As a result, in the revived genre of Constantinopolitan historiography after 1261, the traditional image of a Roman imperial-political community and political Romanness was bound to the state of Nicaea and its emperors for the period between 1204 and 1261. George Akropolites, the only historian who devoted his work to the empire of Nicaea, testifies to this. Beginning his narration with the events of 1204, the author employed the traditional vision of Roman territory as those lands circumscribed by the boundaries of imperial rule. For example, in a reference to the reign of Isaakios II Angelos in the 1190s, Akropolites mentioned that, at that time, the regions of the Bulgarians were still a part of the Roman Empire, for which he used the term *Rhômaîôn eparchía*.[44] In another occasion, he described how the Latin conquerors had divided among themselves the various parts of the *Rhômaîs*, a term denoting here the territory under centralized imperial rule before the sack of Constantinople.[45]

Most interestingly, Akropolites reproduced an image of Roman lands between 1204 and 1261, whose boundaries were imagined as being demarcated by the boundaries of the Nicaean emperors' enforceable authority. For instance, in a reference to the ruler of the state of Epirus, Michael Komnenos, the author mentions that after 1204 he "was ruling over Epirus and a part of the land of the Romans."[46] This is an awkward phrase, which makes little sense if one considers that the Epirotes should be considered as Romans from an ethno-cultural point of view and that Epirus had always been a part of the Roman Empire before 1204. Epirote territory belonged in fact to those western Roman lands that Choniates

---

[44] George Akropolites, *Historical Annales*, I, 11.
[45] George Akropolites, *Historical Annales*, I, 8.
[46] George Akropolites, *Historical Annales*, I, 14.

juxtaposed to the eastern Roman lands in his aforementioned sermons to Theodoros Laskaris.[47] The only way to make sense of Akropolites' statement is to consider that he was hardly interested to project the image of an abstract Roman ethnic homeland. His main incentive was of a political nature and aimed at confining Romanness to those territories that had gradually come under the centralized authority of the emperors of Nicaea after 1204, thus reinforcing the Nicaean emperor's claim as the only true Roman emperors in this period.

This is corroborated by his report on the Nicaean campaign of 1259 against the despotate of Epirus. There, he states that the defeated Epirots:

> drew back as far as their own boundaries, namely the Pyrrenaia Mountains which separate Old and New Epiros from our Hellenic land.[48]

If the reference to a Hellenic land seems confusing here, one should consider that in the writings of the emperors of Nicaea their realm was interchangeably labeled as Hellenic or Roman lands.[49] As a result, what the aforementioned statement aimed at highlighting was once again the distinction between the contemporary lands of the Roman political community (i.e. those lands under the authority of the emperor of Nicaea) and the lands outside contemporary Roman authority (i.e. the territories under the authority of the ruler of Epirus which lay behind the Pindos Mountains). The Epirotes and their lands were deprived of a Hellenic and, by association, a Roman identity in contemporary terms, in the good old Roman imperial fashion due to the fact that they were not loyal to centralized imperial rule.

Akropolites' approach to current Roman territory during the period of the Nicaean state is reiterated in the typikon of the monastery of the Archangel Michael on Mount Auxentios near Chalcedon, commissioned by the emperor Michael VIII Palaiologos. In recounting his period of exile from Nicaea in the sultanate of Rum during the reign of Theodoros II Laskaris, Michael stated:

> I had therefore to leave my native land, that of the Romans, I mean, and I fled to a foreign country. I entered Persian (i.e. Seljuk) territory, facing many dangers along the way, it should be noted, from all of which I was rescued by God ... During the time I spent in Persia I engaged in absolutely nothing, in word, in deed, in plot, or in attempt against the ruler of the Romans at that time, the blessed late emperor, my cousin

---

[47] Cf. nn. 30 and 40 above.

[48] George Akropolites, *Historical Annales*, I, 80.

[49] Angold 1975:64; Papadopoulou 2014:171–172. On the rise of Hellenic identity discourse next to the Roman discourse in Byzantium in the transitional period of the twelfth and thirteenth centuries, see the systematic study of Papadopoulou 2015.

(i.e. Theodore II Laskaris) or against the realm of the Romans [*Rhômaiôn epikrateias*]. Rather, with God's help, I intended and carried out in practice only what would benefit them. The spirit of envy soon dissipated and in a short time I left Persia (i.e. the sultanate of Rum) and again returned to the land of the Romans, subjected myself to the ruler and again loyally performed the services he commanded.[50]

Michael's discourse makes it clear that what constituted the land of the Romans at current time in his view was those territories circumscribed by the imperial authority of the ruler of Nicaea. The political imagery of Roman lands emerging from the texts of Akropolites and Michael VIII, which downplayed the image of a finite ethnic homeland of the *Rhômaíoi* as an ethno-cultural group, reflects how Roman political ideology circumscribed the East Roman power elite's notions of territoriality. Given that shared ethno-cultural identity was not a presupposition for membership in the Roman political community, the latter's territorial boundaries were not imagined as coinciding with ethno-cultural boundaries. These boundaries were demarcated strictly by political allegiance and a subordinate status to centralized imperial rule.

The disintegration of centralized Roman imperial rule in 1204 had brought to the fore an alternative image of the Roman lands as an abstract finite homeland of an ethnic community in the writings of some members of the educated elite. However, the rehabilitation of Roman imperial discourse in Nicaea and, after 1261, in Constantinople contrasted that image and dictated the continuous demarcation of the Roman territorial-political community through the limits of centralized imperial rule. In the discourse of the ruling elite of Nicaea up to 1261, and that of Constantinople afterwards, populations outside the current boundaries of the imperial authority did not qualify as members of the Roman political community irrespective of whether they were classified or self-identified as *Rhômaíoi* in ethno-cultural terms.[51] Equally, territories beyond the boundaries of imperial authority were not viewed as Roman in current terms, but were usually imagined as Roman in terms of their historical status as former possessions and the inheritance of the Roman imperial power of Constantinople, the New Rome.

---

[50] Michael VIII Palaiologos, Τυπικόν, 71; tr. Dennis, '*Typikon* of Michael VIII', 1231.
[51] Page 2008:102–121, 146–158; Macrides 2007:94–94.

Works Cited

Primary Sources

Anna Komnene, *Alexias*: ed. D. R. Reinsch and A. Kambylis, *Anna Comnenae Alexias*. CFHB XL/1. Berlin, 2001.

Arethae Archiepiscopi Caesariaensis Scripta Minora II, ed. L.-G. Westerink. Leipzig, 1968.

Constantine Porphyrogenitus, *De administrando imperio*: ed. G. Moravcsik, 2nd ed. Corpus Fontium Historiae Byzantinae 1. Washington, DC, 1967.

Constantine Porphyrogenitus, *De thematibus*: ed. A. Pertusi. Studi e Testi 160. Vatican City, 1952.

Doctrina Jacobi nuper Baptizati: ed. and trans. V. Déroche, *Travaux et Mémoires* 11 (1991):47–229.

Eunapius, *Fragmenta historica*: ed. L. Dindorf, *Historici Graeci minores*, vol. 1. Leipzig, 1870; English trans. R. C. Blockley, *The Fragmentary Classicizing Historians of the Later Roman Empire: Eunapius, Olympiodorus, Priscus, and Malchus*, vol. 2: *Text, Translation, and Historiographical Notes*. Liverpool, 1983.

Evodius, *Vita martyrum XLII Amoriensum*: ed. P. Vasil'evč Nikitin and V. Grigorévič Vasilievskij, *Skazanija o 42 amorijskich mucenikach*. St. Petersburg, 1906 (61–78).

George Akropolites, *Historical Annales*: ed. A. Heisenberg, *Georgii Acropolitae opera*, vol. 1. Leipzig, 1903; English trans. R. Macrides, *George Akropolites, The History*. Oxford, 2007.

John Kinnamos, *Epitome*: ed. A. Meineke, *Ioannis Cinnami epitome rerum ab Ioanne et Alexio Comnenis gestarum*. CSHB. Bonn. 1836.

Kekaumenos, *Consilia et Narrationes*. In *Sharing Ancient Wisdoms* 2013. https://ancientwisdoms.ac.uk/library/kekaumenos-consilia-et-narrationes/index.html.

Leonis VI, *Tactica*: ed. G. D. Dennis, *The Taktika of Leo VI: Text, Translation, and Commentary*. CFHB XLIX. Washington, DC, 2010.

Michael Choniates, *Letters*: ed. F. Kolobou, *Michaelis Choniatae epistulae*. CFHB 41. Berlin, 2001.

Michael VIII Palaiologos, Τυπικὸν τῆς ἐν τῷ περιωνύμῳ βουνῷ τοῦ Αὐξεντίου μονῆς τοῦ Ἀρχιστρατήγου Μιχαήλ: ed. A. Dmitrievsk, *Typika, Opisanie liturgicheskikh rykopisei* I (1). Kiev, 1895 (769–794).

Michaelis Glycae, *Annales*: ed. I. Bekker, *Corpus scriptorum historiae Byzantinae*. Bonn, 1836.

Niketas Choniates, *Historia*, ed. J. van Dieten, *Nicetae Choniatae historia*, pars prior. CFHB 11.1. Berlin, 1975.

Niketas Choniates, *Sermons and Letters*: J. van Dieten, *Nicetae Choniatae orationes et epistulae*. Corpus Fontium Historiae Byzantinae. Series Berolinensis 3. Berlin, 1972.

Skylitzes, *Synopsis*: ed. J. Thurn, *Ioannis Scylitzae synopsis historiarum*. CFHB 5. Berlin, 1973.

Theodoros Daphnopates, *Letters*: ed. J. Darouzès and L. G. Westenrik, *Théodore Daphnopatès, Correspondance*. Paris, 1978.

Theophanes Continuatus, ed. I. Bekker. Bonn, 1838.

Vita Clementis Ochridensis, in A. Milev, *Gruckite zitija na Kliment Ochridski*. Sofia, 1966.

Secondary Sources

Anderson, B. 2006. *Imagined Communities: Reflections on the Origin and Spread of Nationalism*. London.

Angelov, D. 2003. "Byzantinism: The Imaginary and Real Heritage of Byzantium in Southeastern Europe." In *New Approaches to Balkan Studies*, ed. D. Keridis, E. Bursac, and N. Yatromanolakis, 3–21. Dulles, VA.

———. 2013. "'Asia and Europe Commonly Called East and West': Constantinople and Geographical Imagination in Byzantium." In Bazzaz, Batsaki, and Angelov 2013:43–69.

Angold, M. 1975. "Byzantine 'Nationalism' and the Nicaean Empire." *Byzantine and Modern Greek Studies* 1:49–70.

———. 2003. *The Fourth Crusade: Event and Context*. New York.

Bazzaz, S., Y. Batsaki, and D. Angelov. 2013. *Imperial Geographies in Byzantine and Ottoman Space*. Hellenic Studies 56. Washington, DC.

Cameron, A. 2003. "Byzance dans le débat sur orientalisme." In *Byzance en Europe*, ed. M.-F. Auzépy, 235–250. Paris.

Dagron, G. 1974. *Naissance d'une capitale: Constantinople et ses institutions de 330 à 451*. Paris.

———. 2005. "L'oecumenicité politique: Droit sur l'espace, droit sur le temps." In *Το Βυζάντιο ως Οικουμένη*, ed. E. Chrysos, 47–57. Athens.

Dennis, G. 2000. "*Typikon* of Michael VIII Palaiologos for the Monastery of the Archangel Michael on Mount Auxentios near Chalcedon." In *Byzantine Monastic Foundation Documents. A Complete Translation of the Surviving Founders' Typika and Testaments*, 5 vols., ed. J. Thomas and A. C. Hero, with the assistance of G. Constable, 1207–1236. Washington, DC.

Gaul, N. 2018. "Zooming in on Constantinople: Introductory Notes on the Interplay of Center, Province, and Periphery in the Tenth-Century Byzantine Empire." In *Center, Province, and Periphery in the Age of Constantine*

VII Porphyrogennetos. From De Cerimoniis to De Administrando Imperio, ed. N. Gau, V. Menze, and C. Bálint, 1–22. Wiesbaden.

Gelzer, H. 1833. "Ungedruckte und wenig bekannte Bistumsverzeichnisse der orientalischen Kirche II." *Byzantinische Zeitschrift* 2:22–72.

Hunger, H. 1966. *Reich der neuen Mitte: Der christliche Geist der byzantinischen Kultur.* Graz.

Kaldellis, A. 2017. "The Social Scope of Roman Identity in Byzantium: An Evidence-Based Approach." *Byzantina Symmeikta* 27:173–210.

———. 2019. *Romanland: Ethnicity and Empire in Byzantium.* Cambridge, MA.

Koder, J. 2012. "Die räumlichen Vorstellungen der Byzantiner von der Ökumene (4. bis 12. Jahrhundert)." *Anzeiger der philosophisch-historischen Klasse der Österreichischen Akademie der Wissenschaften* 137:15–34.

Magdalino, P. 1993. *The Empire of Manuel I Komnenos, 1143–1180.* Cambridge.

———. 2000. "The Pen of the Aunt: Echoes of the Mid-Twelfth Century in the Alexiad." In *Anna Komnene and Her Times*, ed. A. Gouma-Peterson, 15–44. New York.

———. 2013. "Constantine VII and the Historical Geography of Empire." In Bazzaz, Batsaki, and Angelov 2013:23–41.

Malatras, Ch. 2011. "The Making of an Ethnic Group: The Romaioi in the Twelfth–Thirteenth Centuries." In *Identities in the Greek World (From 1204 to the Present Day). Proceedings of the 4th European Congress of Modern Greek Studies Granada, 9-12 September 2010*, ed. K. A. Dimadis, 419–430. Athens.

Marciniak, P. 2018. "Oriental like Byzantium: Some Remarks on Similarities between Byzantinism and Orientalism" In *Imagining Byzantium: Perceptions, Patterns, Problems*, ed. A. Alshanskaya, S. Gietzen, and Ch. Hadjiafxenti, 47–54. Mainz.

Noll, R. 1989. "Ein Ziegel als sprechendes Zeugnis einer historischen Katastrophe (zum Untergang Sirmiums 582 n. Chr.)." *Anzeiger der philosophisch-historischen Klasse der Österreichischen Akademie der Wissenschaften* 126: 139–154.

Page, G. 2008. *Being Byzantine: Greek Identity before the Ottomans.* Cambridge.

Papadopoulou, Th. 2014. "The Terms Ῥωμαῖος, Ἕλλην, Γραικὸς in the Byzantine Texts of the First Half of the Thirteenth Century." *Byzantina Symmeikta* 24:157–176.

———. 2015. *Συλλογική ταυτότητα και αυτογνωσία στο Βυζάντιο: Συμβολή στον προσδιορισμό της αυτοαντίληψης των Βυζαντινών κατά την λόγια γραμματεία τους 11ος-αρχές 13ου αι.* Athens.

Simpson, A. 2006. "Before and after 1204: The Versions of Niketas Choniates' 'Historia'." *Dumbarton Oaks Papers* 69:189–221.

Sode, Cl. 1994. "Untersuchungen zu *De administrando imperio* Kaiser Konstantins VII. Porphyrogenitus." *Poikila Byzantina* 13:149–260.

Stouraitis, Y. 2014. "Roman Identity in Byzantium: A Critical Approach." *Byzantinische Zeitschrift* 107:175–220.

———. 2017. "Reinventing Roman Ethnicity in High and Late Medieval Byzantium." *Medieval Worlds* 5:70–94.

———. 2021. "*Scriptores post Theophanem*: Normative Aspects of Imperial Historiography in Tenth-Century Byzantium." In *Historiography and Identity IV: Writing History across Medieval Eurasia*, ed. W. Pohl and D. Mahoney, 219–246. Turnhout.

———. 2022. "Is Byzantinism an Orientalism? Reflections on Byzantium's Constructed Identities and Debated Ideologies." In *Ideologies and Identities in the Medieval East Roman World*, 19–47. Edinburgh.

3

Imagination and Experience in Thirteenth-Century Latin Encounters with the 'Orient'

John of Plano Carpini, the Mongols, and Monsters

ANGUS STEWART

THE CREATION OF THE MONGOL EMPIRE IN THE THIRTEENTH CENTURY, stretching from China in the East to the borders of Syria and of Latin Europe in the West, transformed Western European knowledge of the world.[1] Taking advantage of the so-called '*Pax mongolica*,' Latins were able to travel across the whole of Asia. At first these travels may have been involuntary, but increasingly travelers went freely, and, importantly, were free to return, and report back on their experiences. The most famous of these travelers is, of course, Marco Polo; while some doubts are still expressed as to the reliability of much of his *Travels*, or even as to whether he genuinely journeyed beyond the Black Sea, it is certain that Italian merchants did get to China.[2] In 1951, for example, the gravestone of one Katarina Vilioni, presumably a Venetian, was discovered in the city of Yangzhou; she died in 1342, and her memorial suggests the existence of some sort of Latin community in China at this time.[3] The Florentine Francesco di Pegolotti's guidebook for merchants, the *Pratica della Mercatura*, written 1335–1343, includes detailed advice on the route to China—how to present oneself, how to change money, how best to transport goods, and so on.[4] Even by this time, however, the Mongol window was closing: the breakup of the empire, and more especially the collapse of some of its constituent parts, was making Central Asia increasingly unstable. After the mid-fourteenth century, the overland route to the Orient was once more effectively closed to Western Europeans, apart from a

---

[1]   See e.g. Phillips 1988; Phillips 2014; Legassie 2017.
[2]   Wood 1995; but see Morgan 1996a, de Rachewiltz 1997, Jackson 1998.
[3]   Rouleau 1954.
[4]   Evans 1936:21–23; see 26–31 for an account of Tabriz, and the route there from Ayas/Laiazzo.

few individuals.[5] The accounts left behind from this period remained, however, and stimulated fifteenth-century Portuguese or Italian sailors to seek new ways to get to China or the 'Indies'—without this century or so of European encounters with the Orient, this later 'Age of Discovery' "would have been quite literally inconceivable."[6]

Of course, not all the travelers to the Orient were seeking goods and fortunes; others sought souls. In the period from the mid-thirteenth to the mid-fourteenth century, Roman Catholic missionaries sought to spread the faith. Eventually an ecclesiastical structure was established across Asia. There were mission houses, and even bishops established in Persia, Central Asia, and China, as well as in India. These missionaries and prelates were members of the recently established and increasingly influential mendicant orders—Dominican, and especially Franciscan, friars. For example, the first major mission to China was led by the Franciscan John of Montecorvino, who was made the first archbishop of Khanbaliq (i.e. Beijing) in 1308. As with the mercantile activity, these missions gradually ceased in the mid-fourteenth century: the last archbishop of Khanbaliq that we know of was appointed in 1370; the newly appointed bishop of Zaitun (the Chinese city of Quanchou) was killed in 1362 in Central Asia. While it can be difficult to trace the course of this missionary activity, we do possess letters sent back from the Orient, expressing their challenges, frustrations and (limited) successes. We also possess some longer accounts produced by friars on their return to Western Europe, and among these are some of the most copied texts of their day. While the various versions of the travels of Marco Polo exist in about 150 medieval manuscripts, the Latin narrative of the Franciscan Odoric of Pordenone's journey across the Orient (1320s) survives in 117 manuscripts; and the journey of the Franciscan John of Plano Carpini is recorded in twenty.[7] Other reports of the missions of mendicant friars were copied into popular texts such as the *Speculum historiale* of Vincent of Beauvais (d. 1264). These accounts—the travel narratives of merchants and friars—alongside other much-copied descriptions of the Orient, such as the *Flor des estoires de la terre d'Orient* (1307) by the Armenian prince Het'um of Korykos, were often bound together. They were also among the sources used by the writer of the late medieval bestseller, *The Travels of John Mandeville* (late fourteenth century). The existence and diffusion

---

[5]   Phillips 1988:257. Travel had certainly become less commonplace; after the collapse of the Ilkhanate in the 1330s even the Italian community in Persia, centered on the Ilkhanid capital of Tabriz, eventually evaporated. See Paviot 1997; also Petech 1962.

[6]   Phillips 1988:258.

[7]   Larner 1999:106, 208n3; O'Doherty 2009:200n11; Menestò 1989b.

of this material suggests widespread interest in and appetite for information on the Orient, among both scholarly and popular audiences.[8]

While the later writers may have had access to earlier accounts of travels in the Mongol realm, for the very first travelers it is clear that the voyage East was a voyage into the unknown. In contrast to a later merchant armed with a copy of the *Pratica della Mercatura*, the first mendicant visitors to the Great Mongol Khan were unprepared, not only for the people they would meet but even for the landscape and climate. This sense of entering an alien world is conveyed explicitly by the Franciscan William of Rubruck, the author of the second major account of a journey to Mongolia (1253–1255), who wrote that, only two days after leaving Soldaia (Sudak, on the Crimea), and upon first encountering Mongols, "I really felt as if I were entering some other world."[9] It may be that both William and his predecessor, John of Plano Carpini, were unprepared for their journeys to Mongolia partly because they did not intend to go there. In both cases, they may have intended only to visit the Mongol princes then on the Pontic steppe, only for their missions to be misunderstood, and for them to be forwarded eastwards to the Great Khan. William's motives for his journey are to an extent opaque. At various points he suggests that he wished to find and administer to a group of German miners held captive by the Mongols; he may have been inspired by rumors of the conversion to Christianity of a Mongol prince named Sartaq, based north of the Black Sea; he may have simply wished to gather intelligence. His mission was sponsored by King Louis IX of France, who provided a letter of introduction, and to whom William's account is addressed. Louis had earlier had an uncomfortable experience with an official embassy to the Mongols, which was presented as if an act of submission.[10] The reasons for John of Plano Carpini's journey are, however, more certain.

Latin Europe avoided direct contact with the Mongol empire for the first few decades of its expansion. Despite some warnings, it was unprepared for the attack when it came in 1241.[11] The invasions of both Poland and Hungary, and the subsequent brutal occupation of the latter, were an enormous shock. People reacted in some predictable ways. There were attempts to organize a crusade,

[8] The classic discussion of the activity of the friars in Asia is de Rachewiltz 1971. See also Phillips 1988:83–101. A very useful introduction to the main travelers to the East and their accounts is provided by Phillips 2014. The main narratives and letters produced by the friars are translated in Dawson 1955, available as a mass-market paperback, revealing the continued interest in these accounts.

[9] Jackson and Morgan 1990:71.

[10] According to John of Joinville, King Louis "repented loudly at having sent the envoys": Monfrin 1995:242. While celebrated today, William's account was very little known in the medieval period.

[11] For this invasion, and for the warnings that preceded it, see Jackson 2005:58–71.

and there was some persecution of Jews. Some Western chroniclers—not necessarily those with firsthand experience—described the Mongols in what can only be called apocalyptic terms, as the people of Gog and Magog. This is echoed in the name they are often called in our sources, 'Tartars', as if escaped from Tartarus.[12] In the end, however, there was little practical action. Though the Mongols withdrew from Hungary in 1242, they were still a problem that had to be addressed. It was by no means certain that they would not return to make their rule permanent, as they had in the neighboring principalities of the Rus'. In the aftermath, therefore, of these invasions, Pope Innocent IV sent teams of envoys to make contact with the Mongol armies then known to be operating in the West—in Persia, Asia Minor, and in the former Rus' territory. These envoys were Mendicant friars; while the Dominicans sent to the Middle East, Ascelin and Andrew of Longjumeau, had mixed experiences, the Franciscans sent to Eastern Europe, led by John of Plano Carpini, had an especially eventful time.[13]

John of Plano Carpini and the "Historia Mongalorum quos nos tartaroros appellamus"

Brother John had been born around 1190 at Pian di Carpine (today called Magione), near Perugia in Umbria, central Italy.[14] John had been a companion of St Francis himself, and was a man of great experience, for example leading the Franciscan mission to Germany in the 1220s and 1230s. After 1239, he does not seem to have held any post in the Franciscan order, which perhaps made him free to accept Pope Innocent's commission at Lyons in 1245. He left on Easter Sunday and headed for the Mongols active in the lands north of the Black Sea, picking up along the way a companion, Benedict the Pole, to assist in dealings with Poles and Russians. In contrast to the more abrasive Dominicans, John's very diplomatic attitude seems to have resulted in his positive reception by the Mongol prince Batu, leader of their forces in the west. Perhaps because of the then-delicate state of Mongol imperial politics, the friars were unexpectedly sent on further east to the Mongolian steppe, where they were present when the assembly elected the new great khan, Güyük, in mid-1246. They remained there through the bitter winter. John was able to deliver the letters that he and

---

[12] For some reason the Mongols were known across the Middle East by the name of one of the tribes previously dominant on the eastern steppe, killed off by Chinggis Qan: the 'Tatars'. Because these invaders seemed to the Latins as if from hell, this mutated into 'Tartars', a pun on 'Tartarus', the great hellish abyss in Classical mythology. For a discussion of the Mongols and the apocalypse, see Jackson 2005:142–153.

[13] On these missions, and their wider context, see, e.g., Jackson 1995:25–29.

[14] On John's career, see Menestò 1989a.

the other envoys had been given by the pope, which called for the khan to cease attacking Christians and embrace Christianity. In exchange, he brought back a very threatening response—Güyük summoned the pope to come to submit in person.[15]

In sending out these envoys, Pope Innocent's intention was "without doubt diplomatic, but also exploratory."[16] John's secondary aim, therefore, was to gather intelligence on these Mongols, and this is the basis of the report he produced on his return. This was a systematic, detailed analysis, organized into eight books, looking at Mongol customs, religion, character, history, military methods, and concluding with an assessment of their aims and how best to fight against them. As John traveled back through Europe, early versions of this report were copied down. So keen were people for his story that he was forced to provide an account of his own journey, and this, of great interest, was appended to his report, along with clarifications of details. Other surviving accounts of the journey are based on Benedict the Pole's recollections; the text survives, therefore, in various versions, as John was himself aware.[17] In his final redaction, John concludes with an appeal to any copyists of his work, outlining his principles as a historian, and describing the process of composition:

> We beseech all who read the preceding account to cut or add nothing, for we have written down with complete veracity all that we saw or that we heard from others who we believe are trustworthy, as God is witness, without knowingly adding anything. But because some of those we encountered, in Poland, Bohemia and Germany and in Liège and Champagne, wished to have the above-written account, they copied it before it was finished, and even in wholly abbreviated form, because we had not had a quiet moment to complete it definitively. Therefore no one should wonder that this version is longer and more accurate than earlier ones; because, having some time for repose, we edited the text copiously and completely, or more complete than that which was unfinished.[18]

In this final version, then, John was able to correct the earlier draft, as well as to elucidate material, and provide more detail, especially on his own experiences.[19] The chronicler Salimbene de Adam, his fellow Franciscan, describes how John

---

[15] Jackson 1995:22–23.
[16] Menestò 1989a:56.
[17] Luongarotti 1989; Wyngart 1929:133–134; Painter 1995.
[18] Menestò 1989c:332–333.
[19] Legassie's main interest in the text is in John's attempts to assert authorial integrity, as in this passage—2017:67–71.

read from his book, patiently explaining any confusing material, and this experience doubtless contributed to his final version.[20]

John's expectation was fulfilled. As stated above, the various recensions of his account were widely copied and disseminated. As the first substantial first-hand Western European account of the Mongols, his report may have influenced other accounts from this period. The mostly thematic structure of the *Historia Mongalorum*—the first eight books together represent an intelligence dossier—has allowed readers from its own day to ours to get a sense of various aspects of the Mongols and their culture. John's report is very useful to historians as an eyewitness account of the Mongols in the period of their empire's expansion. This is not the place to discuss his representation of the Mongols; but it is worth pointing out while the portrayal was certainly based on observation, it may also reveal some evidence of the writer placing the Mongols in a preexisting mental framework—such as models for representing the apocalyptic, nomadic barbarian. For example, John reports that:

> They eat all that can be eaten; for they eat dogs, wolves, foxes and horses and, in necessity, they devour human flesh ... They eat that which is emitted by mares with the foals at birth. Indeed, we even saw them eating lice. They said, in fact, "Why should I not eat them, when they eat the flesh of my son and drink his blood?" I have also seen them eat mice ... They do not have bread or greens or vegetables or anything else, except meat ...[21]

Dogs and mice are unclean animals. While John is careful to stress that cannibalism was only *in extremis*, other writers of the time amplified the reports, suggesting that the cannibalism was for pleasure; similarly, other writers amended his equine afterbirth to human. All of this echoes the apocalyptic prophecies of Pseudo-Methodius and the savage peoples of Gog and Magog.[22] John does not seem to go so far. Nevertheless, the fact that the Mongols did not eat bread would have marked them as barbarians, and, in the Biblical tradition, as not quite 'people'. John's statement could, perhaps, be seen as a dehumanizing of the Mongols, which would fit with other descriptions of them—as when the Armenian Grigor Aknerts'i uses a wide range of often rather odd animal imagery to convey a sense of the Mongol appearance.[23] On the other hand, while not eating bread was certainly a marker of the 'barbarian', in this case it

---

[20] Baird et al. 1986:196–203.
[21] Menestò 1989c:248.
[22] Jackson 1995:144–146.
[23] Blake and Frye 1949:294–297.

was not a trait that John imposed on the Mongols, but rather one that reflects their extreme pastoral economy. Moreover, John does not dwell on the elements of the Mongol diet that fascinated contemporaries such as Matthew Paris, whose drawing of Mongols roasting a captive on a spit is well known. Rather, he stresses that these acts are exceptional and that they eat all sorts of other stuff, which could be interpreted as humanizing rather than dehumanizing.[24] However one interprets this passage—straight reportage or coded allusion—the point remains that the *Historia mongalorum* is best understood in the contemporary Western European intellectual context.

What distinguishes the reports of the Mongols provided by the mendicant friars such as John who traveled among them is the absence of some of the wilder rumors recorded by those based in Western Europe. John's stated concern for accuracy and honesty was not an empty promise. Not only his summaries of Mongol characteristics, but also his account of his journey and his experiences, such as his attendance at the ceremonies for Güyük's accession to the imperial throne, are of as great interest to the modern scholar as they were to his contemporaries. The account of his epic journey across the Eurasian steppe, traveling relentlessly by the network of imperial relay stations, is especially impressive. As Dawson has stated, "it would have been an ordeal for the toughest of horsemen, but for an elderly clergyman who was extremely fat and in poor health, it is one of the most remarkable feats of physical endurance on record."[25] This journey left its mark. After leaving Batu's encampment on the Volga on Easter Sunday 1246, John and his companions headed into lands completely unknown to them, "with many tears, for we knew not whether we were going to death or to life."[26]

When placing the land of the 'Tartars' at the beginning of the *Historia*, John places it "in that part of the east in which the east, we believe, joins with the north"; furthermore, "to conclude briefly about this land: it is large, but otherwise ... it is much more abject than we are able to say."[27] John does provide a more detailed overview of the political geography of the lands he passed through in the last book, the account of his experiences. Describing his passage across the lands of the Cumans (now occupied by the Mongols) John seeks to establish geographical relationships with lands already known in the West:

> Cumania has to the north, immediately after Russia, the Mordvins, the Bylers, that is Great Bulgaria, the Bascarts, that is Great Hungary;

---

[24] See Jackson 1995:25 for this interpretation of this passage.
[25] Dawson 1955:xvi.
[26] Menestò 1989c:312.
[27] Menestò 1989c:229, 231.

beyond the Bascarts are the Parossites and the Samogeds; after the Samogeds, those who are said to have faces like dogs and live in the wilderness on the shores of the ocean. To the south, moreover, it has the Alans, Circass, Gazars, Greece, Constantinople, and the land of the Iberians, the Tats, the Brutachi who are said to be Jews and shave their heads, the land of the Sicci, of the Georgians and of the Armenians, and the land of the Turks. To the west it has Hungary and Russia. The aforementioned land [Cumania] is very large and long.[28]

Most of these peoples can be confidently identified. The Cumans are of course the Qipchaks, also known to the Russians as the Polovtsy. Mordvin and Samoyed are names given to Uralic peoples—the former now in the Volga-southern Urals area, the latter further north in Siberia. The name "Byler" may refer to a group of the Volga Bulghars, or to one of their main towns, Bilyar, perhaps their capital in the pre-Mongol period. The Bascarts are presumably the Bashkirs of the Volga-southern Urals region; these are now a Turkic group, and were described as such by Ibn Fadlan in the early tenth century. But it may well be that they retained some connection with the Magyar groups that had settled in the Carpathian basin from the late ninth century—certainly there had been an effort in the early thirteenth century by Hungarian Dominicans to convert their supposed relatives from paganism.[29] The Alans and Circassians (Čerkes) were peoples of the northern Caucasus region, the former possibly the ancestors of modern Ossetians; and Zichia was a territory in this area, on the Black Sea. The Iberians, Georgians, and Armenians are to be found further south in the Caucasus region; the Tats to the east. Further south, the "land of the Turks" is the sultanate of Rum, Anatolia. The shaven-headed, Jewish Brutachi are trickier to place.[30]

Rather more unexpected to the modern reader are the dog-faced men. These are mentioned earlier by John, in an account of the expansion of the Mongols across Siberia to the Arctic.

They came to a land next to the ocean, where they came upon some monsters, we were told for sure, who had an entirely human form but their feet ended in the feet of oxen, and they had human heads, but they had the faces of dogs. Two words they would say like a human and the third they would bark like a dog; and so, for a time, they would

[28] Menestò 1989c:313.
[29] Sinor 1952.
[30] For discussion of these various groups, see Daffinà 1989:453–456, 469–470, 485.

break into barking, yet they would return to the subject, so it was possible to understand what they said.[31]

A little earlier, the Mongols had encountered the Parossites, whose territory was, traveling northwards, between the Bashkirs and the Samoyeds.

> These people have small stomachs and tiny mouths, and we were told that they do not eat but do cook meat; when it is cooked they put themselves over the pot and suck in the vapor; and this is their only nourishment. If indeed they do eat something, it is exceedingly little.[32]

This does not seem to be a detail added late in the text's development. A short account of the mission was related by John's Polish companion Benedict to a cleric in Cologne, and a similar geographical report is provided, bringing together some of the detail provided by John.

> Now as the friars crossed Cumania, on their right they had the land of the Saxi who we [i.e. the scribe] believe are Goths, and who are Christian; afterwards the Alans who are Christian; afterwards the Gazars who are Christian ... then, the Cyrcass and they are Christian. Beforehand in Russia they had the Morduans on their left, who are pagans and they have the back of their heads shaved for the most part; then the Bylers and these are pagans; then the Bascards who are the ancient Hungarians; then the *Cynocephali* who have the heads of dogs; then the *Parocitae* who have small and narrow mouths, nor can they chew anything, but they drink, and receive the vapor of meat and fruit.[33]

The interruption of what seems to be straightforward geography by the obviously fantastical may appear incongruous, or even to undermine the credibility of John's report. John does not, of course, claim that he saw these peoples for himself, but rather that "we were told" about them. This echoes John's appeal to his readers made at the end of the Prologue; if they read "anything which is not known in your parts, do not for this call us liars, for we are bringing back for you that which we saw or that which we heard for certain from others who we believe to be faithful and worthy witnesses."[34] Noting this use of informants, Jackson suggests that John "does appear somewhat gullible."[35] Similarly, Phillips

---

[31] Menestò 1989c:273.
[32] Menestò 1989c:272.
[33] Wyngaert 1929:137–138.
[34] Menestò 1989c:228. Anticipating some disbelief, John concludes that: "it is very cruel for a man to be denigrated by others on account of the good he does."
[35] Jackson 1995:24.

argues that John's problem was "not of false witness ... but credulity."[36] On a few occasions John provides his source for a 'fantastical' detail, as when he was "told by the Russian clerics who live at the Emperor's court" about envoys from the Cyclopedes; or when he was "reliably told at the Emperor's court by Russian clerics and others who had been long among them" about a monstrous people whose women "had the form of a human, but every male had the shape of a dog."[37] These Russian clerics have sometimes been blamed for John's more far-fetched stories, even as if they were deliberately gulling him; or this is seen as evidence of the "jesting nature of the Tartars [*sic*], who probably reveled in misleading the Westerners."[38]

These fantastical elements could be seen to limit the value of the text as a 'source' for historical events. On the other hand, they provide us with an insight into the contemporary Western European imagination, and its understanding of the Orient. It may well be that the elements of the text that modern readers dismiss as revealing only "the incredible gullibility of the medieval travelers to the Mongol capital with their tales of unipeds and shaggy-dog husbands," were not those that John anticipated readers would regard as lies.[39] Could the presence of these stories have served to make John's Orient seem more, rather than less, familiar to his Western audience?

Thirteenth-Century Europe and the Orient

Knowledge of the Orient in the Latin West before the Mongol irruption was patchy at best, and clouded by myth. Latins did not have access to the work of the great Greek geographers of Antiquity, such as Eratosthenes or Ptolemy of Alexandria; nor of their more recent Islamic successors, such as al-Bīrūnī or al-Idrīsī. Ptolemy's work on astronomy had indeed in the twelfth century been translated into Latin via Arabic—hence the name by which it was known, the 'Almagest'; but his geographical treatise was not translated into Latin until the early fifteenth century, from a manuscript brought from Constantinople. While al-Idrīsī worked, in the mid-twelfth century, for a Latin patron, King Roger of Sicily, his treatise had no contemporary impact in Western Europe—composed in Arabic, it was preserved and copied in the Islamic world, and was rediscovered in the West much later.

---

[36] Phillips 2014:192.

[37] Menestò 1989c:274, 259. According to the variant text known as the "Tartar Relation," Friar Benedict believed "for certain that he saw one of the women of the dogs among the Tartars"—identifiable as her sons were monstrous (Painter 1995:73).

[38] Czarnowus 2014:490. Painter 1995:50 also points to their informants—Mongol or Russian—"deluding the friars." For a more general consideration of possible Russian influences on Latin interpretations of the Mongols, see Jackson 2005:147.

[39] Baird 1965:279; this is the review's only comment on the "Tartar Relation."

While the experience of the crusades broadened the perspectives of Latins, as they learned directly about the Middle East, and encountered people there with much broader perspectives, precise geographical understanding remained lacking. This can be seen in the influential *Historia orientalis* composed by James of Vitry (c. 1165/70–1240), bishop of Acre in the kingdom of Jerusalem (1216–1228), and a significant intellectual figure. Despite the more open promise of the title, the focus of the work is Jerusalem and the Holy Land. After a sketch of history from Abraham to Heraclius, the Arab conquest of the Holy Land is described, leading to an overview of Islamic history and doctrine—not entirely even-handed—and an account of Muslim groups and sects (§§2–14). This leads to a history of the First Crusade and the establishment of the Latin states in the region; some attention is given to the sinful nature of their inhabitants and their squabbling, as well as to the other Christian and Jewish inhabitants of the region, whose errors are briefly described (§§15–83). After a brief diversion, the work concludes by returning to the history of Outremer, from Saladin's conquests to the Fourth Lateran council, with its great crusading aims (§§94–102). It is only in the late excursus (§§84–93) that the wider Orient becomes involved. This is a section describing the natural history of the Orient—its weather, its rivers, its flora and fauna, precious stones, and its peoples. Some of this is straightforward—lemons, lions—while some is perhaps less so—the trees in the land of the Seres whose leaves produce a kind of very fine wool, basilisks.[40] Chapter 92 is of especial relevance here—it deals with the peoples of the Orient, the "Amazons, Gymnosophists, Brahmans, and other barbarian and monstrous peoples;" a long chapter, it extends across nearly seventeen pages in the 2008 edition.[41] Most of this reproduces the supposed correspondence of Alexander the Great and Dindymus, the king or chief instructor of the Brahmans.[42] Thereafter James provides a rather breathless catalogue of different peoples, distinguished by their great or limited size, their single eye, their lack of head, their relative hirsuteness, their distinctive dietary practices, and so on. James pauses to justify this diversion from the main theme of his work, explaining that this material was taken "partly from histories of the east and *mappa mundi*, partly from the texts of the blessed Augustine and Isidore, and also from the books of Pliny and Solinus."[43]

James, then, did not base his work on the accounts of travelers passing through his episcopal city, but rather on the authorities of Antiquity preserved in the Latin West, moderated by the Biblical tradition. The first-century Pliny the Elder was the author of the *On Natural History*, an enormous encyclopedia;

---

[40] Donnadieu 2008:344, 352, 350 (presumably a reference to the origins of silk in China), 366.
[41] Donnadieu 2008:348–416.
[42] Donnadieu 2008:386–402, with James's comments extending to the next page.
[43] Donnadieu 2008:406.

the third-century Solinus wrote a compendium *On the Wonders of the World*, some-times known as the *Polyhistor*, or 'very-learned', itself in part based on Pliny. These works in turn influenced that of the seventh-century Isidore of Seville, whose major work, the twenty-volume *Etymologies*, was a vast encyclopedia summarizing the Roman learning of Late Antiquity; two of its volumes dealt with Geography. What this tradition lacked in the scientific rigor of Ptolemy it made up with colorful detail. Building on a separate Classical tradition, the world was divided into various climes, which were peopled by a number of Monstrous Races. These 'Plinian Races' are those described by James, such as the *Blemmyae*, the men with no heads, but with their faces in their chests, so they speak from their stomachs, like lawyers; the *Astomi*, who live off the scent of fruit; or the *Cynocephali*, men with the heads of dogs, who communicate by barking.[44] Stories of such peoples, among other things, informed the medieval West's understanding of the lands of the Orient, as seen in works of scholarship, such as the early eleventh century *Imago Mundi* of Honorius of Autun, or works of entertainment, such as the range of tales encompassed by the term *Alexander Romance*, translated into Western vernaculars from the twelfth century. In these tales, as well as encountering various peoples, such as Amazons, more recognizable animals, such as elephants, and more straightforward mythical beasts, such as griffons, Alexander comes across, and therefore generally fights with, various of these Monstrous Races. Given James of Vitry's clear use of the legendary Alexander material, it could be that this is what he referred to among his sources as a "history of the east."[45]

James also mentions his use of a *mappa mundi*. While one cannot assume that this definitely was a graphic depiction of the world,[46] it may well be that James had in mind something like the thirteenth-century Ebstorf Map, or the later Hereford Map (ca. 1300). While one should not discount an intended prac-tical value, these great *mappaemundi* were not intended to be accurate represen-tations of the world as it was. The world was *not* flat; nor did they display its full extent; rather, they depicted the inhabited or inhabitable portion of the world, which had received Divine Revelation.[47] The central theme of these works was Christian cosmography: Jerusalem is always at the very center, the navel of the

---

[44] For a list of these 'Plinian races', see Friedman 1981, esp. 9–21.

[45] For the more historical sections of the *Historia orientalis* it is clear that James made use of the chronicle of William of Tyre, the *Historia rerum in partibus transmarinus gestarum*, which may be another work covered by 'histories of the east'. On the sources for the *Historia orientalis*, and also on subsequent works that made use of it, see Donnadieu 2008:21–32. For the influence of Augustine on the *Historia orientalis*, see, esp., Donnadieu 2008:36–38. For connections between the *Historia orientalis* and the Alexander Romance, see Schwartz 1949.

[46] Woodward 1987:287–288.

[47] Cf. Scafi, 2006:350.

world—literally so in the case of the Ebstorf Map, where the world is shown as the body of Christ. Geographical accuracy was of secondary importance: the continents fit into a visual scheme where the river Don and the Nile or Red Sea provide a horizontal rule, and the Mediterranean a vertical, so that Europe is at bottom left, Africa bottom right, and Asia across the top. Geographical features—peninsulas, islands, rivers—are arranged to fit into this scheme, with some approximate accuracy, but even so more important areas—the Holy Land—receive disproportionate space. These maps do reveal something about contemporary geographical understanding—for example, the Caspian is generally shown as an inlet of the Arctic Sea—and it may be that they were at least partly intended as an aid to planning itineraries. These maps are, however, about history as much as geography; they are often full of text themselves, and the places marked are often those mentioned in literary histories.[48] The great illustrated *mappaemundi* depict the events of Biblical history, but also secular. The fringes of the world as depicted in the Ebstorf Map, for example, show the adventures of Alexander, peoples such as the Amazons or Gog and Magog, and a variety of monsters, such as the *Cynocephali.*

For an educated Latin at the beginning of the thirteenth century, like James of Vitry, these were the received authorities. The Latin classical tradition of a world peopled by a variety of monstrous races was reinforced by material such as that relating to Alexander; as we see in the *Historia Orientalis* these different strands were deeply intertwined, as also in the *mappaemundi*, the visual counterparts of the literary geographies. This material represents, in perhaps a rather fantastical form, the expectations twelfth-century Latins had of the wider world, and especially the lands of the East; these monstrous peoples were the sort of thing a traveler might find were he to venture, like Alexander, to the extremes of Asia.

But it should not be thought that Latin geographical knowledge was static. The experience of the crusades, of course, led to greater knowledge of the Middle East; it also led to encounters with people there whose horizons were broader still. This was not only Muslims, but also local Christians, such as the Armenians, and, especially, the Syriac-speaking Jacobites and Nestorians. These latter had had much success in Central Asia; even some rulers on the Eastern steppes were nominally Christians, such as the khans of the Kereit confederation. Indeed, it may well have been garbled accounts of such things that led to a further important literary encounter of the Latins with the East: the story of "Prester John." In the middle of the twelfth century a letter arrived in Europe purporting to be from a Christian king in the East—'Prester John', or 'John the

---

[48]   Woodward 1987:289.

Priest'. He assured the recipients that he would soon appear in the Holy Land with his mighty army to join with the crusaders to defeat the Saracens once and for all. The news spread, and when later travelers went East, they sought for Prester John or his realm—which could also be identified with the realm of the Magi of the Gospels—the Three Kings in the Latin version.[49] When the Fifth Crusade was in Egypt, new rumors of the imminent arrival of great reinforcements under Prester John's son, King David, led to the crusaders doing little but wait for two years (1219–1221). These rumors may have been based on a rather garbled account of events in Central Asia—there was indeed a new army approaching, but not that of Prester John.[50] The confusion of these new invaders with older expectations of the east can be seen even later, in 1241, in the rumors at Cologne that this city was the target of those invading Europe from the steppelands to the east—it was thought that they were on their way there to reclaim the relics of the Three Kings housed in Cologne: the legends about Prester John and his Magian descent were still significant.[51]

John of Plano Carpini, the Mongols, and the Monsters

To what extent do Friar John's stories merely reflect this contemporary Latin understanding of the Orient? On one occasion John explicitly refers to the Latin authorities: when describing the Mongol encounter with one-armed and one-legged cartwheeling men, he tells us as an aside that "these are the men Isidore called *Cyclopedes*."[52] More subtly, Khanmohamedi has suggested that the "classifications of culture" that John employed in his descriptions of the life and customs of the Mongols "may well have [been] influenced" by "Isidore's and Solinus's treatment of the Plinian races"; these "classifications … reinscribe much of the same categories that serve as boundaries between the human and the nonhuman in Pliny, Solinus and Isidore."[53] While it may stretch the point to suggest that the Mongols were themselves presented as if a 'monstrous race', it may well be that the method of discussing fantastic peoples had some influence on the seemingly more straightforwardly ethnographic observations made by visitors to the Mongols. Furthermore, it is clear that their dietary and hygienic practices marked them out as 'an unclean people' for their Mendicant guests.[54]

---

[49] See e.g. de Rachewiltz 1996.
[50] See e.g. Richard 1996.
[51] Hamilton 1996; Morgan 1996b:163–164.
[52] Menestò 1989c:274.
[53] Khanmohamedi 2014:22.
[54] Jackson 2001:363.

John certainly shows awareness of more recent knowledge of the Orient. Like many writers on the Mongols, he needed to explain how Prester John fit into the story. For Friar John, Prester John was the king of "Greater India"; when attacked by the Mongols, he had used mannequins filled with Greek Fire to disrupt the Mongol forces:

> He made figures of men of copper, placed in saddles on horses, and put fire inside ... And when they reached the battleground, they sent forward these horses ... The result was that men and horses were burned up by Greek Fire, and the air was blackened by the smoke; and then they shot arrows at the Tartars, of whom many were wounded and killed; and thus in confusion they were thrown out of their territory.[55]

Friar John's method of reconciling the manifest reality of the Mongols with the long-desired Prester John is consistent with the general message of the text— that the Mongols can be defeated. The character of Prester John in this anecdote plays a familiar role, once again embodying the desires of the Latin West for military salvation. This anecdote, however, also reveals less manifest borrowing from the Latin Oriental tradition. Prester John's stratagem is essentially the same as that employed by Alexander in his defeat of King Porus of India, whose army boasted fearsome elephants.[56]

While a story such as this can be seen to have had a didactic purpose— the Mongols can be defeated—very often the rationale for the inclusion of a fantastic element is less clear. Mongol encounters with Monstrous Races often seem to interrupt the flow of John's narrative. For example, his account of the early Mongol conquests follows their defeat of the Qarakhitai with a mention of how Ogedei later founded a city in these lands, near which was "a great desert, in which live wild men for certain, they say, who do not speak at all and nor do their legs have joints." After a couple of sentences describing their camel-hair clothing and use of grass to treat the wounds inflicted by the Mongols, the narrative returns to the how the Mongols turned from the Qarakhitai to the Chinese.[57] Similarly, when describing Chormaghun's campaigns in the Caucasus (1236–1239), we are told that he turned from defeating the Circassians to the Armenians, but on his way he crossed a desert where he encountered *Cyclopedes*, who later sent envoys to the emperor. Then, the main narrative returns— "moving on from there, they came to Armenia."[58] Lacking any obvious purpose, were these stories included merely as entertainments?

---

[55] Menestò 1989c:258–259.
[56] Pritchard 1992:75.
[57] Menestò 1989c:254–255.
[58] Menestò 1989c:273–274.

It should not be assumed, moreover, that these tales of monstrous peoples have their origins in Pliny and the Latin tradition—some of these stories have no clear equivalent there. The strange dog-human hybrids encountered on the retreat from Prester John are *not* simply *Cynocephali*; neither are the dog-faced people with the feet of oxen encountered by the Mongols in northern Siberia.[59] The stiff-legged "wild men" in the Dzhungharian desert also seem different. They do have equivalents in one contemporary text: the Armenian Kirakos Ganjaketsi's narrative of King Het'um I's journey to the Great Khan Möngke in the 1250s.[60] As Peter Jackson has pointed out, these stories relate closely to *Eastern* models—the accounts of eighth-century Uyghur envoys to northern Siberia, and tenth and thirteenth century Chinese travelers on the steppes. Jackson suggests that John "certainly received some of his information from the Mongols."[61] This suggestion might also explain John's rather odd use of the Porus episode from the Alexander Romance—well-known material—passing it off as contemporary history without any comment. It would seem that this was not a conscious borrowing on his part. Rather than a story that he had brought with him to the East, could it have been one that he encountered there?[62] Was this story introduced by John's Russian informants? It has even been suggested that this kind of anecdote might reflect Mongol self-mythologizing: that stories about Alexander circulating *in the east* contributed to the development of a "Chinggis Khan Romance"—though how this defeat at the hands of a king of India fits with this theory is unclear.[63]

John's method of incorporating Prester John in his history of the Mongols proved to be an unusual one. While Prester John is fairly ubiquitous in Latin accounts of the Mongols, he is generally one of the potentates overthrown by the Mongols in their rise to prominence; this approach works better than Friar John's, both explaining his current absence and his failure to turn up as promised in Palestine.[64] But just as it may be that the Mongols might themselves be the source for the stories about Monstrous Races they had encountered, very

---

[59] Menestò 1989c:259–260, 273.

[60] Boyle 1964:181–182 (wild men; and n. 42 for analogues from Islamic world sources), 187 (dog-human hybrids). Cf. Painter 1995:70–71n3.

[61] Jackson 2001:368, and n. 139.

[62] A similar line of argument is used by the late Ruth Macrides to explain some of the apparent inaccuracies in the crusader Robert of Clari's account of Constantinople in 1203–1204; rather than reflecting Robert's own confusion, these reflect the understanding of his Greek informants (Macrides 2002).

[63] See Yourtchenko 1998. Cf. Painter 1995:47–51. A Mongol version of the 'Alexander Romance' was produced, but the surviving fragments date from the fourteenth century: see Cleaves 1959. John's story is closer to the Western European version of Alexander's battle with Porus, as in the tenth-century *Historia de preliis,* than it is to, for example, the version in the *Shāhnāma,* or that found later in the *Iskandarnāma:* see Venetis 2013:57–58, 273, and n. 1165; Pritchard 1992:75.

[64] See e.g. in John of Joinville's *Life of St Louis*—Monfrin 1995:234–240.

quickly they might themselves provide the explanation for Prester John's disappearance. The Mongol envoys who came to Louis IX of France on Cyprus in December 1248 informed the king that the Great Khan Güyük was himself a Christian, through the influence of his mother, the daughter of Prester John.[65] The Latins were looking for Prester John, so the Mongols, helpfully, provided him. Did the enquiries of the Latins distort the answers they eventually received?[66] Does it suggest a significant role as intermediaries between Mongols and Latins for Eastern Christians—Nestorians—whose stories may have contributed to the Prester John legend, and who seem to have been the envoys to Louis in 1248? Or does it suggest that the Mongols themselves were not passive or disinterested—they sought to exploit the expectations of the Latins, to mold them and to use them to promote their own interests, by feeding material back to Latin interlocutors.

It is perhaps too simple to interpret these accounts of Monsters, and Prester John, as merely mental baggage carried with John on his journey. Of course, both he—and the audiences he entertained—would have been preconditioned to accept these stories as at least possible, as advised by James of Vitry, who in the course of his own account of the wonders of the Orient reassured his reader that "if these things seem incredible, we are not compelled to believe them."[67] Not everyone did believe them: a decade later the Franciscan William of Rubruck, back from his own remarkable journey to Karakorum, reports that:

> I enquired about the monsters or human freaks who are described by Isidore and Solinus, but was told that such things had never been sighted, which makes us very much doubt whether [the story] is true.[68]

Such skepticism was anticipated by James of Vitry, who asked whether not all of the works of God are wonders (*mirabilia*). James spends several pages pointing out that various "wonders" are well known to his Latin audience, and even that such matters might seem incredible to Orientals—such as the trees in Flanders that grow birds; Mount Etna's constant eruptions; Charybdis and Scylla; the people in Britain with tails, and those in France with horns, or who bark like dogs; and so on (for several pages).[69] The aim is clearly to make the Orient seem *less* strange, by pointing to the well-known oddities of the Occident. The elements of John of Plano Carpini's political geography of Asia that seem fantastical to the modern reader—monstrous animal-human hybrids, Prester John—may have

---

65   Letter of Odo of Châteauroux to Pope Innocent IV, in Jackson 2007:81.
66   For a more clear-cut example of this, see Jackson 2005:145–146.
67   Donnadieu 2008:406.
68   Jackson and Morgan 1990:201 and n. 5.
69   Donnadieu 2008:408–418.

served a similar purpose: to make an unfamiliar world seem more familiar to his audience. They were intended to reassure, rather than to entertain; they were meant to enhance the text's reputation for reliability, even if today they seem to undermine this reputation. Furthermore, what John's inclusion of these stories reveals is not so much a blinkered imposition of a preconceived Monstrous Orient, but rather John's open-mindedness. They may provide us with a sense of the sort of cultural encounters taking place at the Mongol court. John's background gave him no reason to question the stories of the Russian clerics he cites as sources; that some of these stories seem to reflect Far Eastern legends reinforces, in a way, his reputation as an interlocutor of the Mongol perspective; as his text suggests, these are the stories they seem to tell about themselves.

Works Cited

Aigle, D., ed. 1997. *L'Iran face à la domination mongole*. Tehran.

Baird, J. L., G. Baglivi, and J. R. Kane, eds. and trans. 1986. *The Chronicle of Salimbene de Adam*. Binghamton.

Baird, P. D. 1965. Review of R. A. Skelton, T. E. Marston, and G. D. Painter, *The Vinland Map and the Tartar Relation* (New Haven, 1965). *Arctic* 18:279–280.

Beckingham, C. F., and B. Hamilton, eds. 1996. *Prester John, the Mongols and the Ten Lost Tribes*. Aldershot.

Blake, R. P., and R. N. Frye. 1949. "History of the Nation of the Archers (The Mongols) by Grigor of Akancʻ, Hitherto Ascribed to Matakʻia The Monk: The Armenian Text Edited with an English Translation and Notes." *Harvard Journal of Asiatic Studies* 12:269–399.

Boyle, J. A. 1964. "The Journey of Hetʻum I, King of Little Armenia, to the Court of the Great Khan Möngke." *Central Asiatic Journal* 9:175–189.

Cleaves, F. W. 1959. "An Early Mongolian Version of the Alexander Romance." *Harvard Journal of Asiatic Studies* 22:2–99.

Czarnowus, A. 2014. "The Mongols, Eastern Europe, and Western Europe: The Mirabilia Tradition in Benedict of Poland's *Historia Tartarorum* and John of Plano Carpini's *Historia Mongalorum*." *Literature Compass* 11:484–495.

Daffinà, P. 1989. "Note." In Daffinà, Leonardi, Lungarotti, Menestò, and Petech 1989:401–496.

Daffinà, P., C. Leonardi, M. C. Lungarotti, E. Menestò, and L. Petech, eds. 1989. *Giovanni di Pian di Carpine, Storia dei Mongoli*. Spoleto.

Dawson, C., ed., and Nun of Stanbrook Abbey, trans. 1955. *The Mongol Mission: Narratives and Letters of the Franciscan Missionaries in Mongolia and China in the Thirteenth and Fourteenth Centuries*. London.

Donnadieu, J., ed. and trans. 2008. *Jacques de Vitry, Histoire orientale/Historia orientalis*. Turnhout.

Evans, A., ed. 1936. *Francesco Balducci Pegolotti, La pratica della mercatura.* Cambridge, MA.

Friedman, J. B. 1981. *The Monstrous Races in Medieval Art and Thought.* Cambridge, MA.

Hamilton, B. 1996. "Prester John and the Three Kings of Cologne." In Beckingham and Hamilton 1996:171–185.

Harley, J. B., and D. Woodward, eds. 1987. *The History of Cartography, 1: Cartography in Prehistoric, Ancient, and Medieval Europe and the Mediterranean.* Chicago.

Harvey, P. D. A., ed. 2006. *The Hereford World Map: Medieval World Maps and Their Context.* London.

Jackson, P. 1995. "Early Missions to the Mongols: Carpini and His Contemporaries." *Hakluyt Society Annual Report for 1994*: 15–32.

———. 1998. "Marco Polo and His 'Travels.'" *Bulletin of the School of Oriental and African Studies* 61:82–101.

———. 2001. "Medieval Christendom's Encounter with the Alien." *Historical Research* 74:347–269.

———. 2005. *The Mongols and the West.* Harlow.

———, trans. 2007. *The Seventh Crusade, 1244-1254: Sources and Documents.* Aldershot.

Jackson, P., and D. Morgan, trans. 1990. *The Mission of Friar William of Rubruck: His Journey to the Court of the Great Khan Möngke, 1253-1255.* London.

Khanmohamadi, S. 2014. *In Light of Another's Word: European Ethnography in the Middle Ages.* Philadelphia.

Larner, J. 1999. *Marco Polo and the Discovery of the World.* New Haven.

Legassie, S. A. 2017. *The Medieval Invention of Travel.* Chicago.

Luongarotti, M. C. 1989. "Le due redazioni dell'*Historia Mongalorum*." In Daffinà, Leonardi, Lungarotti, Menestò, and Petech 1989:79–92.

Macrides, R. 2002. "Constantinople: The Crusaders' Gaze." In *Travel in the Byzantine World*, 193–212. Aldershot.

Menestò, E. 1989a. "Giovanni di Pian di Carpine: Da compagno di Francesco a diplomatico presso i Tartari." In Daffinà, Leonardi, Lungarotti, Menestò, and Petech 1989:49–67.

———. 1989b. "La tradizione manoscritta." In Daffinà, Leonardi, Lungarotti, Menestò, and Petech 1989:100–216.

———, ed. 1989c. "Giovanni di Pian di Carpine, *Historia Mongalorum*." In Daffinà, Leonardi, Lungarotti, Menestò, and Petech 1989:225–333.

Monfrin, J., ed. 1995. *John of Joinville, Vie de saint Louis.* Paris.

Morgan, D. O. 1996a. "Marco Polo in China—or Not." *Journal of the Royal Asiatic Society* 6:221–225.

———. 1996b. "Prester John and the Mongols." In Beckingham and Hamilton 1996:159–170.

O'Doherty, M. 2009. "The *Viaggio in Inghilterra* of a *Viaggio in Oriente*: Odorico da Pordenone's *Itinerarium* from Italy to England." *Italian Studies* 64:198–220.

Painter, G. D., ed. 1995. "The Tartar Relation." In Skelton, Marston, and Painter 1995:19–106.

Paviot, J. 1997. "Les marchands italiens dans l'Iran mongol." In Aigle 1997:71–86.

Petech, L. 1962. "Les marchands italiens dans l'empire mongol." *Journal Asiatique* 250:549–574.

Phillips, J. R. S. 1988. *The Medieval Expansion of Europe*. Oxford.

Phillips, K. 2014. *Before Orientalism: Asian Peoples and Cultures in European Travel Writing, 1245-1510*. Philadelphia.

Pritchard, R. T., trans. 1992. *The History of Alexander's Battles*. Historia de preliis, the J1 version. Toronto.

Rachewiltz, I. de. 1971. *Papal Envoys to the Great Khans*. London.

———. 1996. "Prester John and Europe's Discovery of East Asia." *East Asian History* 11:59–74.

———. 1997. "Marco Polo Went to China." *Zentralasiatische Studien* 27:34–92.

Richard, J. 1996. "The *Relatio de Davide* as a Source for Mongol History and the Legend of Prester John." In Beckingham and Hamilton 1996:139–158.

Rouleau, F. 1954. "The Yangchow Latin Tombstone as a Landmark of Medieval Christianity in China." *Harvard Journal of Asiatic Studies* 17:346–365.

Scafi, A. 2006. "Defining Mappaemundi." In Harvey 2006:345–354.

Schwartz, J. 1949. "Jacques de Vitry et l'*Historia de preliis*." *Revue du Moyen Âge Latin* 5:132–133.

Sinor, D. 1952. "Un voyageur du treizième siècle: Le Dominicain Julien de Hongrie." *Bulletin of the School of Oriental and African Studies* 14:589–602.

Skelton, R. A., E. T. Marston, and G. D. Painter. 1995. *The Vinland Map and the Tartar Relation*. 2nd ed. New Haven.

Venetis, E. 2013. *The Persian Prose Alexander Romance*. Saarbrücken.

Wood, F. 1995. *Did Marco Polo Go to China?* London.

Woodward, D. 1987. "Medieval *Mappaemundi*." In Harvey and Woodward 1987: 286–730.

Wyngaert, A. van den, ed. 1929. *Sinica Franciscana*, vol. I: *Itinera et relations Fratrum Minorum saeculi xiii et xiv*. Florence.

Yourtchenko, A. 1998. "Ein asiatisches Bilderrätsel für die westliche Geschichts- schreibung: Ein unbekanntes Werk aus dem 13. Jahrhundert (Der 'Tschingis Khan-Roman')." *Zentralasiatische Studien* 28:45–85.

4

Ottoman Imagined Geography in the Verses of the Court Poets Ahmedi and Abdülvasi (ca. 1402–1414)

Dimitri Kastritsis

THE FIFTEENTH CENTURY WAS A TIME OF TRANSFORMATION not just for the eastern Mediterranean and Middle East, but more generally in global terms. Yet from the perspective of Ottoman history, it remains seriously under-studied. How did early Ottoman authors present the wider world and their place within it, both in terms of broader ideas of social space and with respect to the actual geographies in which they were operating? The present contribution will attempt to address this question by focusing on two historical poems from the early part of the century, which are among the earliest literary works produced in Ottoman courts. The first is Ahmedi's versified account of Ottoman history, which forms part of his *İskendernāme* ('Book of Alexander') completed before 1411. The second is Abdülvasi Çelebi's panegyric on Sultan Mehmed I's 1413 victory over his brother Musa, included in at least one manuscript of his 1414 work *Ḥalīlnāme* ('Book of Halil', i.e. Abraham).[1] More specifically, we will consider the spatial aspects of these works, which can shed light on early Ottoman ideas of political and cultural geography. By the time the poems were written, the Ottoman state had already experienced its first, limited imperial phase, which ended abruptly when Timur crushed the Ottoman armies at the Battle of Ankara (1402). In the aftermath of this disaster, the dynasty and those serving it struggle to legitimize their political claims as relative newcomers to the stage of Islamic history, whose historic centers were further south and east. As we will see, at least part of their justification lay in the idea that they were the

---

[1] For Ahmedi I have used Dankoff 2020; numbers refer to verses rather than pages. I would like to thank Robert Dankoff for sharing his critical edition with me prior to publication. I have also provided verse numbers from Sılay 2004 to assist the reader. For Abdülvasi's poem, I have used Güldaş 1996.

legitimate rulers of the eastern Roman (i.e. Byzantine) lands, which they called following Islamic convention "the land of Rum" (*bilād al-Rūm, diyār-ı Rūm*).[2]

By the time the Ottomans appeared on the historical stage, the name Rum (*Rūm*), an Arabic form of the word "Rome," had long been applied by Muslims to the territories still under Byzantine rule after the early expansion of Islam, particularly Anatolia or Asia Minor. However, from the mid-eleventh century when the Seljuk Turks moved into the Middle East, many parts of Anatolia also came to be ruled by Muslims, despite remaining home to large Christian populations.[3] By the early fourteenth century, when the weakened Seljuks under Mongol domination were replaced by a number of small Turkish emirates (beyliks), Byzantium had lost nearly all its territory in northwestern Anatolia, which came under the rule of the Ottoman beylik. Thanks to a favorable position and Byzantine weakness and division, the Ottomans were gradually able to annex the other beyliks and extend Roman (*Rūmī*) Islamic culture across the straits into the Balkans. For these newly Islamized territories, many of which were captured from Byzantium, they would eventually use the term Rumeli (Rumelia, lit. 'land of the Romans'). As we will see when we examine the two poems, this term (equivalent to Greek *Romanía*) was used literally in the early fifteenth century to refer to regions still associated politically or ethno-linguistically with Byzantium. This usage is in line with that of western Europeans of the time, who used the term Romania for the same regions even when they were under Latin rule. It was only later in the fifteenth century that Ottoman administrative practices extended the use of Rumeli to the bulk of the Balkan Peninsula.[4]

In order to understand Ottoman imagined geography in the early fifteenth century, it is therefore essential to bear in mind the many meanings of the word Rum and its derivatives. In the broadest sense, formerly Byzantine territories in Anatolia and the Balkans could be said to constitute the land of Rum (*bilād al-Rūm, diyār-ı Rūm*). More specifically, parts of the Balkans where Byzantine culture and administration were still dominant were called Rumeli (following the usage of *Romanía* at this time). Finally, to further complicate matters, in our two poems Rum is also used in a more limited sense for the inland Black Sea (Pontus) province of Anatolia around the towns of Amasya, Tokat, and Niksar. The explanation is that in the eleventh century, when Turkish tribes had first moved in, the dynasty of Danişmend, a rival of the Seljuks originally based further south in Sivas, had succeeded in expanding their rule into this still "Roman" (i.e. Greek-speaking) region, much as the Ottomans would do two centuries later in the

---

2   Kafadar 2007:9–10.
3   Peacock and Yıldız 2016:1–3.
4   İnalcık 1994:608.

southern Balkans.[5] For this reason, the Amasya-Tokat region came to be known as the province of Rum, a usage adopted by the Ottomans when they added its territory to their domains in the late fourteenth century.

Before turning to the two poems, it is necessary to have a sense of the complex historical context in which they were produced, to which the poems make reference. Both works date from the era of internecine warfare and political instability known as the Ottoman civil war or interregnum (*fetret devri*, 1402–1413). This was a 'time of troubles' that began with Timur's destruction of the first Ottoman attempt at empire in 1402, and did not fully end until Murad II's elimination of his rivals in 1422, ushering in a period of reconstruction and warfare with Christian Europe that led to the conquest of Constantinople in 1453. In the first two decades of the fifteenth century, when both poems were written, Ottoman society was mostly focused on internal politics and its place within the wider Islamic world. This was largely a response to Timur's action in 1402, which was a direct challenge to Ottoman imperialism under Bayezid I (1389–1402). When Bayezid I came to power upon the death of his father Murad I at Kosovo, he intensified the expansion of the small Ottoman principality into an empire. Making use largely of Christian armies led by his Byzantine and Serbian clients, Bayezid annexed several rival Muslim principalities of Anatolia and added them to his domains. Although his priorities arguably lay in Anatolia and the wider Muslim world, tense relations with local Christians, including Byzantium, forced him to assert his power in Europe as well.[6] He was the first Ottoman ruler to blockade Constantinople, and also defeated a Crusader army at Nicopolis on the Danube (1396). Since the Ottomans had no Muslim rivals in Europe, their successes there earned them prestige in the Islamic world. Nonetheless, Bayezid's expansionist policies in Anatolia brought him into conflict with the Mamluks of Egypt and Syria, and ultimately Timur, eventually resulting in the fateful encounter at Ankara.

When Bayezid was taken prisoner and died in capitivity, Timur intentionally allowed his sons to fight it out for what remained of his domains. The ensuing civil war involved a great many foreign powers, as well as Ottoman factions.[7] In 1402, in the aftermath of Bayezid's defeat and captivity, his son Süleyman managed to take control of the dynasty's territories in Europe. From there, he soon extended his rule to the original Ottoman heartlands, including the capital Bursa and the strategic stronghold of Ankara. This forced his brother Mehmed (the future Mehmed I) to abandon Bursa, which he had previously seized from a third brother named İsa, and withdraw to Amasya in the Black

---

[5] Bosworth 1994:606.
[6] Imber 1990:37–52; Murphey 2014.
[7] Kastritsis 2007.

Sea province of Rum, where he had been governor under his father. From there, Mehmed and his allies were eventually able to overthrow Süleyman by sending a fourth brother, Musa, across the Black Sea to the Danube region, from where he invaded Süleyman's European territories from the north. Once Musa had killed Süleyman and taken control of the Ottoman Balkans, Mehmed was able to retake Bursa and Ottoman Anatolia (1411). The two former allies thus became enemies since each stood in the other's way of becoming the single Ottoman ruler. They fought a series of campaigns in the Balkans, eventually leading to the Battle of Çamurlu near Sofia (1413) in which Musa was defeated and killed: the subject of Abdülvasi's poem.

Now that the necessary historical context has been provided, we may turn to the two poems. The one by Ahmedi (d. 1413) is by far the better known of the two, as it has long been viewed as the first account of Ottoman history to have survived in original form. It was also composed first—so it makes sense to begin here.

Uses of Space in the Ottoman Section of Ahmedi's *İskendernāme*

Ahmedi's poem on Ottoman history forms part of the poet's larger work entitled *İskendernāme* ('Book of Alexander'). This is a wide-ranging composition in the genre of the medieval Alexander Romance, with a long historical section of which the Ottoman poem forms the final part. The work was begun before 1402 and written in stages; the complete version was first presented to Emir Süleyman (d. 1411). The Ottoman poem is based on a lost prose chronicle, traces of which also survive in later histories. However, the events it describes are commented upon and embellished by Ahmedi, making the final result his own work. It is clear that it was intended to praise Süleyman and his forebears, at a time when their authority had been seriously undermined by Timur. Ahmedi's poem is thus panegyric in nature; but like the rest of the *İskendernāme*, it also has didactic aspects. The poem's emphasis on the Ottomans' qualities as holy raiders (ġāzīs) made it a key element in the still dominant if controversial theory of Ottoman origins, known as the Wittek thesis after Paul Wittek, who first proposed it in the middle of the twentieth century.[8] While this is not the place for a detailed discussion of the theory and ensuing controversy, it is worth noting that Ahmedi's poem does indeed emphasize Ottoman raiding in the name of Islam (ġazā). This emphasis is connected to the crisis of Ottoman legitimacy following the disaster of 1402, and as we will see below, forms part and parcel of Ahmedi's presentation of geographical space.

---

[8]   Wittek 1938; Wittek 2012; Kafadar 1995:36–44.

As already discussed, Ahmedi's Ottoman poem is part of a larger historical section in the *İskendernāme*, a work framed in terms of the exploits of Alexander the Great as he had come to be imagined in the medieval world. Specifically in parts of the Islamic world influenced by medieval Persian literature, including the Ottoman domains, the figure of Alexander and his conquests had become a metaphor not just for cosmopolitanism and universal empire, but also for a wisdom quest defined in sufi mystical terms.[9] In the spirit of the original Greek Alexander Romance, which includes among other things an encounter between Alexander and various wise men in Athens, India, and other places, the discourses in Ahmedi also take place in suitably exotic locations.[10] Following the precedent established by Firdawsi's *Shāhnāmeh* (the Persian 'Book of Kings'), Ahmedi presents Alexander as the son of an Iranian king traveling the world in the company of wise men, who present discourses on such areas as astronomy, music, and history. This retinue includes his tutor Aristotle and the prophetic figure Hızır (*Khiḍr*), who represents renewal and rebirth and accompanies Alexander on his quest for the spring of eternal life.[11] Hızır is also responsible for presenting an account of historical events that have not happened, but which will take place after Alexander's death, consisting mostly of Islamic history down to the Ottoman section.

In terms of location, these discourses on history are presented as taking place somewhere in North Africa. However, it is fair to say that apart from the chapters on early Islamic history, Ahmedi's historical account has a distinctly Iranian focus. This is hardly surprising, considering that the poet is writing in the tradition of Islamicate Persian literature. However, it is still striking how much space he allocates to the Ilkhanid Mongols of Iran and the Middle East, who were nominally also the rulers of Anatolia around the time the Ottoman dynasty first appeared.[12] This may strike the modern historian of the Ottoman Empire as unusual, given the fact that in later Ottoman histories the Mongol legacy is almost completely absent. Indeed, even in Ahmedi the seeds of the so-called 'Ottoman dynastic myth' are already present, notably the idea of a power transfer from the Seljuk dynasty to that of the Ottomans.[13] How, then, may we explain the prominent place of the Ilkhanids in Ahmedi's account of world history, especially since the poet's presentation of the Mongols is generally negative? The answer seems to lie in the fact that for Ahmedi, sovereignty

---

[9] Kastritsis 2016.
[10] This geographical focus is clear from the table of contents in Dankoff 2020, which includes sections on Iran, Sistan, India, Egypt, and beyond.
[11] Wensinck 1977; for the Ottoman context, see Boratav 1979.
[12] For Anatolia under the Ilkhanids, see Melville 2009.
[13] Imber 1987.

at a given time always lies primarily with a single ruler or dynasty. This explains the linear nature of his account, which moves from the ancient kings of Iran to the Prophet Muhammad and the Rightly Guided Caliphs, to the Umayyads and Abbasids, to the Ilkhanid Mongols who killed the last Abbasid caliph in 1258, and finally to the Ottomans by means of other petty dynasties and local lords. Above all, such a presentation of history probably reflects literary needs, since it is easier to focus on a single ruler at a time. But more or less intentionally, it also creates the impression of a single sovereignty passing from ruler to ruler, and from dynasty to dynasty. Of course, not all rulers are equal in merit: although the Ilkhanid Mongols did eventually convert to Islam, Ahmedi makes it clear that they were tyrants, unlike the Ottomans who were true Muslims and restorers of sovereignty and justice.[14]

Let us now consider the Ottoman section of Ahmedi's *İskendernāme* from the perspective of imagined geography. After presenting the history of the Mongol Ilkhanate and its fragmentation, with occasional references to the Seljuks of Rum, the scene is set for the arrival of the Ottomans.[15] The dynasty is presented as having started out as clients of the Seljuk sultan Alaeddin—an idealized figure not unlike Charlemagne or King Arthur. According to the story, this Seljuk sultan is engaged in holy raiding (*ġazā*) against the infidels (i.e. Christian Byzantines) in the borderlands to the northwest of his domains, when he is forced to return to his capital Konya to face the Mongol threat in that region. As he departs, he appoints Ertuğrul, the father of the Ottoman founder Osman, to lead the struggle against Christendom, granting him some recently captured lands in Bithynia near Constantinople, which will later become the core of the Ottoman dominions. Although this story is fictitious and serves a legitimizing purpose for the Ottoman dynasty, nonetheless it is worth including here because of its role in setting up the geography of the rest of Ahmedi's Ottoman poem. From the outset, the poet places the dynasty in the shifting borderlands between the Islamic and Christian worlds, where the Ottomans fulfill the role supposedly assigned to them by the Seljuk sultan, carrying out holy raids for the expansion of the domains of Islam. Ahmedi's emphasis on this sacred role allows the poet to shift his geographical focus from Iran, Iraq, and other central lands of Islam to the land of Rum, the Ottoman sphere of operations. However, the wider Islamic world does continue to feature, albeit from a new, more Roman perspective. Although the protagonists of the Ottoman section (notably, members of the dynasty) are still presented in distinctly Persian and Islamic terms, it is clear that their native land is eastern Rome, the land of Rum.

---

[14] Dankoff 2020:7539–7544; Sılay 2004:3–8.
[15] Dankoff 2020:7561–7586; Sılay 2004:25–50. For an earlier appearance of the Seljuks, see Dankoff 2020:7288–7589.

After a very brief account of the reign of the first ruler Osman (?–1324?), which discusses his struggles with the infidel Christians (*kāfir*) and his conquest of some towns in northwest Anatolia (i.e. Bithynia), the poet turns to the reign of Osman's successor Orhan (r. 1324–1362).[16] Since it was under Orhan's rule that the Ottomans first rose to prominence and crossed the straits to the Balkan Peninsula in Europe, he receives a much more generous treatment consisting of two long, separate chapters. The first concerns his conquests in Bithynia before crossing the straits, and the second is devoted to events in the Balkans following this important event. Ahmedi waxes eloquent about Orhan's piety and struggles against the infidel, as well as his justice, for which he is compared to the early Islamic caliph Umar (r. 634–644 CE). He mentions Orhan's conquest of the important Byzantine towns of Bursa (Prousa, 1326) and Nicaea (İznik, 1331), with an emphasis on their supposed Islamization. Although the language in this chapter is overwhelmingly that of Islamic piety and holy raiding (*ġazā*), the poet also draws on the Persian epic tradition to describe Orhan's bravery in battle. The final verse of the first chapter provides a suitable transition to the second, in which the geographical emphasis shifts to Europe:

> Lāz'a düşmiş idi andan velvele
> Üngürus'uŋ éllerine zelzele

> Because of him (Orhan) the Serbs (Laz) were overcome by tumult
> The lands of the Hungarians were struck by an earthquake[17]

Needless to say, this is little more than rhetoric. Serbia was powerful until the death of Stefan Dušan in 1355, *after* the Ottomans had already crossed to Europe and captured Gallipoli. So neither the Serbs, nor of course the more distant Hungarians, would have felt threatened while the Ottoman domains were still limited to the Asian side of the straits. Here Ahmedi is merely anticipating the following chapters, which discuss Ottoman operations in the Balkans. For our purposes, what is interesting here is the poet's presentation of the new lands located on the European side of the straits.

Ahmedi's account of Murad I's reign (1362–1389) allows us to explore these themes in further detail. Since it was under Murad that the Ottomans first emerged as the main power in the region, the poet devotes a full four chapters to describing his exploits, which are presented as an outcome of his sincere faith and devotion to holy raiding.[18] Ahmedi states that "he was the first to extend

---

[16] Dankoff 2020:7587–7671; Sılay 2004:51–135.
[17] Dankoff 2020:7629; Sılay 2004:93. All translations are my own.
[18] Dankoff 2020:7672–7789; Sılay 2004:136–253. This includes the Islamic version of the story of David and Goliath, which is used to show the power of sincere faith.

his hand to Rum" and that as a result "many perils were reaching the Caesar."[19] It is clear that what is meant here by "the Caesar" (*Ḳayṣer*) is the Byzantine emperor; however, a broader reading of the poet's work reveals another, very different instance of a Caesar. When recounting the story of Alexander's birth early in the *İskendernāme*, Ahmedi elaborates on the *Shāhnāmeh* version of the story by adding a distinctive element: the figure of Caesar, the ruler of Rum, who is defeated and killed by Alexander's biological father, the Persian king Dara (*Dārā*, i.e. Darius). After becoming master of Rum, Dara appoints Philip (*Feleyḳūs*) to govern Greece (*Yūnān*) on his behalf, who raises Alexander as his own son.[20] Thanks to this story, when Ahmedi's audience encountered the name Caesar in reference to the Byzantine ruler threatened by Murad, they would presumably have made the connection. The message is clear: since ancient Rome and its Caesar had once fallen to the armies of Iran, it was only a matter of time before Byzantium would also fall to the Ottomans.

In short, when Ahmedi makes use of the term Rum, he clearly has in mind the legacy of Rome represented by Byzantium. The fact that, like Alexander's father, Murad represents a young warrior challenging an ageing Caesar gives him legitimacy in the Islamic world, since he and his dynasty represent the ideal of just war against the infidel. Like Alexander in Firdawsi's Persian version of the Alexander legend, which Ahmedi follows, Murad is by right of conquest the true owner of the Roman tradition, even though his roots may ultimately lie further east. This justifies Ottoman challenges not only to Christian Byzantium, but also to other Rumi Muslim states: notably Karaman, against which Murad wages war in one of Ahmedi's chapters. To discredit the Karamanids, whose rival claims were serious not least because they controlled the old Seljuk capital of Konya, Ahmedi presents them as supported by Mongols (Tatars) as well as Turkish tribes.[21] This is partly based on reality, since Karaman did indeed have an important tribal base; but more importantly, it fits the poet's overall presentation of history, in which the Mongols represent injustice. After defeating Karaman, Murad is free to turn his attention once more to the conquest of new territory on the European side of the straits. For this European field of action broadly defined, the poet consistently uses "the far bank" (*ısra yaḳa*) and "the side across" (*ısra geçe*), rather than the term Rumeli (*Rūm éli*), which was not yet fully established in its later sense.[22] On the rare occasions when Ahmedi does use it, he does so more literally:

---

[19] Dankoff 2020:7692; Sılay 2004:156: *Evvel ol idi ki Rūm'a ṣundı el / Ḳayṣer'e érürdi çoḳ dürlü zelel.*
[20] Dankoff 2020:319–405. See also Kastritsis 2016:266–269.
[21] Dankoff 2020:7696–7697, 7702; Sılay 2004:160–161, 166.
[22] It is worth noting that Rumeli does appear in the later, broad sense in other sources from this time. Several examples may be found in Kastritsis 2017:121, 129, 132, 135–154, which incorporates

Rūm élini çün musaḫḫar eyledi
Beglerin gendüye çāker eyledi

Lāz'a daḫı étdi ṭamaʿ encām-ı kār
Ara yérde düşdi lā-büd gīr ü dār

Gebr ü Tersā ġarba degin her ne var
Lāz'a leşker vérbidiler bī-şümār

When he subdued the land of Rum (Rūm éli)
He made its lords his own servants

In the end, he also coveted (the land of) Lazar (Lāz)
So inevitably, conflict and warfare arose between them

As far as the west, all the infidels (lit. Zoroastrians) and Christians
Sent countless armies to (the assistance of) Lazar[23]

From these verses, it is clear that in this case, the term Rumeli is being used in a literal sense to mean 'land of the Romans' (Greek *Romanía*), a definition that excludes Moravian Serbia under Murad's adversary Lazar (*Lāz*: the knez Lazar Hrebeljanović, r. 1373–1389). In fact, this is the only instance of the term Rumeli in Ahmedi's Ottoman poem. However, the poet does use the same term in other parts of the *İskendernāme*, to mean literally 'the Roman lands'.[24]

In the verses we have just considered, despite Ahmedi's overwhelmingly positive treatment of Murad I and his exploits, it is possible to discern a note of criticism in the phrase "he coveted (the land of) Lazar." Given the fact that it was Murad's campaign against Lazar that led to the Battle of Kosovo and the death of both rulers, as well as Ahmedi's wider concern with the vanity of worldly ambition, this critique is worth noting, especially because it anticipates the following section on Murad's successor Bayezid I. Unlike Murad, who died a martyr for Islam, Bayezid's ambition was directed against other Muslim states, leading to his downfall at the hands of Timur. Ahmedi's presentation of his reign divides neatly into two parts, the first positive and the second much more critical. The easiest explanation for the disparity is that the first section was written during

---

a prose epic first composed under Mehmed I. Perhaps, then, this was a matter of style, with court poets preferring more nuanced ideas of space.

[23] Dankoff 2020:7771–7773; Sılay 2004:235–237.
[24] E.g. 1140 where Alexander leads the armies of 'the land of Rum'. In Islamic tradition, Alexander is thought of as Roman (*Rūmī*) because he is associated with Hellenism and eastern Roman space.

the reign of Bayezid, when Ahmedi first joined the Ottoman court, while the second was composed in the aftermath of his defeat by Timur in 1402, when Bayezid was dead and the failure of his empire-building project was apparent to all. In line with the general didactic tone of Ahmedi's entire work, it is thus intended as a cautionary tale; not for Bayezid himself, as has been suggested, but rather for his son and successor Emir Suleyman, Ahmedi's ultimate patron who had little choice but to pursue a less aggressive foreign policy.[25]

With this overall context in mind, we may now consider the role of geography in Ahmedi's presentation of Bayezid I's reign. After describing Bayezid's rise to the throne following his father's death at Kosovo, Ahmedi compares him favorably to his ancestors in matters of justice and good administration. Then he turns to his foreign policy, discussing his campaign against Sivas and Tokat in northern Anatolia:

> Rūm'dan Sivas u Toḳat'ı aldı ol
> Canik'i alup Samsun'a geldi ol
>
> From (the region of) Rum he took Sivas and Tokat
> He took Canik and came to Samsun[26]

There is no need to discuss here the specifics of the campaign in question. For our purposes, the important point concerns Ahmedi's use of the term Rum for the inland region around Sivas and Tokat, distinguished from the coastal strip called Canik to its north. As already discussed, this is a holdover from the twelfth century when this region was under the Turkish dynasty of Danişmend. In the verses that follow, Ahmedi continues to recount Bayezid I's annexation of most of Muslim Anatolia, leading up to his confrontation with Timur. First Bayezid returns to Bursa, referred to as 'his capital' (*dār-ı mülk* 'abode of sovereignty').[27] And indeed, contrary to a still common perception that the European town of Edirne (Adrianople) had replaced Bursa when it was conquered sometime in the 1360s, there is ample evidence that when Ahmedi was writing Bursa was still considered the main Ottoman capital.[28]

---

[25] While largely agreeing with my own conclusions about Ahmedi's presentation of Bayezid I and other rulers, Lowry 2003:15–31 has suggested that the Ottoman section of the *İskendernāme* is a mirror for princes (*naṣīḥatnāme*) originally intended for Bayezid. In my view, the Ottoman poem as a whole (including its emphasis on holy raiding) can only be understood in the context of 1402. On Bayezid, see also Emecen 2014.

[26] Dankoff 2020:7796; Sılay 2004:260.

[27] Dankoff 2020:7797; Sılay 2004:261.

[28] Kastritsis 2007:79–110; Kastritsis 2022.

According to Ahmedi's account, from Bursa, Bayezid conquered all towns and territories down to the frontier of Antalya on the Mediterranean coast.[29] His conquests included the Byzantine town of Philadelphia (Alaşehir), which had managed until then to remain independent, as well as the rival Turkish principalities (beyliks) of western Anatolia.[30] As in the earlier case of Moravian Serbia, called Laz even after the death of Lazar in 1389, in most cases the names of the Anatolia regions remained those of the beylik dynasties from which they were conquered. However, Ahmedi does mention some towns by name: Kastamonu, the capital of another rival principality, and also Konya and Larende, the two main cities of Karaman. After all this campaigning, Ahmedi presents Bayezid as returning to his capital Bursa, called once again "the abode of sovereignty" (*darü'l-mülk*). Following a common literary trope, the Ottoman ruler is presented as sitting on his throne and administering justice to his subjects, who are thus able to busy themselves with making the entire land prosperous:

> Bu ḳamu Rūm içre bir yėr ḳalmadı
> Kim anuŋ ʿadliyle maʿmūr olmadı

> No place remained within all of Rum
> which was not made prosperous by his justice[31]

In this case, the term Rum is being used in its most general sense to mean the entirety of the lands associated with the Byzantine legacy, namely most if not all of the Anatolian and Balkan peninsulas.

Having thus described Bayezid I's unification of the entire land of Rum under his rule, Ahmedi devotes the rest of the first chapter to the ruler's piety, justice, and consolidation of Ottoman administration. Then he moves on to the second, more critical chapter on Bayezid. Here the geographical focus moves outside the lands of Rum, a fact that is key to understanding the poet's negative presentation of Bayezid's imperial overextension and consequent demise. Upon hearing of the death of the Mamluk sultan Barkuk ("the Sultan of Egypt") Bayezid sets his sights on Syria and the rest of the Mamluk domains:

> Bunı işidüp Şām'a ol ḳaṣd eyledi
> Mıṣr benüm oldı dėyü söyledi

> Hearing this, he set his sights on Syria.
> He proclaimed "Egypt is now mine!"[32]

---

[29]   Dankoff 2020:7798, Sılay 2004:262.
[30]   Dankoff 2020:7799; Sılay 2004:263.
[31]   Dankoff 2020:7805; Sılay 2004:269.
[32]   Dankoff 2020:7817; Sılay 2004:281.

In the verses that follow, Ahmedi meditates on the inevitability of death and the folly of trying to take advantage of an enemy's demise. Then he returns to Bayezid's conquest of Malatya (*Mildenī*, Melitene), which he presents as a prelude to a future invasion of Mamluk Syria.[33] Given the fact that the next event described is Timur's campaign against Rum, it is difficult to avoid the conclusion that Bayezid's downfall was directly connected to his attack on Mamluk territory. The implication here is that this was a direct result of the hubris of trying to extend his power outside the lands of Rum to the foreign regions of Syria and Egypt. Given this overextension, it is fitting that Bayezid's downfall comes from Timur, also an outsider to the lands of Rum.

In the final chapter of his account, Ahmedi presents his patron, Bayezid's son Süleyman, as possessing moral qualities greater than all of India and its river Jumna (*Cevne*, Yamuna), a major tributary of the Ganges.[34] Although Süleyman could supposedly have conquered any territory in both East and West, like Alexander's son in a later chapter of the *İskendernāme*, he is presented as having no interest in worldly dominion due to a generous and philosophical disposition.[35] Although these are literary tropes through which the poet is seeking to praise his patron, it is still worth drawing attention once again to Ahmedi's use of geographical references. As we have seen, Ahmedi perceives the lands of Rum as the natural Ottoman sphere of action, while neighboring non-Rumi regions such as Syria or Egypt are emblematic of Bayezid I's excessive ambition. On the other hand, in the spirit of the Alexander Romance, more distant and exotic lands like India may still function as symbols of universal empire and therefore be used as literary tropes by the poet to make wishes for his patron. As we will now see, the same functions of space are also discernible in the verses of Ahmedi's contemporary Abdülvasi.

Uses of Space in Abdülvasi's Epic Account of the Battle of Çamurlu

The second work we will be considering is a historical panegyric by Abdülvasi Çelebi (fl. 1414), another court poet roughly contemporary to Ahmedi.[36] As in the case of Ahmedi's poem about Ottoman history, which forms part of his larger *İskendernāme*, Abdülvasi's panegyric is also included in a larger work about the

---

[33] Dankoff 2020:7824–7826; Sılay 2004:288–290.
[34] Dankoff 2020:7836; Sılay 2004:300. The Jumna (Yamuna) feeds into the Ganges (Ganga) and is the longest tributary river in India today.
[35] Dankoff 2020:7838–7843; Sılay 2004:302–307. For Alexander's son İskenderūs, see Dankoff 2020:8679–8699.
[36] Güldaş 1996; Kut 1988. For a full translation, see Kastritsis 2007:221–232.

life of the Prophet Abraham. The work in question is entitled *Ḫalīlnāme*, from the prophet's Islamic epithet Ḫalīl Allāh, 'friend of God'. Broadly speaking, the romance belongs to the "Tales of the Prophets" genre (*ḳıṣaṣu 'l-enbiyā*), a popular one in fifteenth-century Turkish vernacular literature aiming to provide entertainment, moral edification, and religious education.[37] Needless to say, there were also political benefits for the patrons of such works. The stories they contained about prophets and other leading figures of Islamic civilization could be used to reinforce existing power structures, since the struggles of these figures could be compared to those of current Ottoman rulers. In Abdülvasi's work, the panegyric on Mehmed I's 1413 victory at Çamurlu over his brother Musa is inserted immediately after a section describing the victory of Abraham over the unjust king Nimrod, creating a clear comparison between Abraham and Mehmed on the one hand, and Nimrod and Musa on the other.

Abdülvasi begins by providing an overview of the decade of dynastic wars leading up to the decisive battle that is his main subject. Here is how he describes prince Mehmed's situation upon his father Bayezid I's death:

> Bu Rūm élinde sulṭān olmış idi
> Bu él anuŋla şādān olmış idi
>
> Aŋa ʿOs̱mān éli mīrās̱ atadan
> Ḳalup dururdı şerʿ ile Ḫudādan
>
> He had become sultan in this land of Rum (Rūm éli)
> This land had become glad with him
>
> The land of Osman (ʿOs̱mān éli) had been left to him as inheritance
>   from his father
> By the will of God, in accordance with sharia law[38]

These verses bring us once more face to face with the fluidity of geographical terms in this period of Ottoman history. In fact, in this case the ambiguity is probably being used intentionally to send a political message. As is clear from another contemporary account, following Timur's 1402 victory over the Ottomans, Mehmed had to fight to regain control of the province of Rum around Amasya and Tokat, where he had been governor under his father.[39] From there he extended his rule to the Ottoman ancestral lands around Bursa ("the land of

---

[37] Grenier 2018:43–46; Kastritsis 2017:11–13, 21, 50.
[38] Güldaş 1996:1748–1749.
[39] Kastritsis 2017:14, 34–35, 97–112; Kastritsis 2007:28–33, 63–77.

Osman"), claiming that it was the will of Bayezid that he should have them as well. In other words, the above verses agree with what we know of Mehmed's fortunes and political claims in the years following 1402. Taken more broadly, however, they also reflect his broader claims after 1413: "this land of Rum" (*bu Rūm éli*) could also mean all of Anatolia and the Balkans, and "the land of Osman" (*'Osmān éli*), the largest extent of the Ottoman state during the reign of Bayezid I.

After setting the scene, Abdülvasi goes on to describe in summary form Mehmed's struggles against his two brothers İsa and Süleyman. Once again, his account more or less agrees with what we know from other sources.[40] However, he skips over the details and jumps ahead to a later point in the war, when Süleyman is forced to abandon Anatolia because Musa has seized his Balkan territories. In describing Süleyman's abandonment of Anatolia, Abdülvasi presents it as a retreat before Mehmed's armies, employing once again some interesting geographical terms:

> Bunun azmine ḳatlanmadı ḳaçdı
> Ḳodı 'Osmān élin ucāta geçdi
>
> Yüridi ṭutdı hep ol éli Sulṭān
> Bunı dilerdi 'Osmān ile Orḫan
>
> (Süleyman) could not bear (Mehmed's) advance and fled
> He abandoned the land of Osman and fled to the borderlands
>
> The Sultan advanced and occupied that entire province
> That was what Osman and Orhan (would have) wanted[41]

In these verses, Mehmed is presented as a conquering sultan whose advances would have pleased the dynasty's founders (called in the next verse "those gazi beys").[42] In this case, "the land of Osman" (*'Osmān éli*) may refer either to Bursa and Bithynia or to all of Anatolia, contrasted with the European side of the straits, which the poet calls "the borderlands" (*ucāt*). This is similar to Ahmedi's terms "the far bank" (*ısra yaḳa*) and "the side across" (*ısra geçe*), especially in the context of his emphasis on the Ottomans' role as holy raiders (*ġāzīs*). Although Abdülvasi's poem does not focus on holy raiding as such, his use of the term "borderlands" (*ucāt*) for the entire Balkan Peninsula is striking nonetheless. While the battle he is describing is between two Ottoman princes, it takes place

---

[40] Güldaş 1996:1750–1754; Kastritsis 2007:79–123.
[41] Güldaş 1996:1755–1756.
[42] Güldaş 1996:1757 (*Ol ġāzī beglerüŋ şād oldı rūḫı*).

near Sofia at the very center of the Ottoman Balkans, and as we will see below the victorious Mehmed is presented as a champion of Islam asserting his power over a borderland region.

The same opposition between Anatolia and the Balkan 'borderlands' may be seen in the verses that follow. After Süleyman's departure, Mehmed occupies his father's throne in Bursa, "leaving only the borderlands (*ucāt*)."[43] Meanwhile, Süleyman is defeated and killed by Musa, who takes his place in "the land across" (*ısra yér*).[44] Musa's success makes him conceited, so that he does not content himself with ruling the borderlands, but desires his father's throne. As in Ahmedi, it is clear that this refers to Bursa:

> Yüzin çevürdi ata taḫtın ister
> Ne ata taḫtı dünya baḫtın ister

> Diler berü geçe ṭuta cihānı
> Begenmez berü geçedeki ḫānı

> He turned his attention elsewhere, now he wants his father's throne
> Not just his father's throne, he wants the fortune of this Earth

> He wishes to cross to the other side and conquer the world
> He does not like the ruler on the side across[45]

Here the perspective has shifted to Musa, whose excessive ambition is described in terms similar to the ones Ahmedi had used for Bayezid. From Musa's perspective in the Balkans, Anatolia and its ruler are on "the side across" (*berü geçe*); whereas two verses earlier, we saw that the poet had described Musa's rise to power as taking place "in the land across" (*ısra yérde*) relative to Anatolia, as in Ahmedi. This perspective shift is not without interesting spatial implications. For however great the significance of the Balkan "borderlands" (*ucāt*) for the prestige of the Ottoman dynasty in this period, for the Ottomans the center of the world is still clearly on the Asian side. Not only is it the location of their capital and the ancestral "land of Osman," but these in turn are connected to established Islamic centers in more distant parts of Anatolia, such as the old Seljuk capital Konya, itself the gateway to a wider Islamic Middle East. Abdüvasi presents Musa as boasting that he would conquer all these regions:

---

[43] Güldaş 1996:1758.
[44] Güldaş 1996:1762.
[45] Güldaş 1996:1763–1764.

Ol él daḫı benümdür uş geçerem
Baŋa kim ḳarşu ṭurur çün göçerem?

Eger cemˁ eylesem yüz biŋ kişim var
Varursam Kaˁbeye degin işüm var

That land is mine, now I will cross over
Who will stand against me as I advance?

If I gather (my army) I have one hundred thousand men
Once I get there, I have business as far as the Kaaba[46]

In Abdülvasi's presentation of Musa's supposed desire to expand his domains as far as the holy Kaaba in Mecca, we have a striking parallel to Ahmedi's earlier claim that Musa's father Bayezid wished to extend his power to Syria and Egypt. From the perspective of those living in the land of Rum, all these places are foreign and represent the still legendary, if not entirely unfamiliar, Arab heartlands of Islam. This allows them to become symbols of unbridled ambition.

Having set up the confrontation as one between a greedy and ungrateful youth challenging a legitimate older brother, Abdülvasi is now able to proceed with describing the battle and its aftermath, which takes up the rest of the poem. Once again, ideas of space and geography are essential to his presentation. Mehmed's decision to cross the straits and face his brother is supposedly met with disapproval by his viziers, who urge caution given the fact that Mehmed's army is not yet large enough. For he is still awaiting the assistance of distant allies:

Bizüm leşker daḫı cemˁ olmamışdur
Iraḳdan ulu begler gelmemişdur

Our army has not yet assembled
The great lords have not yet come from afar[47]

Once again, we are dealing here not only with literary tropes, but also with some of the realities of Mehmed's 1413 campaign. From another source, we know that Mehmed's armies assembled in Bursa and waited for reinforcements before crossing the straits. These came from Dulkadir, a tribal confederacy in eastern Anatolia with which Mehmed had forged a marriage alliance, as well as in the

---

[46] Güldaş 1996:1769–1770.
[47] Güldaş 1996:1777.

form of other Turkmen and Mongol tribal contingents from the Black Sea coast and central Anatolia.[48]

Upon crossing the straits, Mehmed was received by the Byzantine emperor Manuel II Palaiologos, whose assistance was essential to the success of his campaign. Abdülvasi makes no effort to hide the Byzantine emperor's involvement, but presents the so-called "Tekfur of Istanbul" as Mehmed's loyal client:

> Duʿāyı pīş idüp ʿazm étdi ol şāh
> Ėrişdi girü İstanbul'a nāgāh
>
> Revān işitdi İstanbul Tekūrı
> Gelüp ḫıdmet ḳılup ḳıldı ḥubūrı
>
> Bir iki günde geçdiler deŋizi
> Sürüp Edreneye ṣaldılar izi

> Leading with prayers, that shah (Mehmed) advanced
> All of a sudden, he reached Istanbul
>
> As he was moving, the lord (tekūr/tekfūr) of Istanbul heard
> He came and made obeisance, showing his delight
>
> In one or two days, they had crossed the sea
> They advanced, casting their trail toward Edirne[49]

Apart from the political implications (the two rulers were united by a common enemy), what is noteworthy here is the admission that Byzantine ships were needed to ferry Mehmed's army across the straits.[50] This brings home the fact that in the early fifteenth century, from an Ottoman perspective, the Balkans were still very much 'the other side' when it came to military campaigns. The Ottoman navy was very small at this time, and in civil conflicts the few Ottoman ships that did exist were often in enemy hands. Thus it is a recurring theme in the literature of the time for Byzantium, Genoa, and other Christian powers to ferry Ottoman armies across the straits separating Asia from Europe.[51]

---

[48] Kastritsis 2017:146–151; Kastritsis 2007:188–194.
[49] Güldaş 1996:1785–1787.
[50] On the role of Byzantium in this campaign, see Kastritsis 2007:188–190.
[51] Another example is Murad II's reliance on the Genoese in the struggle against his uncle Mustafa (Kastritsis 2017:158).

According to the poem, after reaching Edirne, Mehmed's army "moved around for five or ten days within the province" reaching first Serbia (*Lāz*) and then Wallachia (*Eflāḵ*).[52] These regions are described as "provinces with very harsh terrain" (*ṣarp muşkil éller*) in which Alexander and Caesar would have been afraid to campaign, but Mehmed was brave enough to set up camp. This description may seem odd to the modern reader, given the fact that the historic Alexander the Great and Julius Caesar had in fact ruled over some of these same regions. However, we must bear in mind that the literary context here is similar to that of Ahmedi's *İskendernāme*, in which both figures are associated with Rum, a region thought of as Anatolia or at best the Greek-speaking (i.e. Byzantine) parts of the Balkans. Serbia and Wallachia therefore belong to a different category for Abdülvasi, as had been the case with Serbia and Hungary for Ahmedi:

O yére varmadı hergiz ulu ḫān
Meger dedesi Ḫᵛāndgār-ı bin Orḫān

Müsaḫḫar kıldı ol Eflāḵ u Lāzi
Olara gösterüp çoḵ dürlü bāzī

Ṣanasın Ḥamza Kūh-i Ḵāf'a düşdi
Ḵatına dürlü dürlü dīvler üşdi

ᶜAcāyib ḵorḵular key müşkil éller
ᶜAceb ṣūretler ü key tuḥfe diller

No great khan had ever been there before
Except perhaps (Mehmed's) grandfather, the Lord (Murad I) son of
    Orhan

He charmed those Wallachians and Serbs into submission
Showing them all kinds of tricks

As if he were Hamza falling upon Mount Qaf
All sorts of demons (dīv) gathered around him

What strange perils, what treacherous lands,
What wondrous faces and what rare languages![53]

---

[52] Güldaş 1996:1788–1789.
[53] Güldaş 1996:1795–1798.

Here in addition to the Ottoman ruler Murad I (known as *Hüdāvendigār*, 'the lord'), who had died after battling Serbs and Bosnians at Kosovo, Mehmed is being compared to the epic hero Hamza, the protagonist of the epic *Ḥamzanāme*.[54] A conflation of personages and stories from Iranian and early Islamic tradition, the *Ḥamzanāme* cycle was especially popular in Indo-Muslim and Turkish literature, probably because it features a Muslim hero fighting infidels, as well as marvelous journeys to far-flung places. Like Alexander, Hamza's adventures take him to the far reaches of the earth, including the legendary Mount Qaf, where he helps the good fairies (*perī*) in their struggles against the evil demons (*dīv*).[55] In Abdülvasi's verses, the inner Balkan regions are compared to this imaginary mountain; and like Hamza, Mehmed is able to subdue the strange peoples living there and recruit them in his struggle against Musa. Although Mehmed did indeed rely on Byzantine and Serbian allies in his struggle against his brother, here the mention of Wallachians is probably just a literary device, allowing the poet to create the impression of a strange and foreign land ("Wallachians and Serbs," *Eflāḳ u Lāz*). The main point is that, thanks to the Islamic character of the *Ḥamzanāme* cycle, Mehmed's use of Christian troops against his brother can be cast in a positive light: for Abdülvasi presents him like Hamza as a warrior for just religion, whose ultimate aim is to subdue the infidel "borderlands" (*ucāt*).[56]

In the early fifteenth-century Ottoman literary imagination, then, the Balkan interior could be presented as a foreign place, inhabited by strange peoples speaking exotic tongues. We may contrast this presentation to that of Byzantium, which forms part of a more familiar Roman (*Rūmī*) space. This exotic view of the Balkan interior is not really based on geographical distance, since it is not so far from the Ottoman homeland around Bursa; or even lack of familiarity, as the Ottomans had already been engaging with Serbs and other Balkan peoples for decades. Instead, the novelty of these places seems to have been based on their perceived non-Roman character and foreign status from the perspective of Persianate and Islamicate literature. The wider spatial and literary context described above is essential for understanding the references in both Ahmedi and Abdülvasi. In the verses that follow, part of the section that builds up to the final confrontation between Mehmed and Musa, Abdülvasi turns once again to geographical references to show Musa's pride. After supposedly bragging that he could easily have subdued Alexander and other legendary heroes, Musa adds:

---

[54] Hanaway 2003.

[55] Prior 2009. Although the supposed location of Mount Qaf varies, it was usually thought of as being in either the Caucasus or Central Asia.

[56] For Mehmed's reliance on Serbs and other Christians, see Kastritsis 2007:188–194.

> Semerḳand éline varam dérem ben
> Ḥorāsān éllerin uram dérem ben
>
> I say, I will go to the province of Samarkand
> I say, I will attack the province of Khorasan[57]

As with earlier examples, the places mentioned here are famous but distant regions of the wider Islamic world: in this case, located on either bank of the Oxus river, which is the boundary between Iran and Central Asia. When the verses were written, both places were associated with the Timurid dynasty: Samarkand had been Timur's capital until his death in 1405, and Herat (known as "the pearl of Khorasan") was the capital of Timur's successor Shahrukh. With this in mind, what Abdülvasi is implying is that Musa boasted of attacking the Timurids, the dynasty that had crushed his father just ten years before and whose representatives still considered themselves the Ottomans' overlords.[58]

Having set up the confrontation between the two brothers in these terms, the rest of Abdülvasi's poem is spent describing Musa's preparations, the ensuing battle between the two brothers, and the aftermath of Mehmed's victory and elimination of his brother.[59] These verses contain few geographical references, beyond the claim that Mehmed's sword made blood flow like the Oxus (*Ceyhūn*) and his mace could have turned Mount Qaf into putty (*maʿcūn*).[60] More detailed uses of space only return at the end of the poem, when the poet describes the aftermath of Mehmed's victory:

> Varup Mehdī gibi ucāt'ı ṭutdi
> Bu Rūm u Lāz u Ulġar élin utdı
>
> Firenk, Eflāḳ u Sırf u Engürusı
> Daḫı Ḳıfçaḳ u Tatar u Urusı
>
> Musaḫḫar ḳıldı, ḳarşu geldi begler
> Tekūr u Gencelusı daḫı yégler
>
> He arrived like the Mahdi (Islamic Redeemer) and captured the
>   borderlands
> He conquered these lands of the Rum, Laz, and Bulgarians

[57] Güldaş 1996:1810.
[58] For Mehmed's position as a Timurid client, see Kastritsis 2007:198, 203–205.
[59] Güldaş 1996:1813–1924.
[60] Güldaş 1996:1859.

> The Franks, Wallachians, Serbians, and Hungarians,
> The Kıpchak, Tatars, and Russians,
>
> He charmed into submission. And lords came before him,
> The Tekfur, the Consul, and their betters[61]

As in the earlier case from Ahmedi ("this [land of] Rum"), here the use of the definite article *bu* suggests that despite their differences, the territories referred to (Rum, Serbia, Bulgaria) are all part of the Ottoman world, to a greater or lesser degree. On the other hand, the names that follow are used mostly for literary effect, to suggest a multitude of foreign nations living in the wider region (what we would call today central and eastern Europe). "The Tekfur" is the Byzantine emperor, while "the Consul" (*Gencelus, consolus*) is presumably a generic term for the consuls of Venice, Genoa, and other Latin powers. The verses that follow enumerate the tribute all of these nations and rulers supposedly brought to Mehmed following his victory, creating the impression of an overlord with many clients enriched by lively trade throughout his domains.

Such imperial imagery notwithstanding, however, Abdülvasi is careful not to present Mehmed as bent on extending his rule beyond the land of Rum, broadly defined. Although he mentions Kipchaks, Tatars, and Russians, vague references to the northern Black Sea regions, when he was writing, any thought of Ottoman influence in these regions was mostly wishful thinking. Along the same lines, later the poet expresses the desire that one day God would extend Mehmed's rule even further:

> Anun hukmine Şīrāz u Semerḳand
> Muṭīʿ olsun Mıṣır u Şām u Derbend
>
> May Shiraz and Samarkand submit to his rule
> As well as Egypt, Syria, and Derbent[62]

Given the poet's earlier, negative presentation of Musa's alleged desire to extend his power as far as Samarkand, Khurasan, and Mecca, it is surprising to see him make similar claims for his patron Mehmed. The mention of Derbent is especially intriguing, as this fortified Caspian town was seen as the gateway to the northern Caucasus, associated in the Persian epic tradition with the boundaries of the inhabited world. Given the literary context of the Alexander Romance and *Ḥamzanāme*, in which Abdülvasi is writing, this would probably

---

[61] Güldaş 1996:1881–1883.
[62] Güldaş 1996:1911.

evoke Mount Qaf, as well as Alexander's barrier against the unclean nations—identified with Gog and Magog in the Islamic tradition.[63] With all this in mind, it is clear that Abdülvasi is making a wish for his patron to attain universal empire, expressed in terms of the broadest possible imagined geography. This is reinforced two verses later, where the poet wishes that, like Solomon, Mehmed may one day conquer the whole world and rule over both humans and demons (*dīv*).[64] However, despite the grandiosity of these verses, there is an essential difference between them and those attributed to Musa earlier in the poem. Fundamentally, this is a question of perspective: the verses supposedly uttered by Musa portray the hubris of a prince claiming the right and power to conquer the world, whereas those about Mehmed are merely the wishes of a court poet for his patron. No matter how great Mehmed's bravery and suitability for world empire, in Abdülvasi's poem, there is little doubt that his real field of action is "this clime of Rum, the land of Osman, the borderlands" (*bu Rūm iklīmi, ʿOsmān éli, ucāt*).[65]

Conclusion

Having examined the geographical references in Ahmedi and Abdülvasi's histor-ical poems, we may now proceed to some general conclusions. The first concerns the many meanings of Rum and its derivatives among early fifteenth-century Ottoman authors. As we have seen, the term has a long history in the Islamic world, but is invariably associated with medieval, Greek-speaking eastern Rome (Byzantium) and its territory, particularly Anatolia (Asia Minor). This explains why the Ottomans called the Greek language 'Roman' (*Rumca*) into modern times, and why Alexander, the founder of Hellenistic civilization, was known to Muslims as 'the Roman' (*İskender-i Rūmī*). At the same time, the expansion of Islam into Anatolia and beyond led to a variety of more specific meanings as well. In the broadest sense, territory that had been Byzantine in medieval times before becoming part of the 'abode of Islam' was still referred to as 'the land of Rum' (*bilād al-Rūm, diyār-ı Rūm*) regardless of whether it was under Christian or Muslim rule. To the confusion of the modern scholar, however, in a more limited sense the term was applied within these territories to areas that were especially Roman in character. In the twelfth century, the Turkish Danişmend dynasty referred to the Amasya-Tokat region in this way, and minted coins with

---

[63]   Van Donzel and Ott 2001.
[64]   Güldaş 1996:1913. For the place of Solomon in fifteenth-century Ottoman legends and debates about empire, see Yerasimos 1990:49–61.
[65]   Güldaş 1996:1904.

Greek inscriptions.[66] So when the Ottomans conquered it much later, they also called it "the province of Rum." At the same time, they expanded the process of Islamization to the Aegean and Balkan regions, parts of which were now considered 'Roman land' (*Rūm éli*, cf. Greek *Romanía*). It is clear that this name was meant literally at first, since the authors we have considered made a distinction between Roman and other parts of the Balkans, which they called by other names (*Lāz, Sırf, Ulġar*, etc.).

We have also seen that along with the two poets' use of the term Rum for Roman or Byzantine territory, they generally consider the land of Rum and its borderlands to be the Ottoman dynasty's natural field of action. In other words, like the Rum Seljuks before them, the Ottomans are presented as the rightful Muslim heirs to the Roman legacy. Already in the early fifteenth century, this idea seems to have resulted in the use of the term Rumeli more loosely to refer to all of the Balkans, even if our two poets shied away from this particular usage. The same idea would eventually fuel Mehmed the Conqueror's claims to not only Constantinople and the Byzantine legacy, but even the original city of Rome.[67] As far as the rest of the Islamic world was concerned, the Ottomans were indeed the lords of Rum, since that was the term used by other Muslims for the region in which their empire was based.[68] The desire to be defined as Muslim Romans partly explains Ottoman attempts to create a connection with the Seljuks of Rum (already apparent in Ahmedi's account) as well as their interest in the medieval Alexander Romance (the *İskendernāme*). At the same time, the exotic nature of the inner Balkan Peninsula and the lands beyond lent itself to other literary comparisons, especially for poets writing in the long shadow of the Persian epic tradition. By studying the works of Ahmedi, Abdülvasi, and other court authors of the early fifteenth century, it is possible to gain insight into Ottoman identity and imagined geography at a time when the empire and its culture were still in the process of formation. At this time, these new Romans were trying to define themselves culturally and politically in the larger world of late medieval Anatolia, Byzantium, southeastern Europe, and the greater post-Mongol Islamic Middle East. It would take another century for this process of self-definition to produce what would come to be thought of as classical formulations of Ottoman identity, which would themselves undergo further transformation into the modern period.

---

[66] E.g. Georganteli 2012:149–150.
[67] Necipoğlu 1991:12–13.
[68] See the chapter by Andrew Peacock in the present volume.

Works Cited

Boratav, P. N. 1979. "Khiḍr-Ilyās." *Encyclopaedia of Islam*, 2nd ed., vol. 5:5.

Bosworth, C. E. 1994. "Rūm: 2. Relations between the Islamic Powers and the Byzantines." *Encyclopaedia of Islam*, 2nd ed., vol. 8:602–606. Leiden.

Chrissis, N., and M. Carr, eds. 2014. *Contact and Conflict in Frankish Greece and the Aegean, 1204-1453*. Farnham.

Dankoff, R., ed. 2020. *Ahmedî, İskendernâme: İnceleme—Tenkitli Metin*. 2 vols. Ankara.

Emecen, F. 2014. "İhtirasın Gölgesinde bir Sultan: Yıldırım Bayezid." *Osmanlı Araştırmaları* 43:67–92.

Fleet, K., ed. 2009. *The Cambridge History of Turkey: Byzantium to Turkey, 1071-1453*. Cambridge.

Fowden, E. K., S. Çağaptay, E. Zychowicz-Coghill, and L. Blanke, eds. 2022. *Cities as Palimpsests? Responses to Antiquity in Eastern Mediterranean Urbanism*. Oxford.

Georganteli, E. 2012. "Transposed Images: Currencies and Legitimacy in the Late Medieval Eastern Mediterranean." In Harris, Holmes, and Russell 2012:141–179.

Grenier, C. 2018. "The Yazıcıoğlu Brothers and the Textual Genealogies of Ottoman Islam." *Turcica* 49:37–59.

Güldaş, A., ed. 1996. *Abdülvasi Çelebi, Halilname*. Ankara.

Hanaway, W. L., Jr. 2003. "Ḥamza-nāma: i. General." *Encyclopaedia Iranica* XI/6:649.

Harris, J., C. Holmes, and E. Russell, eds. 2012. *Byzantines, Latins, and Turks in the Eastern Mediterranean World after 1150*. Oxford.

Imber, C. 1987. "The Ottoman Dynastic Myth." *Turcica* 19:7–27.

———. 1990. *The Ottoman Empire, 1300-1481*. Istanbul.

İnalcık, H. 1994. "Rūmeli." *Encyclopaedia of Islam*, 2nd ed., vol. 8:607–611.

Kafadar, C. 1995. *Between Two Worlds: The Construction of the Ottoman State*. Berkeley.

———. 2007. "A Rome of One's Own: Reflections on Cultural Geography and Identity in the Lands of Rum." *Muqarnas* 24:7–25.

Kastritsis, D. 2007. *The Sons of Bayezid: Empire and Representation in the Ottoman Civil War of 1402-1413*. Leiden.

———. 2016. "The Alexander Romance and the Rise of the Ottoman Empire." In Peacock and Yıldız 2016:243–283.

———. 2017. *An Early Ottoman History: The Oxford Anonymous Chronicle (Bodleian Marsh 313)*. Liverpool.

———. 2022. "Ottoman Urbanism and Capital Cities before the Conquest of Constantinople (1453)." In Fowden, Çağaptay, Zychowicz-Coghill, and Blanke 2022:287–306.

Kut, G. 1988. "Abdülvâsi Çelebi." *Türkiye Diyanet Vakfı İslâm Ansiklopedisi*, vol. 1:283–284.

Lowry, H. 2003. *The Nature of the Early Ottoman State*. Albany.

Melville, C. 2009. "Anatolia under the Mongols." In Fleet 2009:51–101.

Murphey, R. 2014. "Bayezid I's Foreign Policy Plans and Priorities: Power Relations, Statecraft, Military Conditions, and Diplomatic Practice in Anatolia and the Balkans." In Chrissis and Carr 2014:177–215.

Necipoğlu, G. 1991. *Architecture, Ceremonial, and Power: The Topkapı Palace in the Fifteenth and Sixteenth Centuries*. New York.

Peacock, A. C. S., and S. N. Yıldız, eds. 2016. *Literature and Intellectual Life in Fourteenth- and Fifteenth-Century Anatolia*. Würzburg.

Prior, D. 2009. "Travels of Mount Qāf: From Legend to 42° 0' N 79° 51' E." *Oriente Moderno* 89.2:425–444.

Sılay, K. 2004. *Aḥmedī, History of the Kings of the Ottoman Lineage and Their Holy Raids against the Infidels*. Cambridge, MA.

Van Donzel, E., and C. Ott. 2001. "Yādjūdj wa-Mādjūdj." *Encyclopaedia of Islam*, 2nd ed., vol. 11:231–234.

Wensinck, A. J. 1977. "Al-Khaḍir (Al-Khiḍr)." *Encyclopaedia of Islam*, 2nd ed., vol. 4:902–905.

Wittek, P. 1938. *The Rise of the Ottoman Empire*. London.

———. 2012. *The Rise of the Ottoman Empire: Studies in the History of Turkey, Thirteenth–Fifteenth Centuries*, ed. C. Heywood. Milton Park.

Yerasimos, S. 1990. *La fondation de Constantinople et de Sainte-Sophie dans les traditions turques*. Paris.

5

Mapping the Safavid/Bijapur/Mughal/ Savanur/Mysore/St Andrews Qur'an

A Diachronic Life History[1]

Keelan Overton

A TYPICAL LABEL FOR A MANUSCRIPT ON DISPLAY in a museum or gallery of Islamic art—whether in Tehran, Doha, London, or New York—opens with a tombstone listing its most basic identifying features: title, place, date, and perhaps the name of the calligrapher, illuminator, and/or painter. This convention is drawn from museological models devoted to the display of European and American art, wherein such historical data is viewed as relatively fixed and finite (e.g. Van Gogh painted this oil on canvas in Arles in 1888). Over the last few decades, and taking their cue from anthropologists and archaeologists, art historians have begun to explore the biographies and life histories of objects— that is, everything that unfolded after original production. The tombstone is no longer viewed as the be-all and end-all of an object's story, but rather the launching point for subsequent histories. Specialists of medieval and early

[1] Acknowledgments: I am sincerely grateful to Dr. Dimitri Kastritsis and the Center for Anatolian and East Mediterranean Studies (CAEMS) for the invitation to present at the "Imagined Geographies" workshop. Dr. Paul Churchill also deserves thanks for his administrative assistance with the workshop, which was essential to its success. A related fellowship from CAEMS allowed me to finalize my study of the St Andrews Qur'an manuscript with Kristine Rose-Beers. Further thanks are due to the staff of Special Collections at the Library of the University of St Andrews for their ongoing support and permissions. Finally, I am indebted to Kanika Kalra for allowing the reuse of her maps, originally drawn for Overton 2020a, and for amending Map 2 to indicate the travels of the 'St Andrews Qur'an'. Additional images of the manuscript can be found in my two contributions to "Echoes from the Vault: a blog from the Special Collections at the University of St Andrews" (2016 and 2018), in print (Overton, Rose-Beers, and Wannell 2020), and the recent online exhibition by Special Collections (https://exhibit.so/exhibits/N0GUNXZ00OoxNGRZGL5c).

Figure 1. Single-volume Qur'an manuscript copied by Muhammad Mu'min b. 'Abdullah al-Murvarid, probably Herat or Tabriz, ca. 1520–1540. University of St Andrews, MS O 19. Photo: Keelan Overton.

modern manuscripts must often address production and afterlife in tandem, for the latter can have a seminal impact on the ability to get to the root of original context (the so-called Ur-moment). In the case of the Great Mongol *Shahnama* (or Demotte *Shahnama*) and Tahmasp *Shahnama* (or Houghton *Shahnama*), the book's afterlife was such a seminal factor in its physicality that, for a time, it became its leading designation. In parentheses above are the individuals responsible for the dismemberment of each manuscript.[2]

Unlike these renowned *Shahnamas*, the single-volume Qur'an manuscript that I will be discussing here, which is preserved in Special Collections at the University of St Andrews (henceforth 'the St Andrews Qur'an'), can thankfully still be appreciated as a complete sacred text (Figure 1). This is not to say, however, that the codex has not undergone profound transformation. Having recently completed and published an intensive multi-year (2016–2019) archaeological excavation of the manuscript, I suggest that nothing short of the following label would do it justice:

> Single-volume Qur'an manuscript, Herat or Tabriz, early Safavid period, ca. 1520–1540, copied by Muhammad Mu'min b. 'Abdullah al-Murvarid (fl. 1520–1540), probably made for a Safavid royal patron or elite, with a composite Timurid-Safavid frontispiece, a tampered colophon (antiquated to the Timurid Abu Sa'id [r. 1451–1469]), and a composite Perso-Deccani binding, ca. 1600–1800, restored in 1988. Provenance and intervention: Bijapur, northern Deccan, under Ibrahim 'Adil Shah II

---

[2] Grabar and Blair 1980; Blair 2019.

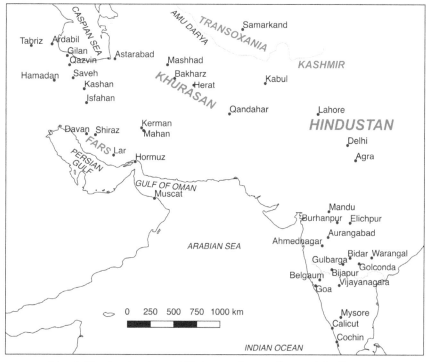

Map 1. The Persianate world between Greater Iran and the Deccan.
Drawn by Kanika Kalra.

(r. 1580–1627); imperial Mughal library, likely in the northern Deccan, under Shah Jahan and 'Alamgir (between ca. 1638–1659 and probably as late as 1699); Savanur state in the western Karnatak, Deccan (ca. 1699–1786); Srirangapatna, kingdom of Mysore, southern Deccan, under Tipu Sultan (r. 1782–1799); Calcutta and London, headquarters of the East India Company (1799–1806); and University of St Andrews (August 1806–present).[3]

The reader will immediately note two points about this theoretical label: the manuscript's constituent parts require contextualization in time and place (we are not dealing with a Safavid manuscript in toto), and four of its 'homes' on the Indian subcontinent were in the Deccan, a region that requires its own deconstruction. In its broadest definition, the Deccan refers to the majority of peninsular India south of the Narmada River and flanked on either side by

---

[3] Overton, Rose-Beers, and Wannell 2020. I direct readers to this much longer article for all details of the codex, including a table devoted to its biography (pp. 271–273), which is the basis of the geographical sections here.

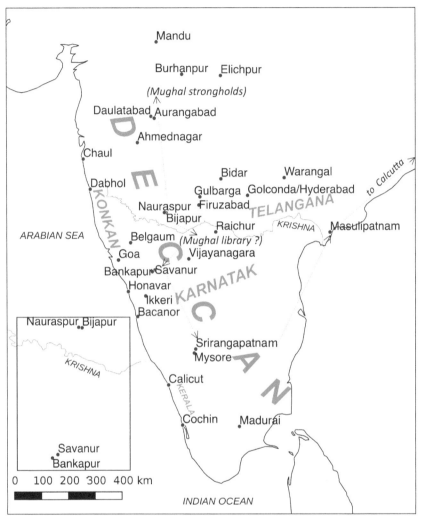

Map 2. The travels of MS O 19 (the St Andrews Qur'an) on the Indian subcontinent, ca. 1600–1805. Drawn and annotated by Kanika Kalra.

mountain ranges (Western Ghats and Eastern Ghats).[4] The region is typically divided into northern and southern zones separated by the Raichur *doab*, a fertile strip of land between the Krishna and Tungabhadra rivers. The capital cities of the Deccan's Islamic sultanates (ca. 1347–1687) were located in the northern Deccan and included Bahmani Gulbarga and Bidar, Nizam Shahi Ahmadnagar, 'Adil Shahi Bijapur, and Qutb Shahi Golconda and Hyderabad. Each sultanate

---

4   Joshi 1973.

engaged in expansions and campaigns into the frontier, which shifted over time and included Telangana, the Raichur *doab*, the Karnatak to the south, and the western Konkan coast. The latter was home to ports like Goa, Dabhol, and Chaul that connected the region to maritime networks traversing the Arabian Sea, Indian Ocean, Persian Gulf, and beyond (Maps 1–2).

The goal of this essay is ostensibly simple: to retrace the St Andrews Qur'an manuscript's two centuries of travels across the Indian subcontinent (Map 2) and allow it to map itself, as opposed to imposing an 'imagined geography' or taxonomy upon it. Depending on the eye of the beholder/reader, the spaces and places listed in the label above will be more or less familiar, and perhaps with a bit of a twist. Early modernists rooted in the comparative Gunpowder Empires framework will hone in on the Safavid and Mughal contexts, but the physicality of the latter space—in the Deccan versus the more familiar Hindustan—may raise eyebrows. Those trained in the classical Persian manuscript tradition may gravitate to the Timurid-Safavid layers and continuities. The so-called golden age of Bijapur under Ibrahim 'Adil Shah II will be familiar to experts of the Deccan sultanates, but the book's subsequent life on the Deccan plateau may introduce a host of new, or at least alternative, trails and actors.

The latter observation is based on personal experience, for I first approached the manuscript almost exclusively through its Bijapur provenance, a layer preserved on its binding. As I studied the book more and more as a complete object—binding and textblock, and the two in relation—its additional owners and sojourns steadily revealed themselves, and I quickly hit a number of gaps in my own knowledge base. What could have happened to the manuscript between the fall of Bijapur in 1686 and its presence in Tipu Sultan's Mysore kingdom by around 1786? What exactly did the Deccan plateau look like during this period? Who were the players, and what were the potential push and pull factors informing the circulation of precious books? Once I allowed the manuscript to tell *its own* story and reveal *its own* geography, I had to struggle to keep up. It is not an exaggeration to say that the St Andrews Qur'an manuscript challenges and nuances most if not all of the taxonomies of conventional Islamic art history, including such terms and concepts as Indo-Persian, Islamic South Asia, Deccan sultanates versus Deccan studies, center versus periphery, and late medieval/early modern versus everything else (the rest).[5]

---

[5]   For a recent discussion of the term Indo-Persian, see Peacock 2021. While this term is at times problematic and overused, it is probably the simplest way to describe the manuscript in question. As we shall see, it is ultimately an Arabic Qur'an manuscript in the Timurid-Safavid Persian tradition with profound Deccani layers and interventions, some of which enable us to explore the specificity of Muslim practice in an individual Indian court (Tipu's Mysore). In her study of Qutb Shahi Hyderabad, Ruffle 2020, p. 271, uses the term "Indo-Shiism" and explains why she prefers this to "Indo-Persian," which "privileges the Persianate linguistic and cultural tradition."

The beauty of the St Andrews Qur'an manuscript is that it bears the evidence to write most of its own history and in doing so liberates us from our fields' arbitrary boundaries and semantics. For Islamic art history, it throws into sharp relief some of the historiographic challenges facing the discipline. This ongoing identity crisis was exemplified by the call for papers for the 2021 biannual Historians of Islamic Art Association conference:

> How do we write histories of Islamic art and architecture, and in the service of what interests? ... The aim of this conference is to focus on moments of "regime change" in Islamic art history and to also direct attention to "regimes" that structure our own field, raising questions of interpretation and method. We invite new research focusing on art and architecture after clear political ruptures (e.g., invasion, occupation, conversion); on the replacement of one symbolic order with another (e.g., public inscriptions in the urban space, changes in sartorial codes, new gender norms); and on the transfer of resources (e.g., artists, objects, libraries, treasuries) from one power to another.[6]

The life history of the St Andrews Qur'an manuscript is precisely one of "regime change" and transfer from "one power to another." Its "regimes" span both the well known and the lesser known, and accordingly challenge the "regimes" that have structured Islamic art history. A quick perusal of museum resources dedicated to Islamic art and some of the field's most popular university-level surveys reveals that the overarching rubric of Islamic art history is indeed the dynasty, but there are widespread disparities and unevenness in which dynasties make the cut.[7]

Despite a surge in publications, exhibitions, dissertations, and even guidebooks, the Deccan's Islamic courts generally remain an afterthought or sidebar in mainstream Islamic art narratives.[8] This is attested by the single essays on

---

[6] "CFP—HIAA Biennial Symposium. Regime Change, Oct. 29–Nov. 1, 2020," https://networks.h-net.org/node/7636/discussions/4756762/cfp-hiaa-biennial-symposium-regime-change-oct-29-nov-1-2020. Due to the COVID-19 pandemic, the conference was held by Zoom in April 2021.

[7] Blair, Bloom, and Ettinghausen 1994; Ettinghausen, Grabar, and Jenkins 2001; Wagoner and Necipoğlu 2017; David Collection, "Islamic dynasties," https://www.davidmus.dk/en/collections/islamic/dynasties; Metropolitan Museum of Art, "Timeline of Art History," https://www.metmuseum.org/toah/keywords/islamic-art/.

[8] Over the last two decades, nearly a dozen dissertations have been completed on the late medieval and early modern Deccan. In 2015, the sultanates were the focus of major exhibitions at the Metropolitan Museum of Art, New York (Haidar and Sardar 2015) and the National Museum, New Delhi (https://artsandculture.google.com/exhibit/nauras-the-many-arts-of-the-deccan-national-museum-delhi/UgJSsSkMl8_LJw?hl=en; Ramaswami and Singh 2015). For a review of the literature, see Overton 2020b (many more academic works have been published since).

the region in two recent compilations: the two-volume *A Companion to Islamic Art and Architecture* (more than fifty essays total) and *The Empires of the Near East and India: Source Studies of the Safavid, Ottoman, and Mughal Literate Communities* (thirty-three essays total).[9] The opening map in the latter volume underscores the Deccan's anonymity in the grander Gunpowder Empires scheme. The entire Indian subcontinent is punctuated by small white dots indicative of the Mughal empire, and the main cities of the Deccan sultanates (Ahmadnagar, Bijapur, Bidar, Golconda, etc.) read as merely Mughal, despite the fact that official Mughal hegemony in the region did not occur until 1636, when Golconda and Bijapur signed the deed of submission (*inqiyad nama*). Such a map also obscures the critical fact that it was only *after* Mughal suzerainty that Golconda and Bijapur reached their greatest territorial extent, pushing far into the southern Karnatak. Even though this exceptional sourcebook seeks to highlight voices outside of "empire builders," it nonetheless falls prey to the unilateral 'Mughalization' of the subcontinent. This suggests the question: How can we better map the Indo-Persian world?

The Geographies of the St Andrews Qur'an

Inspired by a number of methodologies that have gained currency in art history over the last decade—the social lives of things, histories of collecting, global history, network analysis—scholars who work on manuscripts produced in and around the historical Islamic world have become increasingly attuned to diachronic histories of the mobile and mutable codex. Arguably the best known Safavid Persian manuscript on the move and in flux is the aforementioned two-volume Tahmasp *Shahnama,* which was a diplomatic gift from Tahmasp (r. 1524–1576) to Selim II (r. 1566–74) and remained 'quiet' in the Topkapı treasury until 1800–1801, when commentaries in Ottoman Turkish were glued in to face the paintings.[10] The manuscript next resurfaced in Paris in 1903 and was ultimately ripped apart by Arthur A. Houghton Jr. and dispersed between the 1960s and 1990s. Seventy-six illustrated folios were donated to the Metropolitan Museum of Art, many were sold piecemeal on the market, and the "carcass" or "remains" of the codex returned to Iran in 1994 in a well-known swap for a Willem de Kooning.[11] In the related yet distinct field of Armenian manuscript studies, Heghnar Zeitlian Watenpaugh has retraced the tragic story of the Zeytun Gospels (1256), a sacred "survivor object" of the

---

[9]   Khafipour 2019 (see the final essay, Overton and Benson 2019); Flood and Necipoğlu 2017 (see chapter 31, Wagoner and Weinstein 2017).
[10] Blair 2019, esp. 531–534.
[11] Quoting Blair 2019:534. See also Soucek 1994; Melikian 1996.

Armenian Genocide that remains split between Yerevan's Matenadaran (the mother/parent manuscript) and the J. Paul Getty Museum (the Canon Gospels, four parchment bifolium), as settled in Los Angeles County Superior Court in 2015, the centennial of the Armenian Genocide.[12]

In terms of peripatetic Qur'an manuscripts, Sheila Blair has explored the peregrinations of Sultan Öljeitü's (r. 1304–1316) 30-volume Qur'an—typically known as 'Öljeitü's Baghdad Qur'an'—which was produced in Baghdad between 706–710/1306–1311 and endowed to Öljeitü's monumental tomb at Sultaniyya in northwest Iran. After the Ottoman occupation of Sultaniyya in October 1534, sections of the manuscript were seized as booty and transferred to Istanbul, where they were dispersed to various repositories including the tomb of Şehzade Mehmed (d. 1543), as endowed by Rüstem Pasha in 1544, and the Topkapı treasury.[13] One reconstituted volume traveled with the Ottoman army to the siege of Vienna in 1683, was apparently stolen from the camp of the Grand Vizier (hence a second round of transfer as military booty), and ended up in the hands of a German book publisher who in turn presented it to the Senate Library in Leipzig in 1694.[14]

Like Öljeitü's Baghdad Qur'an, the St Andrews Qur'an was a luxury codex of its day, changed hands multiple times as a coveted trophy of war, and requires investigation as both a sacred text and site of political contest. Unlike many luxury manuscripts that were effectively frozen on the shelf once they entered royal treasuries or were endowed as *waqf* to religious institutions, the St Andrews manuscript remained resolutely mutable during its two centuries of peregrinations on the Indian subcontinent between roughly 1600 and 1805 (Map 2). It therefore presents a rare glimpse of what it means to be Indo-Persian from the ground up and object out. *It* reveals its trails, networks, owners, users, and locales, and the result is a decidedly personal map that is fundamentally rooted in place and space and liberated from what *we* might impose or imagine.

---

[12] Watenpaugh 2019.
[13] Blair (2023) also describes a brief period of preservation in Mihrimah's first mosque complex at Üsküdar. My thanks to Sheila Blair for sharing this essay in advance of publication.
[14] Blair (2023) describes the TIEM volume as the "parent" and Leipzig as the "offspring." Other volumes that traveled with the Ottomans on campaign experienced similar fates and ended up in repositories in Dresden and Sarajevo. Adam Olearius (d. 1671), who visited Sultaniyya in 1637, seems to have been responsible for the transfer of the two folios now in Copenhagen.

Figure 2. Detail of a typical text panel and gold-flecked margin in the
St Andrews Qur'an manuscript. University of St Andrews, MS O 19.
Photo: Keelan Overton.

1. Tabriz or Herat, Greater Iran, ca. 1520–1540

Based on the quality and style of the St Andrews Qur'an, the biography of
its scribe Muhammad Mu'min (known to have worked under Isma'il [r. 1501–
1524] and Tahmasp in both Tabriz and Herat), and the sectarian nature of its
colophon, we can suggest that the manuscript was copied in Tabriz or Herat
at some point between 1520 and 1540.[15] Its fairly large size (a single page
measures 34.2 x 23.3 cm), luxurious materials (paper, ink, pigments, gold),
exemplary execution in all categories (gold-flecked margins, rulings, illumination, calligraphy), and association with an illustrious early Safavid scribe
suggest that it was likely made for a royal patron or an elite of comparable
means and resources (Figures 1–2).

Like many other manuscripts of the early Safavid period, the St Andrews
Qur'an is replete with bridges and allusions to the Timurid past. These include
the Timurid pedigree of the scribe himself (the son and grandson of renowned
Timurid statesmen and artist-savants) and the tampering of the colophon to
the Timurid Abu Sa'id (r. 1451–1469) at some point during the sixteenth or

---

[15] What follows synthesizes and slightly expands what was earlier presented in Overton, Rose-
Beers, and Wannell 2020.

seventeenth centuries.[16] Additionally, the book's double-page illuminated frontispiece was carefully crafted in relation to a salvaged fragment likely dating to the late Timurid period (see the current right-hand page with sura *al-Fatiha*). In sum, the manuscript celebrates the Timurid past on multiple levels: personal lineage (the scribe), meticulous recycling, stylistic continuity, and fictive dynastic memory (Abu Saʻid).[17]

2. Bijapur, northern Deccan, ca. 1580–1627

At some point after its probable creation in Safavid Tabriz or Herat, the St Andrews Qurʾan traveled to the Indian subcontinent. Although we will likely never know the exact push and pull factors informing its movement east, we can observe that the book was both luxurious and portable (a single-volume codex of large but not unwieldy size), and hence a coveted commodity subject to transfer within established political, commercial, and personal networks. During the lengthy reign of Ibrahim ʻAdil Shah II (r. 1580–1627), the book entered the royal library of Bijapur. By virtue of the many works of art, architecture, and literature associated with the sultan directly or created during his rule, Ibrahim-era Bijapur is regarded as a 'golden age' of the Deccan sultanates (Figure 3). At this time, the Deccan sultanates comprised three main rival dynasties—the ʻAdil Shahs of Bijapur, Qutb Shahs of Golconda and Hyderabad (1591), and Nizam Shahs of Ahmadnagar—each of whom contended against the encroaching Mughals. Ahmadnagar fell the earliest, in 1636, and Bijapur and Hyderabad in turn pushed south into the Karnatak frontier.

The St Andrews Qurʾan's presence in Ibrahim's library is confirmed by the elaborate scalloped medallion (H: 95 mm) decorating each doublure (interior cover) of its binding.[18] The epigraphic design of these medallions (Q 2:130) closely replicates Ibrahim's royal seal used for impression on paper.[19] Due to their protected placement on the inside of the book, the medallions are in excellent condition, and there can be little doubt that they were applied to signal the ruler's proud ownership of such an illustrious codex. Ibrahim is becoming increasingly known as an avid bibliophile-collector-patron, and although we

---

[16] For images of the tampered colophon, see Overton, Rose-Beers, and Wannell 2020, figs. 10.3–10.5.

[17] On the Cairo *Bustan* of Saʻdi's production in Timurid Herat (1488) and subsequent move to Safavid Tabriz, where it received a new folio with verses from the *Iskandarnama* (Book of Iskandar) transcribed at the end of March 1513, see Balafrej 2019:215–216. The verso of this added page bears the seal of Shah ʻAbbas II (r. 1643–1666) dated 1053/1643–1643, thus confirming the manuscript's later sojourn in Isfahan. Balafrej's epilogue discusses many issues of mobility (Herat-Tabriz) and continuity (Timurid-Safavid) that are relevant to the original production of the St Andrews Qurʾan, aspects of which remain elusive and ambiguous.

[18] Overton, Rose-Beers, and Wannell 2020, figs. 10.5–10.6.

[19] See the many images of this seal in Overton 2016b.

Figure 3. View of the northwest side of the Bijapur citadel from the roof of the Sat Manzil, looking over the Jalamandir and toward the back of the Gagan Mahal (1561). Photo: Keelan Overton.

still do not know the exact route of the manuscript's travels from Greater Iran to Bijapur—by sea from the Persian Gulf to the Konkan coast or overland to Hindustan and then down to the Deccan?—it is not at all surprising that it ended up in sultanate Bijapur.

During Ibrahim's reign, Bijapur was a pole of attraction to a variety of human talents, adventurers, and entrepreneurs from the European and Islamic worlds, whether Dutch, Portuguese, Armenian, Iranian, Afghan, or many options in between. Here it is worth restating Sanjay Subrahmanyam's conclusion in his essay in the catalog of the Metropolitan Museum of Art's 2015 exhibition on the Deccan: "In sum, even if the great centers of the Mughal north, such as Delhi, Agra, and Lahore, may have attracted a greater number of such figures [Europeans], there is little sense in seeing the Deccan as a terra incognita for these wandering Europeans of the seventeenth century."[20] Indeed, just because the Deccan is routinely positioned as a sidebar in contemporary scholarship (recall the volumes cited above) does not mean that it was a disconnected

---

[20] Subrahmanyam 2015:312.

unknown in its own day. Quite the opposite, in fact. Ibrahim's library included standard European prints and books alongside universally coveted Arabic and Persian volumes, and we can imagine that the St Andrews Qur'an could have easily arrived in Bijapur as an official state gift or through more fluid and personal channels.[21] The latter conduits could include any one of the many Iranian elites who were lured to Bijapur during Ibrahim's reign, including the calligrapher Khalilullah (d. ca. 1625, a favorite of Shah 'Abbas [r. 1588–1629]), the poet Kalim (d. 1651, who later moved to the Mughal court), the historian Rafi' al-Din Shirazi (d. 1620), and the prime minister Shah Navaz Khan (d. ca. 1611, himself a collector). These Iranian savants marked the tail end of two centuries of elite migration from Iran to the Deccan that had begun in the early 1400s, a century before the founding of the Mughal empire.[22]

3. Mughal imperial library, likely in the northern Deccan, ca. 1638–1699

At some point around 1638–1639, the St Andrews Qur'an manuscript entered the imperial Mughal library. This is confirmed by approximately a dozen seal impressions and inscriptions preserved on the opening and closing flyleaves of the manuscript. This goldmine of ownership evidence is not visible to the naked eye but instead hidden under a sheet of paper laminated (adhered) to the original underlying surface.[23] This deliberate concealment occurred at some point during the book's later life on the Indian subcontinent, but the technologies of the present—specifically the use of transmitted light, or viewing of the pages over a light sheet—enable us to see what lies beneath.

These Mughal ownership marks confirm that the St Andrews Qur'an was in the imperial library between circa 1638 and 1659, and probably as late as 1699, meaning during the reigns of Shah Jahan (r. 1628–1658) and 'Alamgir (r. 1658–1707). This period coincided with heightened Mughal hegemony in the Deccan, and as noted above, Bijapur and Golconda signed the deed of submission in 1636. Although the precise circumstances of the transfer from the Bijapur library to the Mughal library remain unknown, it is conceivable that the book would have been offered as tribute (*pishkash*) from the Bijapuri *khan* (a demotion of *shah*)

---

[21] Overton 2020b; Overton 2016a.

[22] For a preliminary prosopography tracking forty-eight such figures, including those mentioned above (nos. 39, 46, 33, 34), see "Appendix: Iranian Elites in the Deccan, ca. 1400–1700," in Overton 2020b:49–58.

[23] Overton, Rose-Beers, and Wannell 2020, figs. 10.7–10.10. These ownership marks are detailed in Overton et al. 2020, Table 2, 274–275.

to the Mughal *padishah*.[24] The critical point to remember is that the Mughal court was firmly entrenched in the Deccan by this time, and the book need not have traveled north to Hindustan. Based on its next owner (see below), it likely remained on the move with the imperial war machine or entered a fixed repository in a Mughal settlement in the northern Deccan such as Burhanpur or Aurangabad. Such cities are replete with baths, tombs, gardens, and palaces patronized by Mughal emperors, princes, and nobles, and it is in such spaces that we might logically imagine this stage of the manuscript's life.[25]

4. Savanur, western Karnatak, Deccan, ca. 1700–1786

While the Mughal-controlled Deccan is now part and parcel of Deccan studies and cities like Aurangabad and Burhanpur populate virtually all of the region's maps, the same cannot yet be said about the St Andrews Qur'an manuscript's next sojourn: Savanur. Savanur is located about 150 miles south of Bijapur in the western Karnatak, a lusher and cooler frontier region vied for amongst the northern Islamic sultanates and other regional powers. To my knowledge, it is not labeled on any of the maps featured in the canonical publications of Deccani art history.[26] Despite its general anonymity in art historical circles, Savanur and its earlier sister city of Bankapur are fundamental locales in historical studies devoted to autonomous households and territorial conquests in the Karnatak.[27] In this context, two points warrant (re)emphasis. First, it was in the decades following Mughal suzerainty (1636) that Bijapur and Hyderabad reached their greatest territorial extent and partitioned the southern frontier. Second, the travels of objects like the St Andrews Qur'an manuscript did not simply cease with the conclusion of the sultanates in 1687. What then were the push and pull factors shaping the mobility of objects and individuals on the Deccan plateau from the 1680s onward?

The nawabs of Savanur were members of the Afghan (Pathan) Miyana household, hence also known as the 'Savanuri Miyanas.'[28] During the seventeenth century, the Miyanas established strongholds at Bankapur and Savanur and rose to high positions in the Bijapur administration. As described by Subah

---

[24] On Bijapur-Mughal political relations and the associated material record, see Alam and Subrahmanyam 2012; Overton 2014.

[25] Haidar and Sardar 2015:281–287; Michell and Philon 2018:216–237 and 380–407.

[26] For example, Michell and Zebrowski 1999; Haidar and Sardar 2015; and Michell and Philon 2018.

[27] Chitnis 2000; Dayal 2016 (see the map at the opening of chapter 2, 86); and Archambault 2018 (see map 1, 27; map 2, 49). In these maps, Bankapur is highlighted but not Savanur. Ursula Sims-Williams's ongoing research of the Tipu Sultan collection in the British Library will continue to yield important findings about Savanur as a manuscript entrepôt. See her important recent study, Sims-Williams 2021.

[28] Archambault 2018:203.

Dayal, Bankapur was a "frontier city" of the Bijapur sultanate comparable to what Burhanpur was to the Mughals—in other words, a home base for launching military campaigns.[29] Muhammad 'Adil Shah (r. 1627–1656) himself marched with the Bijapur army to Bankapur in January 1644, in the days leading up to a seminal battle at Ikkeri. In 1672, Sikandar 'Adil Shah (r. 1672–1686) awarded 'Abd al-Karim Khan Miyana (d. 1678) the jagir of Bankapur. 'Abd al-Karim had commanded the Bijapur army and served as regent for the young Sikandar, and he would become vizier of the sultanate late in life (1675–1678).

The third nawab of Savanur—'Abd al-Ra'uf Khan Miyana (r. 1686–1720)—played a key role in the negotiations between 'Alamgir and Sikandar. Upon the fall of Bijapur in 1686, he was awarded the Mughal title "Dilir Khan" and a rank (*mansab*) of 7,000, and established his capital at Savanur. The Savanur state reached its greatest territorial extent under the fourth nawab, 'Abd al-Majid Khan Miyana (r. 1726–1754), but then steadily lost much of its territory to the Marathas. Under 'Abd al-Hakim Khan Miyana (r. 1754–1794), Savanur was caught in the middle of bitter campaigns between the Marathas and Mysore kingdom of Haidar 'Ali (r. 1761–1782), and then Tipu Sultan. As we shall see, it was this tenuous circumstance that led to the St Andrews Qur'an's next transfer.

The evidence for the manuscript's tenure in Savanur is not found in the codex itself but rather a booty list written by an officer of the East India Company at Srirangapatna (Seringapatam) on December 28, 1799, hence about eight months after the defeat and death of Tipu Sultan (May 4–5, 1799).[30] The description of the volume reads: "Koran in three different characters ... This Koran was purchased by Nabob Dillair Khan of Sanoor [Savanur] for three thousand pagodas, and came into the possession of the late Sultaun with the plunder of that place." The Savanur nawab in question could be 'Abd al-Ra'uf "Dilir Khan," titled as such by 'Alamgir in 1686, or one of his successors, perhaps 'Abd al-Majid or 'Abd al-Hakim. As traced by Ursula Sims-Williams, the Savanur nawabs owned codices linked with Safavid Iran, the Deccan sultanates, and the Mughals. Thanks to the presence of his seal dated 1145/1732–1733, the known collection of 'Abd al-Majid currently stands at thirteen manuscripts.[31]

Although we may never know which Savanur nawab purchased the St Andrews Qur'an manuscript at some point between 1699 (the latest probable date of one of the recovered Mughal inscriptions) and 1786 (a seminal battle to which we shall soon return), we can observe several critical points about

---

[29] Dayal 2016:132. I am grateful to the author for sharing this chapter of her dissertation in advance of publication. Her monograph, *The Household State: Engaging the Mughals in Seventeenth-Century South India*, is in progress.

[30] Ogg 1799, fols. 81v–82v. Thanks to Ursula Sims-Williams for sharing this critical source.

[31] Sims-Williams 2021:295–298 and fig. 5.

the Savanur state. Despite its relative academic anonymity today, Savanur was connected to virtually every single major polity on the central Deccan plateau—first the Bijapur sultanate, then the Mughals as of 1686, and finally caught in between the Marathas and Mysore from about 1750 onward. In many ways, the shifty (by necessity) life story of this Afghan household parallels that of the St Andrews Qur'an. Both household and manuscript negotiated conflicting actors and interests on the Deccan plateau, moved readily between contexts, and do much to expand a tunnel vision understanding of the Islamic Deccan rooted in the northern sultanates alone. That the Savanur nawabs were important biblio-philes in the seventeenth and eighteenth century Deccan should come as little surprise, and future codicological research will identify more codices once in their possession.[32]

5. Srirangapatna, Mysore kingdom, southern Deccan, ca. 1786–1799

For the kingdom of Mysore, Savanur was a major conflict zone in ongoing campaigns against the Marathas.[33] From 1756 onward, when the Marathas controlled about half of the Savanur state, both Haidar 'Ali and then Tipu Sultan launched attacks against Savanur city. In October 1786, Tipu won a decisive victory at Savanur, and he may have plundered the Qur'an manuscript in question during this occupation (recall that the December 1799 EIC list records that it "came into the possession of the late Sultaun with the *plunder of that place* [Savanur]).[34] Additional support for this assertion is found in Charles Stewart's 1809 catalog of Tipu's collection. In his introduction, Stewart observes: "Very few of these books had been purchased by Tippoo or his father. They were part of the plunder brought from Sanoor [Savanur], Cuddapah [Kadapa, or Neknamabad], and the Carnatic."[35] His section on the St Andrews Qur'an manuscript reads, "… said to have cost the Nabob Dilēr Khan, of Sanūr, Three Thousand Pagodas, and was plundered from him by Tipoo Sultān."[36]

At some point after its acquisition (aka plunder) in Savanur, the St Andrews Qur'an traveled another two hundred miles south to the kingdom of Mysore, where it presumably entered a workshop-library in Srirangapatna, Tipu's

---

[32] On the collections of their nearby relatives, the Nawabs of Kadapa (Cuddapah or Curpah), see Sims-Williams 2021:298–301.
[33] Chitnis 2000:53–58; Archambault 2018:212–216.
[34] Chitnis 200:56–58.
[35] Stewart 1809:v.
[36] Stewart 1809:167 (no. xxxiii). If we choose not to read the EIC list and Stewart as ironclad accounts, we must leave open the possibility that Haidar 'Ali could have acquired the manuscript during one of his earlier battles at Savanur. On this ambiguity, see Overton 2020b:322n41.

fortified island capital along the Kaveri River.[37] We know that Tipu personally viewed the manuscript, for he wrote a note on its front cover restating
the salient historical 'facts' of the colophon—that is, the patron Abu Sa'id (r.
1451–1469) and corresponding date of 845/1441–1442 (we now know that these
lines were deliberately antiquated to the Timurid period). In the Srirangapatna/
Mysore workshop, the manuscript underwent a series of significant interventions, including structural and aesthetic modifications to its binding, the addition of marginal inscriptions dictating the proper recitation and division of the
Qur'anic text, and the addition of endpapers inclusive of prayers. These latter
interventions in the service of localized use set the manuscript apart as a living
sacred text and contribute to our knowledge of religious practice in Tipu's court.

We can also presume that the Srirangapatna/Mysore workshop deliberately concealed the flyleaves bearing Mughal seals and inscriptions by covering
them with new sheets of paper (lamination). This obliteration of provenance
speaks volumes about how the St Andrews Qur'an manuscript was not just a
well-used sacred text and beloved prestige manuscript but also a physical stage
for the performance of potent geopolitics, an observation that can be made
about Tipu's library in general.[38] In Islamic manuscripts, it is not uncommon to
encounter seals and inscriptions that have been vigorously effaced, and Ibrahim
II's large Qur'anic seal was particularly subject to this fate. This acknowledged,
the use of lamination as a deliberate and theoretically more effective tool of
erasure warrants further research.

6. Calcutta, College of Fort William, 1799–1805

The St Andrews Qur'an manuscript's reduction to a pawn in political contest
likewise marked the next stage of its life. If we agree that Tipu plundered the
manuscript at Savanur in October 1786, then it only took about twelve years for
him to lose it in a similar fashion. Upon Tipu's death and defeat at Srirangapatna
in early May 1799, his library of around three to four thousand volumes fell into
the hands of the East India Company.[39] Along with many other manuscripts, the
St Andrews Qur'an was sent to the College of Fort William in Calcutta, where it
was assessed by Charles Stewart and a local scribe who may have corrected some
errors in original transcription. A series of additional endpapers were also added
at this time, and one was inscribed with a note signaling its imminent departure from the subcontinent: "For the University of Saint Andrews, From Tippoo's

---

[37] On Srirangapatna, see chapter 3 in Nair 2011.
[38] On the politics, prestige, and function of Tipu's Srirangapatna library, much of which was
amassed through plunder, see Ehrlich 2020:482–485.
[39] Ehrlich 2020:481–482.

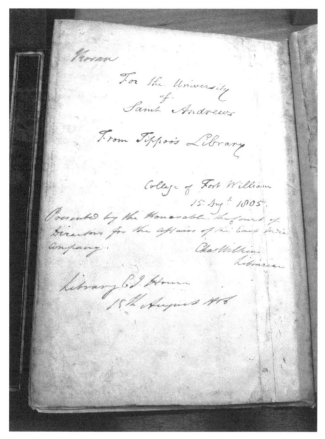

Figure 4. East India Company inscriptions, dated 15 August 1805 (Calcutta)
and 15 August 1806 (London), on endpapers added to the front of the
St Andrews Qur'an manuscript. University of St Andrews, MS O 19.
Photo: Keelan Overton

Library. College of Fort William, 15 August 1805" (Figure 4). Like all of the other books and precious loot acquired at Srirangapatna, the St Andrews Qur'an became part of a much larger program of imperialist distribution.[40] Most of Tipu's manuscripts were sent to universities, libraries, and collections in Oxford, Edinburgh,

---

[40] Stronge 2009:50–57.

Cambridge, Windsor, and London (about six hundred volumes are in the British Library).[41] A select few found their way to the United States.[42]

It is worth noting that the battle of Srirangapatna was far from the only instance when manuscripts changed hands between Tipu Sultan and the British. The Library of the Royal Botanic Garden in Edinburgh preserves a volume of notes taken by Francis Buchanan during the botanical lectures delivered by Professor John Hope at the garden in the summer of 1781.[43] Buchanan lent his lecture notes to a shipmate named Alexander Boiswell on his voyage to India in 1785. Boiswell subsequently lost them in 1790 at the battle of Sittimungulum (Sathyamangalam), when Tipu defeated the East India Company. The ruler and/ or his librarians clearly recognized the value of the notes, which represented the most advanced botanical knowledge in Europe at the time, and had them bound in a simple yet familiar Mysore style. This cherry-red leather binding features a central tooled medallion with axial pendants and four corner pieces and is further embellished with gold-painted lines and a large four-petal flower. Ironically but not necessarily surprisingly, the newly bound notes—now a true manuscript—soon found their way back into British hands. Just nine years later, in May 1799, they were among the loot won by the East India Company at Srirangapatna. Buchanan's inscription on the flyleaf is dated May 23, 1800, following the repatriation.

7. London, Library at East India House, 1805–1806

By August 15, 1806, the Qur'an manuscript had made its way to the Library of the East India Company in London. There, the librarian Charles Wilkins penned the following note below the Calcutta one of exactly a year earlier: "Presented by the honorable Court of Directors for the affairs of the East India Company. Charles Wilkins, Librarian, Library East India House, 15 August 1806" (Figure 4).

[41] On Tipu's collection in the British Library, see Sims-Williams 2021 and her many contributions to the *Asian and African Studies* blog, https://blogs.bl.uk/asian-and-african/. For the politics of Tipu's library within the East India Company and 'British India' at large, see Ehrlich 2021:485–492.

[42] Consider the illustrated *Gulshan-i 'Ishq* of 1155/1742–1743 in the Philadelphia Museum of Art (1945-65-22). According to typed and handwritten notes appended to its binding, it "was found in the Zanana [variously "Harem"] of Tipoo Sahib at Seringapatam when it was taken in 1799." The binding is visible online at https://www.philamuseum.org/collections/permanent/49733.html.

[43] I am grateful to the late Bruce Wannell for bringing these notes to my attention in 2016 and Dr. Henry Noltie for providing additional information and images. See also Overton, Rose-Beers, and Wannell 2020:330–331n160 and Ehrlich 2020:484–485.

St. Andrews University Library

Koran of Abu Said

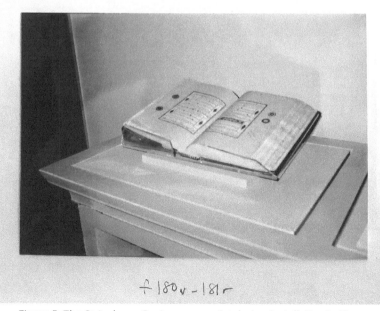

f 180v - 181r

Figure 5. The St Andrews Qur'an manuscript during installation in *Timur and the Princely Vision* (1989), opened to folios 180v–181r. Photo: Archive of Special Collections, Library of the University of St Andrews.

LACMA — July 89

Figure 6. The St Andrews Qur'an manuscript on display in *Timur and the Princely Vision*, Los Angeles County Museum of Art, 1989. Photo: Archive of Special Collections, Library of the University of St Andrews.

8. St Andrews, Library of the University of St Andrews, Special Collections, 1806–present

A few weeks later, the codex reached its final destination: the University of St Andrews. According to the Senate Minutes, the "magnificent present" arrived on August 27, 1806 with a letter from Charles Wilkins addressed to the Revd. Dr. Trotter, Rector of the University.[44] In the late twentieth century, the manuscript made its international debut in two major exhibitions: *The Qur'an* (London, 1976) and *Timur and the Princely Vision* (Washington, DC and Los Angeles, 1989) (Figures 5–6).[45] At that point, it was best known as the "Koran of Abu Said" (see the annotation in Figure 5), meaning its colophon was read at face value. Prior to the Timur exhibition, the manuscript was significantly restored, to include both rebacking in new leather and resewing of the textblock.[46] In recent years, it has undergone select imaging and restoration treatments in the United Kingdom.

---

[44] Senate Minutes 1806:61–62. I thank Maia Sheridan for providing a scan of these pages.
[45] Lings and Safadi 1976; Lentz and Lowry 1989. The opening displayed in the Washington, DC show was 180v–181r, "not the frontispiece as originally requested" (Gallop 1989).
[46] See the final section entitled "Binding" in Overton, Rose-Beers, and Wannell 2020:304–314.

Cartographic Alternatives: Interdisciplinarity, Diachronism, and Liminality

A review of the most common maps used in the fields of early modern Islamic, Indo-Persian, and Deccan studies reveals a range of conscious choices and inevitable omissions, as with any cartographic exercise. For many, especially students, the study of the early modern period is governed by the Gunpowder Empires map.[47] Adjacent blocks of red, purple, and yellow (or variously green, peach, and purple) delineate the Ottoman, Safavid, and Mughal empires and are easily read. The general emphasis on the Mughals and Safavids has led to a framing of Indo-Persian relations as a predominately northern relationship centered on and around Hindustan, and conventional narratives focus on Humayun (r. 1530–1556) and Tahmasp, Jahangir (r. 1605–1627) and Shah 'Abbas, disputed territories like Qandahar, and Persian poets and language at the Mughal court.

As for the Deccan, the region is typically divided into northern versus southern zones or mapped according to dynastic periodization and opposing political authorities.[48] A more recent approach, as demonstrated in Map 1 here, seeks to integrate the Deccan into the much larger Persian cosmopolis and hence stretches north to the Amu Darya and modern-day Uzbekistan and west to encompass all of Iran and the Persian Gulf.[49] A final method, alluded to above and encapsulated in Map 2 here, approaches the Deccan as a holistic region covering virtually all of peninsular India from the Narmada River to Madurai and includes well-known capital cities and settlements alongside frontier spaces and paths of conquest. The questions remain: Do any of these maps sufficiently capture the ground realities of the liminal people and things that crisscrossed the Gunpowder Empires, Indian Ocean, Indo-Persian worlds, Indian subcontinent, Deccan sultanates, and Deccan plateau? Do fixed maps jibe with the betwixt and between?

---

[47] Ottoman, Safavid and Mughal Empires | World History | Khan Academy: https://www.youtube.com/watch?v=hNpcQEGw3S4.

[48] The two front-matter maps in Michell and Zebrowski 1999 divide the region into northern and southern zones and are extremely detailed. Haidar and Sardar 2015 includes three maps: "India circa 1400" (Bahmani sultanate versus Vijayanagara to the south), "India, late 16th century" (indicating the zones of the five sultanates), and "The Deccan, 17th century" (comparable to the former but also highlighting foreign interests and strongholds), xii–xiv. Temporal division is also favored in Michell and Philon 2018 (four excellent maps covering 1350–1500, 1500–1600, 1600–1700, and 1700–1750).

[49] Flatt 2018, fig. 2.1; Eaton 2019, map 1, 12; Green 2019, maps 1–3; Overton 2020a, map 1, front matter.

As we have seen, the life of the St Andrews Qur'an manuscript on the Indian subcontinent spanned circa 1600 to 1805 and five distinct locales: 'Adil Shahi Bijapur in the northern Deccan, the Mughal library likely on the move in the north-central Deccan, Savanur state in the western Karnatak, Srirangapatna (kingdom of Mysore) in the southern Deccan, and the East India Company headquarters in Calcutta. While Map 2 charts the manuscript's confirmed and speculative trails via a series of arrows, it provides little indication of the expansive timeframe in question, which the reader only gleans from the provided caption. The book's dizzying and at times ambiguous and perplexing peregrinations can be compared to those of the human itinerant, especially Iranian elites who circulated between multiple courts in search of better opportunities and patronage. To offer one of many contemporary examples, the aforementioned poet Kalim was born in Hamadan, studied in Kashan, lived in Ibrahim's Bijapur for about two decades (1601–1618), returned to Shah 'Abbas's court for two years (1618–1620), next set his sights on Jahangir's Agra (1621), became *malik al-shu'ara* (poet laureate) under Shah Jahan, and ultimately died in Kashmir.[50]

As historians, art historians, and literary specialists alike become increasingly concerned with objects, talents, and cultural norms in motion across the Persian cosmopolis, it seems that an alternative form of mapping is in order. Our fields might be well served by transitioning from fixed print maps to virtual interactive databases that better capture the complexities of personal experience (a ground-up view), versus the overarching polity (a top–down view), while tracing relationships and transmissions across vast swathes of time and space. We can imagine clicking on Bidar, for example, and pulling up subsections devoted to individuals, objects, aesthetics, and literatures associated with the city. The Sufi saint Shah Khalilullah (d. ca. 1442–1454) would link the user to his tomb in Bidar, the nearby tomb of the Bahmani ruler Ahmad I (r. 1422–1436), who was a devotee of the saint's father Shah Ni'matullah Vali (d. 1431), and that pir's shrine complex in Mahan, which was originally patronized by Ahmad I.[51] The literary trail would lead the user to the resonance of Shah Ni'matullah's poetry in Deccani contexts, including the painted interior of Ahmad I's tomb, and manuscripts known to have been in the Ni'matullahi family collection, which would in turn lead to the contemporary Shiraz school of philosophy and painting, later collectors like Ibrahim II of Bijapur, and still later collectors who absorbed Bijapur collections ('Abd al-Majid of Savanur, Shah Jahan and 'Alamgir, Haidar 'Ali and Tipu Sultan).[52] The *qutb* of the order succeeding Shah Khalilullah,

---

[50] Overton 2020b, no. 46, 57.
[51] Overton 2020b, figs. 1.4–1.6 (Mahan); Firouzeh 2020, figs. 5.1–5.9 (Bidar).
[52] Firouzeh 2020, figs. 5.1–5.9 (Bidar) and fig. 5.10 (a Bidar/Ni'matullah to Bijapur/'Adil Shah manuscript).

Shah Muhibullah (d. ca. 1506), would link to the famous merchant-cum-prime minster of Bidar Mahmud Gavan (d. 1481) and in turn the architecture and tile-work traditions of Central Asia and Khurasan—reconfigured in his own Bidar madrasa (876/1471–1472)—and Herati savants like Jami (d. 1492).[53] Such an interdisciplinary and diachronic platform would address the human case study (prosopography), umbrella geopolitics, historical watersheds, the built environment, and patterns of mobility and mutability in a truly networked fashion. It would do better justice to objects like the St Andrews Qur'an manuscript, which we must thank for challenging and expanding our imagined, and at times all too convenient, geographies.

To close this essay, we must interrogate the all too convenient moniker used throughout to describe the manuscript at hand: 'the St Andrews Qur'an'. This title is an arbitrary matter of simplicity, given that the volume's production, ownership, refurbishment, and use flowed between at least six major contexts. Identifying the manuscript by its present owner is not without fault, however, especially since its final destination in the United Kingdom is the product of a moment of profound imperialist violence and plunder. As contested objects and collections of all kinds continue to be scrutinized, we must consider the difficult question: Whose manuscript, or patrimony broadly speaking, is it anyway? Appropriately, the ever-elusive codex skirts a clear-cut answer to this question. Tipu Sultan left the most indelible mark on the manuscript as a used sacred text, but he too acquired it through plunder and to his mind, it was the Qur'an of Abu Sa'id. Ibrahim II of Bijapur, the Mughals, and the nawabs of Savanur all claimed it and left a mark, but it is ultimately a luxury product of early-sixteenth century Safavid Tabriz or Herat. Perhaps it would be best to sidestep ownership altogether and identify the codex by its esteemed calligrapher, that is, 'the Qur'an of Muhammad Mu'min b. 'Abdullah al-Murvarid'. But if we want to capture its diachronic history and many layers, we will have to attempt something of the tongue twister titling this essay.

Works Cited

Alam, M., and S. Subrahmanyam. 2012. "The Deccan Frontier and Mughal Expansion, circa 1600." In *Writing the Mughal World: Studies on Culture and Politics*, 165–203. New York.

Archambault, H. L. 2018. "Geographies of Influence: Two Afghan Military Households in Seventeenth and Eighteenth Century South India." PhD diss., University of California, Berkeley.

---

[53] On Mahmud Gavan's madrasa, see Blair and Bloom 2020.

Balafrej, L. 2019. *The Making of the Artist in Late Timurid Painting*. Edinburgh.

Blair, S. 2019. "Reading a Painting: Sultan-Muhammad's *The Court of Gayumars*." In Khafipour 2019:525–538.

———. 2023. "Sultan Öljeitü's Baghdad Qur'an: A Life Story." In *The Word Illuminated: Form and Function of Qur'anic Manuscripts*, ed. S. Rettig and M. Farhad, 97–122. Washington, DC.

Blair, S., and J. Bloom. 2020. "From Iran to the Deccan: Architectural Transmission and the Madrasa of Mahmud Gavan at Bidar." In Overton 2020a:175–202.

Blair, S., J. Bloom, and R. Ettinghausen. 1994. *The Art and Architecture of Islam, 1250–1800*. New Haven.

Chitnis, K. N. 2000. *The Nawabs of Savanur*. Delhi.

Dayal, S. 2016. "Landscapes of Conquest: Patrons and Narratives in the Seventeenth Century Deccan, c. 1636–1687." PhD diss., University of California, Los Angeles.

Eaton, R. E. 2019. *India in the Persianate Age: 1000–1765*. Oakland.

Ehrlich, J. 2020. "Plunder and Prestige: Tipu Sultan's Library and the Making of British India." *South Asia: Journal of South Asian Studies* 43:478–492.

Ettinghausen, R., O. Grabar, and M. Jenkins. 2001. *The Art and Architecture of Islam, 600–1250*. New Haven.

Firouzeh, P. 2020. "Dynastic Self-Fashioning and the Arts of the Pen: Sufi and Calligraphy Networks between Fifteenth-Century Shiraz and Bidar." In Overton 2020a:145–174.

Flatt, E. 2019. *The Courts of the Deccan Sultanates: Living Well in the Persian Cosmopolis*. Chapel Hill.

Flood, F., and G. Necipoğlu. eds. 2017. *A Companion to Islamic Art and Architecture*. 2 vols. Hoboken.

Gallop, A. T. 1989. Letter from Annabel Teh Gallop, British Library, to Robert Smart, St Andrews University Library, April 20, 1989. Archive of Special Collections, Library of the University of St Andrews.

Grabar, O., and S. Blair. 1980. *Epic Images and Contemporary History: The Illustrations of the Great Mongol Shah-Nama*. Chicago.

Green, N., ed. 2019. *The Persianate World: The Frontiers of a Eurasian Lingua Franca*. Oakland.

Haidar N. H., and M. Sardar, eds. 2015. *Sultans of Deccan India, 1500–1700: Opulence and Fantasy*. New York.

Joshi, P. M. 1973. "Historical Geography of Medieval Deccan." In *History of Medieval Deccan, 1295–1724*, ed. P. M. Joshi and G. Yazdani, vol. 1:3–28. Hyderabad.

Khafipour, H., ed. 2019. *The Empires of the Near East and India: Source Studies of the Safavid, Ottoman, and Mughal Literate Communities*. New York.

Lentz, T. W., and G. D. Lowry. 1989. *Timur and the Princely Vision: Persian Art and Culture in the Fifteenth Century.* Los Angeles.

Lings, M., and Y. H. Safadi. 1976. *The Qur'ān: Catalogue of an Exhibition of Qur'ān Manuscripts at the British Library, 3 April–15 August 1976.* London.

Melikian, S. 1996. "Destroying a Treasure: The Sad Story of a Manuscript." *New York Times*, April 27, 1996.

Michell, G., and M. Zebrowski. 1999. *Architecture and Art of the Deccan Sultanates. New Cambridge History of India*, pt. 1, vol. 7. Cambridge.

Michell, G., H. Philon, and A. Martinelli. 2018. *Islamic Architecture of Deccan India.* London.

Nair, J. 2011. *Mysore Modern: Rethinking the Region under Princely Rule.* Minneapolis.

Ogg, Captain S. W. "Addition to the Selected Manuscripts." Seringapatam (Srirangapatna), December 28, 1799, British Library, Mss Eur E 196.

Overton, K. 2014. "*Vida de Jacques de Coutre*: A Flemish Account of Bijapuri Visual Culture in the Shadow of Mughal Felicity." In *The Visual World of Muslim India: The Art, Culture, and Society of the Deccan in the Early Modern Era*, ed. Laura Parodi, 233–264. London.

———. 2016a. "Book Culture, Royal Libraries, and Persianate Painting in Bijapur, circa 1580–1630." *Muqarnas* 33:91–154.

———. 2016b. "From an Enigmatic Binding Stamp to a Holistic Reassessment: The St Andrews Qur'an." *Echoes from the Vault: a blog from the Special Collections of the University of St Andrews*, December 12, 2016, https://special-collections.wp.st-andrews.ac.uk/2018/07/16/the-st-andrews-quran-part-two-deconstructing-a-frontispiece-mapping-an-insert/.

———. 2018. "The St Andrews Qur'an Part Two: Deconstructing a Frontispiece, Mapping an Insert." *Echoes from the Vault: A Blog from the Special Collections of the University of St Andrews,* July 16, 2018, https://special-collections.wp.st-andrews.ac.uk/2018/07/16/the-st-andrews-quran-part-two-deconstructing-a-frontispiece-mapping-an-insert/.

———, ed. 2020a. *Iran and the Deccan: Persianate Art, Culture, and Talent in Circulation, 1400–1700.* Bloomington.

———. 2020b. "Introduction to Iranian Mobilities and Persianate Mediations in the Deccan." In Overton 2020a:3–76.

Overton, K., and J. Benson. 2019. "Deccani Seals and Scribal Notations: Sources for the Study of Indo-Persian Book Arts and Collecting (c. 1400–1680)." In Khafipour 2019:554–596.

Overton, K., and K. Rose-Beers, with contributions by B. Wannell. 2020. "Indo-Persian Histories from the Object Out: The St Andrews Qur'an Manuscript between Timurid, Safavid, Mughal, and Deccani Worlds." In Overton 2020a: 256–335.

Peacock, A. C. S. 2021. "Indo-Persian Manuscripts." *Iran: Journal of the British Institute of Persian Studies* 59:147–150.

Ramaswami, P. B., and K. Singh. 2015. *Nauras: The Many Arts of the Deccan*. New Delhi.

Ruffle, K. 2020. "Gazing in the Eyes of the Martyrs: Four Theories of South Asian Shiʻi Visuality." *Journal of Material Cultures in the Muslim World* 1:268–290.

Sims-Williams, U. 2021. "Collections within Collections: An Analysis of Tipu Sultan's Library." *Iran: Journal of the British Institute of Persian Studies* 59: 287–307.

Soucek, P. 1994. s.v. "Demotte *Šāh-nāma*." *Encyclopaedia Iranica*.

Stewart, C. 1809. *A Descriptive Catalogue of the Oriental Library of the Late Tippoo Sultan of Mysore*. Cambridge.

Stronge, S. 2009. *Tipu's Tigers*. London.

Subrahmanyam, S. 2015. "Europeans in the Deccan." In Haidar and Sardar 2015: 309–312.

Wagoner, P., and L. Weinstein. 2017. "The Deccani Sultanates and Their Inter-regional Connections." In Flood and Necipoğlu 2017, vol. 2:777–804.

Watenpaugh, H. Z. 2019. *The Missing Pages: The Modern Life of a Medieval Manuscript from Genocide to Justice*. Stanford.

6

Pan-Islamic Plot or Colonial Paranoia?

Ottoman Policies towards Southeast Asia, 1824–1916

A. C. S. Peacock

IN 1915, AS THE FIRST WORLD WAR GROUND ON, the Muslim Indian soldiery based in Singapore mutinied; it was only with French, Russian, and Japanese support that the British, who had left their eastern territories seriously underdefended, were able to suppress the revolt. Subsequent official British reports into the mutiny attempted to play down both the threat it presented and the motivation. A misunderstanding over the regiment's next assignment was credited, for the Muslim mutineers feared they were being sent to fight their coreligionists in Turkey. Yet officials suspected a much more worrying and insidious threat— that the mutineers were in fact inspired by a pan-Islamic ideology propagated by the Ottoman Empire and possibly directly aided by outsiders.[1] The position of the Ottoman sultan as Caliph, a claim implying a status as leader of all Muslims everywhere, which had been increasingly emphasized from the reign of Sultan Abdülhamid II (1876–1909), gave further fuel to these fears, especially given the Ottoman declaration in 1914 that the War was a jihad. The British were not alone in their anxiety about pan-Islamic influences, although they were rather late to the party. Perhaps their long alliance with the Ottomans, seen as vital to the security of India, led them to downplay the threat, at least compared to the Dutch, who, at least since the 1870s, had evinced grave concern about Ottoman pan-Islamic influence on their subjects in the East Indies.[2] Such concerns were intensified by the warnings of the prominent scholar Snouck Hurgronje, advisor

---

[1] By pan-Islam, for the purposes of the present discussion I follow Reid's definition: "a movement is taken to be pan-Islamic if it provides an ideological basis for cooperation between, or beyond, individual political units in a political struggle under the banner of Islam" (Reid 1967:267).

[2] Reid 1967.

on Islamic affairs to the Dutch Indies government, who saw pan-Islam as a real and growing danger, propagated by Ottoman influence over Muslims worldwide through the position of Caliph.[3]

The reality of pan-Islamism as political phenomenon was questioned both by some contemporaries as well as by some modern researchers.[4] However, the idea of a plot by the Ottomans, in cahoots with their German allies, to undermine colonial regimes through pan-Islamism, continues to resonate in much recent scholarship. To take the example of a recent history of Southeast Asia in the First World War, the author writes:

> Ottoman and German diplomats and activists sought to undermine colonial rule in Southeast Asian colonies by providing aid or support to pan-Islamists, the Ghadar party, or Indochinese nationalists, depending on the time and place. This story, then, is dotted with conspiracies to subvert colonial rule with the help from allies near and far.[5]

A similar view is expounded by Tim Harper in his study of the global connections of the 1915 mutiny:

> After the declaration of jihad by the Sheikh-ul-Islam in Istanbul on behalf of the Ottoman Caliph on 14 November 1914, the Allies seemed to face "a revolt of Islam". This possibility was both imagined and real. Turkish and German propaganda attempted to conjure it into being across Asia and Africa.[6]

Studies based on Dutch sources have reached a similar conclusion. The historian of the First World War in the Dutch Indies, Kees van Dijk, describes a "conspiracy" coordinated by Berlin, constituting a "Turco-German effort to incite a Holy War and subvert allied rule in British and French colonies."[7]

The crisis of the First World War is seen by many scholars as a formative moment in linking various Asian and Islamist movements, which were becoming increasingly prominent from the 1870s onwards. As Reid puts it:

> A mind-set which we might today call jihadist or Islamist, and attribute to the global projection of struggles in Palestine and Iraq, do [sic] in fact have a long history in Southeast Asia. The twentieth century rise of nationalism not only marginalized such thinking, which colonial

---

[3] van Dijk 2008:291–293; cf. Kadı 2021.
[4] E.g. van Dijk 2008:290–293; Kadı 2015.
[5] Streets-Salter 2017:11.
[6] Harper 2013:1789.
[7] van Dijk 2008:ix.

writers labeled "pan-Islamic", but made it seem quixotic, its importance exaggerated by colonial paranoia. A century later, with nationalism again vigorously challenged by concepts of solidarity with a
global umma, the situation looks very different. This current must be
seen as a continuing one within the Islamic world, emerging with far
greater salience at some periods, such as the present, than at others.
The period between 1870 and 1918 was another such period when
the solidarity of the umma loomed particularly large in the region at
another time of Muslim frustration.[8]

Even scholars who are skeptical about the earlier commitment of the Ottoman
Empire to pan-Islamist policies view the First World War as a moment of change,
when the empire embraced an avowedly pan-Islamic outlook to ensure its own
survival.[9] As Aydın puts it, "The wartime Ottoman government mobilized pan-
Islamic activists and ideas to foment Muslim disobedience against its Christian-
colonizer enemies."[10] But he goes on to caution that, "Although the Ottoman
center turned to pan-Islamism when its relationship with Western powers dete-
riorated and it needed an alternative alliance to strengthen its international
position, it did not invent pan-Islamism but rather utilized already existing
ideas and emotions."[11] Whatever Istanbul's own intentions, frequent reference was made by a wide variety of anti-colonial activists to their Ottoman
connections. A revolt in Kelantan on the east of the Malay Peninsula in 1915
was claimed by some to be Ottoman-inspired,[12] while even after the First World
War, nearby Terengganu was shaken in 1928 by a rebellion that raised the
Turkish flag, the 'Bendera Stambul.'[13] Similarly, in the Dutch East Indies, revolts
in 1915–1916 from Sulawesi to Sumatra hoped for Turkish support to oust the
colonial power.[14] This was the legacy of a much longer tendency of Southeast
Asian rulers and individuals to resort to Istanbul's aid that stretched back the
nineteenth century and beyond.[15]

Nonetheless, most research to date—including that of Reid in his important
study of nineteenth-century pan-Islamism in Southeast Asia,[16] and almost all
work on the First World War in the region—has relied on the admittedly rich

---

[8] Reid 2014:101.
[9] E.g. Aydın 2007:93–94, 106–111.
[10] Aydın 2007:109.
[11] Aydın 2007:111.
[12] Kheng 2006.
[13] Malhi 2015.
[14] van Dijk 2008:310.
[15] See essays in Peacock and Gallop 2015 for an overview.
[16] Reid 1967.

and valuable material in colonial archives. Such archives contain not just the accounts of colonial administrators but also the testimony of their subjects; for example, the evidence provided by the Singapore mutineers of 1915 after their arrest. This often supports the interpretation of a pan-Islamic, Ottoman-inspired conspiracy. For example, a letter written by one of the mutineers explains the regiment had decided to mutiny on hearing that the Kaiser had converted to Islam and married his daughter to the heir to the Sultan of Turkey, while a Muslim sympathizer with the mutineers was executed for attempting to summon aid from the Turkish consul in Rangoon.[17] Yet it is necessary to move beyond the colonial archive that constitutes the main prop of historians, with its inevitable limitations. If the imperial view was the view 'from the boat' (and, as has rightly been observed, there were also other boats),[18] one such view escapes easy categorization: that of the Ottomans in this period, who were an imperial power but at the same time shared many of the concerns of the colonized. The Ottoman archives constitute the main source for this paper,[19] but I also draw on Malay texts in order to paint a rather more nuanced picture than available in some of the existing literature. The evidence of these sources challenges the idea of an Ottoman 'conspiracy,' and, more fundamentally, the proposition that pan-Islamism or the Caliphate was an especially influential ideological factor on either the Ottoman or Southeast Asian side. This, in turn, may suggest reconsidering the extent to which the period from the 1870s to the First World War does indeed represent a turning point in bringing together trans-Asian movements, and giving more attention instead to the enduring prevalence of older loyalties and ideas. If pan-Islam was little more than a figment of the imagination of some colonial administrators, as one tendency in scholarship has argued,[20] how then can we explain the undoubted political links of disparate parts of the Muslim world to the Ottoman Empire, which certainly went far beyond conventional diplomatic relations? To enable us to address this question, we must briefly sketch the background to Ottoman involvement in Southeast Asia, which stretches back to the sixteenth century.

---

[17] Harper 2013:1789–1790.

[18] Ho 2004.

[19] Here for brevity I cite the translations only of documents published in Kadı and Peacock 2020; the original text in transliteration alongside a complete translation, details of the call-numbers of the original documents and in many instances their facsimiles can be found in the full publication. Almost all documents discussed are held in the Cumhurbaşkanlığı Devlet Arşivleri in Istanbul (formerly the Başbakanlık Osmanlı Arşivi).

[20] E.g. Kadı 2015; Kadı 2021.

The Sixteenth-Century Relationship and Its Nineteenth-Century Revival

The entry of the Portuguese into the Indian Ocean after their rounding of the Cape of Good Hope in 1498 and subsequent establishment of their empire in the east, the Estado da Índia, coincided with Ottoman expansion towards the same region. Initially as allies of the Mamluks who controlled Egypt, the Ottomans were increasingly drawn into the struggle against the Portuguese. With the Ottoman conquest of the Mamluk territories in Egypt and the Red Sea from 1517 onwards, the empire found itself in control of the western terminus of the trans-Indian Ocean trade routes that the Portuguese sought to dominate for themselves. Portuguese raids on Ottoman-controlled Jeddah and other towns in the Red Sea demonstrated that doing nothing was not an option. An Ottoman report from Jeddah written in 1525 shows that Ottoman officials were already aware of the Portuguese presence in Southeast Asia.[21] Probably as early as the 1530s, some sort of alliance had been established between the Ottomans and the sultanate of Aceh. In the second half of the sixteenth century, as Portuguese aggression increasingly targeted Aceh, the latter sent a series of ambassadors to Istanbul seeking military aid, apparently offering in return acceptance of Ottoman suzerainty. In 1566, the Acehnese sultan 'Ala al-Din Kahhar is claimed to have written to the Ottoman sultan:

> We sincerely request that your Imperial Majesty should no longer consider me, your servant in this land, to be an independent ruler, but instead to accept him as a poor, humble and downtrodden slave who lives thanks to the charity of your Imperial Majesty, Refuge of the World and Shadow of God [on Earth], in no way different from the governors of Egypt and Yemen or the beys of Jeddah and Aden.[22]

The question of the authorship and significance of this letter, preserved in the Topkapı Palace Archive with shelfmark E.8009, is highly problematic.[23] However, irrespective of the exact circumstances in which this document was composed, a memory of such Ottoman suzerainty was somehow upheld in Southeast Asia into the nineteenth century, despite the absence of direct political contacts with the Ottomans in the intervening period. The Ottoman sultan, or Raja Rum, became an important figure in Malay literature, where what has been described as a 'Turkic-Turkish theme' developed as a major preoccupation of many

---

[21] Lesure 1976.
[22] Kadı and Peacock 2020, vol. 1:48.
[23] See Gallop, Peacock, and Kadı 2020:27–30, and Casale 2005.

writers from the seventeenth century onwards.[24] Yet that does not suffice to explain the startling claim made by the Sultan of Kedah, on the west coast of the Malay Peninsula, in an 1824 letter addressed to Istanbul seeking help against the Siamese invaders from whom he had been forced to take refuge in the British-controlled island port of Penang:

> God exalted prompted us to explain our situation to you, which is that, sire, may it not be hidden from you that: I was the sultan of one of the lands of Jawa, which is beneath the equator, called Kedah, which has belonged to us since ancient times. We have there 15 ancestors, all of them sultans there. We inform you of this only because of our long association with you, for in our beginnings, our lands were only conquered and became part of the land of Islam because of your exalted zeal.[25]

Kedah is entitled to Ottoman aid, then, owing to the alleged Ottoman role in the Islamization of the region. This claim, of course, has no factual basis: whatever the Ottoman relationship with Aceh, there is no evidence of any earlier Ottoman involvement in the Malay Peninsula. However, the claim may reflect the prestige of the Raja Rum in Kedah traditions, and a particular traditional association of Kedah with Turan, the word for Turkish peoples in the Persian *Shahnama* (compiled ca. 1010), of which some elements may have filtered into Malay literary traditions. According to the traditional history of Kedah, the *Hikayat Merong Mahawangsa*, which was put into writing in its current form at roughly the same time as this letter was composed, the sultans of Kedah claimed descent from a Turkish Prince, Merong Mahawangsa, who was a subject of the Raja Rum. In the *Hikayat,* Kedah itself is described as "the Turkish land" (Kedah Zamin Turan), and Islam is said to have been brought by a holy man from Arabia who bore the suggestive name Shaykh Nur al-Din Turan.[26]

By circa 1824, then, an association with Turks seems to have been especially valued in the Kedah courtly circles who were the audience for the *Hikayat*, and where doubtless the letter to the Ottomans was also composed. Kedah was not unique in this regard. Claims of royal ancestry stretching back to the mythical Raja Rum could be found in many sultanates in Southeast Asia, starting with the prestigious rulers of Palembang and Minangkabau;[27] indeed, even beyond the Malay world, connections to Rum are mentioned in the foundation myths of the island polities of Buton and Madura, as well as Java. In both Javanese and Madurese legend, it was the ruler of Rum who in ancient times had first sent

[24] Braginsky 2015.
[25] Kadı and Peacock 2020, vol. 1:77.
[26] Falarti 2014:35–62; Braginsky 2015:111–126.
[27] Braginsky 2015.

men to clear the lands of evil spirits, allowing Java and Madura to be populated; while in the Butonese version, the ruler of Rum appears in association with the Sharif of Mecca who first dispatches men to bring Islam to the island.[28] Prince Dipanagara, leader of the great Javanese revolt against the Dutch that collapsed in 1830, assumed the name Ngabdulkamit (i.e. 'Abd al-Hamid or Abdülhamid) perhaps both in emulation of the historical Ottoman sultan Abdülhamid I (r. 1774–1789), and simultaneously to evoke the ruler of Rum's task in Javanese legend of ridding Java of malign beings.[29] Legends of Rumi involvement in cannon-casting are found in several traditional Malay histories of Southeast Asia, such as the *Hikayat Patani*, and may also reflect a memory of the sixteenth-century Ottoman involvement in the region, when cannon casters were indeed dispatched from Istanbul to Aceh.[30] Indeed, even in distant Sulawesi, Bugis texts refer to the both spiritual and technical prowess of Hacı Bektaş, the patron saint of the Janissaries,[31] reflecting the quasi-sacred status that cannon were assigned in premodern Southeast Asia, endowed with supernatural powers.[32] It was not, then, a mere exaggeration when the Acehnese embassy to Istanbul in 1850 presented the Ottomans with a map of Southeast Asia depicting the Malay Peninsula as 'Anadol', an Anatolia displaced by several thousand miles to project itself into the heart of the archipelago.[33] Southeast Asia's connection to Rum through legitimatory legends of state formation, dynastic ancestry, and cannon must have made this visual projection of Anatolia on the Acehnese map seem less startling to its authors than it did to its audience. Yet the Kedah connection to Rum does seem especially strong: no other traditional history puts quite the same emphasis on a specifically Turani/Turkish connection in terms of both royal ancestry and conversion myth.

Despite the failure of Kedah's approach—the letter arrived during the Greek War of Independence and was filed away with no action taken—the search for Ottoman allies continued during the second half of the nineteenth century,

---

[28] Ricklefs 1974:241–244; Zahari 2017; Aswinna 2018.
[29] Ricklefs 1974:241, 244.
[30] Kadı and Peacock 2020, vol. 1:67.
[31] British Library MS Add. 12,358, folios 21r–27r. The same tract also seems to be present in British Library, MS Add 12365, folios 10r–17r. Regrettably this treatise remains wholly unstudied. According to the description provided to the British Library by Dr Cense, it comprises "Teachings of Haji Bankatasi chief artillerist in Istanbul, a native of An[a]doli (Turkish Anadolu, i.e. Anatolia), whose mother was a jin and whose father was a Rūḥ (? Rūm) named Ayinggasi (?). Certainly Haji Bektash, the famous founder of the Bektashi order and the spiritual source of inspiration of the corps of Janissaries, is meant." The manuscript itself evidently comes from the royal library of Bone, late eighteenth to early nineteenth century. See also Ricklefs, Voorhoeve, and Gallop 2014:29.
[32] Cf. Crucq 1941; Andaya 2011.
[33] Kadı and Peacock 2020, vol. 1:104; detailed discussion in Kadı, Peacock, and Gallop 2011.

as the sultanates of Riau, Aceh, and Jambi dispatched letters and envoys to Istanbul seeking allies against Dutch encroachment. The Acehnese repeatedly asserted that, on the basis of the sixteenth-century relationship, they were in fact already Ottoman subjects, as can be seen in the letter sent in 1850 by the Acehnese sultan Mansur Shah to Istanbul:

> We, the people of the region of Aceh, indeed all the inhabitants of the island of Sumatra, have all been considered subjects of the Sublime Ottoman State generation after generation, since the time of our late lord Sultan Selim Khan son the late sultan Süleyman Khan son of the late sultan Selim Khan the Conqueror—may God's mercy and favour be upon them. That is proved in the sultanic record-books. This great, long island [Sumatra] contained a number of regions each of which had a governor subject to the Sublime Ottoman State, although every governor had the title of sultan and king according to their custom, seeing as each one was independent in governing the people of his region, in which no one opposed him. Their affairs were in order because of his late excellency the vizier Sinan Pasha who settled the sultan of each region in rule of its people.[34]

The same claim was repeated in a letter sent by Mansur Shah in 1869, which reiterates the story that evidence of Aceh's ancient attachment to the Ottomans was to be found in Aceh's records,[35] while a petition sent by Acehnese ministers in 1873 also sought to 'renew' the ancient relationship.[36] As late as 1893, when the remnants of the Acehnese resistance to the Dutch from their hideaway of Kota Keumala again sought Ottoman assistance, this claim was reiterated.[37] Less ambitiously, the sultans of Jambi, Riau, and Tembusai sought to be recognized as Ottoman subjects, again with the explicit aim of seeking protection from Dutch aggression, while the Sultan of Brunei tried to hand over his entire territory to the Ottoman sultan to protect himself from the British, although his letter never reached Istanbul.[38]

Southeast Asian rulers were not the only group to assert an affiliation to the Ottomans. The substantial Hadrami diaspora in Southeast Asia also claimed Ottoman citizenship on the basis of the sixteenth-century conquest of Hadramaut by Sultan Selim (an event with only a most tenuous connection to reality). In a letter delivered to the Ottoman consulate in Batavia in 1898,

[34] Kadı and Peacock 2020, vol. 1:102; cf. Kadı 2021.
[35] Kadı and Peacock 2020, vol. 1:170–171.
[36] Kadı and Peacock 2020, vol. 1:195.
[37] Kadı and Peacock 2020, vol. 1:291.
[38] Kadı and Peacock 2020, vol. 1:142–148, 153–155, 243–256, 320–325.

seeking Ottoman support against the Dutch authorities, the Hadrami community of Java reminded Istanbul that:

> The one who became amir of Hadramaut on behalf of the Sublime State
> through a sultanic firman was [the Kathiri ruler] Badr b. ʻAbdallah,
> known as Abu Tuwayraq. Many firmans were sent to him through the
> governor of Sanʻa. Among them was the sultanic firman of Sultan Selim
> [sent] via the governor of Sanʻa.[39]

None of the initiatives to obtain Ottoman assistance ever bore fruit in terms of
concrete military aid, and indeed even requests for vassal status were treated
with extreme caution by the Ottomans for fear of provoking the wrath of the
Dutch. Nonetheless, these approaches do seem to have encouraged the Ottoman
Empire to take an interest in the region. Although the so-called 'pan-Islamic'
policy is generally associated with Sultan Abdülhamid II, in fact as early as 1856
the Ottomans had started negotiations with the Dutch to establish a consulate
in Batavia.[40] It seems likely that this was prompted by the recent Acehnese
mission, which we know was take extremely seriously at the highest echelons of
the Ottoman state.[41] However, it was only around 1865 that an Ottoman honorary
consul was appointed to Singapore, and not until 1883 was a full salaried consul
sent to Batavia.[42] The Ottomans' interest in the region was also signaled by
their attempts in 1873 to mediate between the Dutch and the Acehnese in the
Aceh war. The diplomatic note from the Sublime Porte to the Dutch Embassy in
Istanbul made it clear, however, that the attempted Ottoman mediation, which
the Dutch firmly rebuffed, was inspired by Aceh's claim to being part of Ottoman
territories on the basis of its ancient relationship with the Sublime Porte:

> The abovementioned [Mansur] Shah [of Aceh], basing himself upon the
> relations that were established in ancient times between the Sublime
> State and the Acehnese government, requested the inclusion of the
> countries under his rule into the sovereign [Ottoman] dominions as
> an autonomous province. Following the example of his ancestors, he
> recognized the Sublime State as the one to be mentioned in the Friday
> sermon, and himself as the executor of the commands of the Caliphate
> of Islam. These requests of the Sultan of Aceh were approved, and an
> exalted [Ottoman] imperial order was issued to that effect.[43]

[39] Kadı and Peacock 2020, vol. 2:805.
[40] Kadı and Peacock 2020, vol. 1:419–420.
[41] Kadı, Peacock, and Gallop 2011.
[42] Kadı and Peacock 2020, vol. 1:426–427, 432–436.
[43] Kadı and Peacock 2020, vol. 1:229.

The Ottomans also repeatedly intervened with the Dutch authorities to try to gain recognition for the Hadramis as Ottoman subjects, which in turn should have meant that they were treated as Europeans rather than Asians in the racially differentiated legal system of the Dutch Indies—or at least, so the Ottomans tried to argue.[44] Again, the Dutch were hardly receptive to such arguments; but the fact that the Ottoman authorities raised them repeatedly indicates the seriousness with which the Hadrami claim was taken in Istanbul. It probably helped, too, that this coincided with the Ottoman reestablishment of control over much of Yemen in the second half of the nineteenth century, if not in reality Hadramaut.

Thus both Southeast Asian rulers and Hadramis based their efforts to gain Istanbul's attention and support not on vague pan-Islamic pieties, but on the claim that their ancestral lands already formed part of the Ottoman Empire. The attempts of Riau and Jambi, which were both couched in a language of pan-Islamic solidarity, to attract Ottoman interest met rather shorter shrift in Istanbul. Raja 'Ali bin Ja'far of Riau, who had requested to be recognized as an Ottoman subject in 1858, was simply awarded a rather lowly Mecidiye medal third class and given permission to mention the Caliph's name in Friday prayers.[45] The envoy of Jambi was sent off from Istanbul in 1859 with a cash gift and an assurance that "the imperial favour of His Majesty the Caliph to all Muslims is completely applicable to the people of that region as well but it would not be appropriate to act in the way they requested."[46] In other words, the evidence from the Ottoman archives suggests that while a vocabulary of pan-Islam was certainly regularly deployed by both Ottoman and Southeast Asian rulers, it had little impact in practice. Much more effective were Acehnese and Hadrami efforts to convince the Porte that they were in fact already Ottoman subjects. Indeed, even when confronted by a mysterious (but rather transparent) imposter, a certain Sharif 'Ali who made his way to Istanbul in 1891 purporting to be a member of the Acehnese royal family, his claims were taken seriously at the highest level, and discussed by the Ottoman sultan, the Foreign Ministry and the Ministry of Defence. Sharif 'Ali claimed that Aceh was an island located in the Red Sea—certainly the most egregious attempt to play on Ottoman sentiments of obligation to their own territories.[47] That his claims were nonetheless extensively debated at the top of Ottoman politics is testimony both to this sentiment, and to the Ottomans' enduring uncertainty as to their own territorial expanse, for at this date, the Ottomans controlled (at least in name) the entirety of the Red Sea.

[44] Kadı and Peacock 2020, vol. 2:822–828, 842–862; in general see Kathirathimby-Wells 2015.
[45] Kadı and Peacock 2020, vol. 1:151.
[46] Kadı and Peacock 2020, vol. 1:158.
[47] Kadı and Peacock 2020, vol. 1:264–287.

Ottoman Activities in Southeast Asia, ca. 1883–1913

As the Sharif 'Ali episode suggests, Istanbul's policy did not change dramatically in the reign of Sultan Abdülhamid II, who is generally credited as the most active proponent of pan-Islam. Nonetheless, an increased emphasis on the Caliphate can be observed from this period. An insight into Istanbul's priorities can be obtained from the reports of her consuls in Batavia—very little evidence indeed survives from the short-lived consulates in Rangoon, Manila, and Singapore. In a report sent after the end of his term of office, Galip Bey, the first Ottoman consul to Batavia who served from 1883 to 1887, explained how he interpreted his duties:

> During this period, I deemed it my primary function to explore the means of strengthening the obedience of the hundreds of millions of Muslims in the said region, and due to its proximity in India and Indochina, to the centre of the great Caliphate. I was the first [consul general] sent by the Imperial Sultanate to the Indian Islands [i.e. the Dutch East Indies].[48]

In a sense, then, Galip Bey's activities were 'pan-Islamic'; but it is worth reviewing in more detail of what they actually consisted. Galip Bey's primary activity seems to have been encouraging the use of the Caliph's name in the khutba, but he also persuaded Istanbul to have Qur'ans printed and distributed "to create a good impression" on leading Javanese, as Istanbul Qur'ans were considered more accurate and prestigious than their Egyptian competitors.[49] However, an attempt by Galip Bey to persuade Istanbul to invest funds in building a mosque in Batavia that would serve to promote the Ottoman dynasty's prestige fell on deaf ears.[50] On a later occasion, the consul asked for 200 copies of an Arabic translation of a book detailing Ottoman victories over Greece in the 1897 war.[51] This was evidently considered sensitive and likely to provoke Dutch wrath, so it was asked that the books be sent under cover. However, even the most Islamic of activities were not necessarily motivated by pan-Islamic sentiments. In 1891, the Ottoman government decided to award a medal to an individual who had been particularly active in distributing Istanbul Qur'ans and building mosques in Sumatra, a certain Monsieur Herring, who was a citizen of Saxony and land-owner in the Asahan region.[52] There is no indication that he was a convert to

---

[48] Kadı and Peacock 2020, vol. 2:588.
[49] Kadı and Peacock 2020, vol. 2:574–575, 590–592, 600–601, 612–616.
[50] Kadı and Peacock 2020, vol. 2:601–603.
[51] Kadı and Peacock 2020, vol. 2:614–615.
[52] Kadı and Peacock 2020, vol. 2:590–597.

Islam, or indeed of his motivations, beyond, presumably, wishing to promote locally his own image.

The most concrete token of Ottoman interest in Southeast Asia was the dispatch in 1889 of the frigate *Ertuğrul*. The ship bore gifts and medals from Ottoman Sultan Abdülhamid II to the Japanese Meiji Emperor, intended to cement relations between two of the principal non-Christian but modernizing powers of Asia that had retained their independence. However, en route to Japan, the *Ertuğrul* made stops in South and Southeast Asia, where it was greeted with considerable excitement by local Muslims, who sought to use it to convey both petitions for help and messages of esteem to the Ottoman sultan. The commander of the *Ertuğrul*, Osman Pasha, entertained various local Muslim dignitaries during his stop in Singapore, who, he reported, "talk about the oppression which their overlords, the British, Dutch, and Siamese governments, deem suitable to inflict upon Muslims, and [express their] hope that we will remedy their situation."[53] Nonetheless, Osman Pasha was also on guard that these might be *agents provocateurs* sent by the colonial authorities. Further, the visit of the *Ertuğrul* seems in fact to have been successfully turned by the Dutch into a public relations disaster for the Ottomans. Perhaps mindful of the dangers of upsetting the Dutch authorities, the *Ertuğrul* visited only Singapore and Saigon before continuing on her way to China. As Kosta Karaca Pasha, the Ottoman ambassador to The Hague, complained, the visit had generated great hopes and expectations among local Muslims, which were dashed when the *Ertuğrul* failed to materialize. Indeed, at Dutch instigation, newspapers in the Indies ran stories that "spread slander and lies about the position of Great Caliphate which may undermine the fame of the Imperial Government." Karaca Pasha suggested that the Ottomans make amends by including Batavia on the return leg of the *Ertuğrul*'s journey, although he indicated Aceh was too politically sensitive.[54] The sinking of the ship just off the Japanese coast aborted these hopes, but it is interesting that they were more or less an afterthought, and not part of the original plans for the *Ertuğrul*'s itinerary, in which pan-Islamic concerns were evidently of minor importance.

The reference to Siamese Muslims in Osman Pasha's dispatch from Singapore also suggests the limitations of Abdülhamid's pan-Islamic interests, when push came to shove. Osman Pasha had described the condition of the Siamese Muslims as "helpless and wretched in all respects ... The local government absolutely prohibits the performance of their religious rituals," and forwarded to Istanbul a petition detailing their desperate plight.[55] Yet in the

---

[53] Kadı and Peacock 2020, vol. 1:246.
[54] Kadı and Peacock 2020, vol. 1:583–584; vol. 2:580–583.
[55] Kadı and Peacock 2020, vol. 1:246–247.

last years of the nineteenth century, Siamese royals became regular visitors to Istanbul, starting with the visit of prince Damrong in 1891, followed by trips by prince Chakrabongse in 1897, and later prince Borowadet in 1909.[56] There is no indication that the status of Siam's Muslims was raised in any of these visits, which were initiated by the Siamese with the intention of finding out more about the Ottomans, as a rare example of another Asian empire of the period that had withstood colonialism and modernized. Given Siam's precarious independence, squeezed as it was between encroaching French and British colonial powers, it is scarcely surprising that they saw the Ottomans as a possible source of inspiration. It is rather harder to see what was in these visits for the Ottomans, but certainly any pan-Islamic solidarity with Siam's benighted Muslims did not stand in the way of the lavish receptions with which the Siamese delegations were greeted.

Istanbul's rather distant attitude towards local Muslim movements is also reflected in the consular reports from Batavia sent in 1913 concerning the formation of Sarekat Islam, the Muslim association that came to play a prominent part in colonial political life in Indonesia. While these reports go into some detail on the reasons for the establishment of Sarekat Islam, they do not indicate any effort whatsoever to contact the leaders of the movement, or indeed anyone involved in it. The only discussions the consular dispatches mention on the issue are with Dutch officials.[57]

Islamic Legitimacy or Simply Tourism? Sultan Abu Bakar of Johor in Istanbul

A good example of the relative ineffectiveness of pan-Islam as a political instrument for either side is provided by the case of the Sultan of Johor, Abu Bakar, the only Malay ruler actually to make it to Istanbul in person. As is well known, Sultan Abu Bakar was pro-British and a regular visitor to England; but he also had strong Ottoman connections, having allegedly married an Ottoman princess.[58] More importantly, perhaps, Abu Bakar incorporated Ottoman law into that of Johor through his adoption of the Ottoman legal code, the *Mecelle*, in 1893, the year of his visit to Istanbul.[59]

Unsurprisingly, the idea that Abu Bakar's visit to Istanbul was motivated by political reasons, such as a desire to obtain Ottoman recognition, is found in the

---

[56] Kadı and Peacock 2020, vol. 1:328–416; Kadı 2018.
[57] Kadı and Peacock 2020, vol. 1:548–556.
[58] Abdullah 2010.
[59] Hussin 2013.

secondary literature,[60] where it is even claimed that Abu Bakar depended upon the Ottoman Empire for its nominal protection against the British as well as for the legitimacy of his dynasty.[61] Yet curiously, although the Ottoman archives do indeed mention the visit in passing, there is no evidence of any interest in the Malay sultan. In fact, the visit seems to have been more or less serendipitous, if we are to believe the account of Wilfred Blunt, the British anti-imperialist and resident of Egypt who encountered Abu Bakar in Cairo shortly before his visit to Istanbul:

> I took the Sultan of Johore to Sheykh el Bekri [a senior religious figure in Cairo], acting for him as interpreter … The truth is they were at cross purposes. What el Bekri wanted to find out was whether the Sultan had any panislamic ideas, whether he wanted to see Abdul Hamid at Constantinople for a political purpose, and whether he would encourage panislamic missionaries at Johore. The old man, on the other hand, only wanted a little personal sympathy as a Mohammedan from Mohammedans. He was too humble-minded to expect much notice from Abdul Hamid, and had nothing of any importance to say to him … [Abu Bakar said he] had never had the smallest communication with Constantinople, and the Ottomans looked on them as Kaffirs. A Turkish man-of-war [the *Ertuğrul*] had once come and stayed some time at Singapore on her way to Japan, and it was not till just before she sailed that they discovered that Johore was Mohammedan. Then everybody had been delighted. That was the only communication that had ever taken place with the Turks … As to missionaries, he would be delighted if the Sheykh would send them a professor to teach them their religion. They were all Shafais at Johore. They said their prayers in Arabic, but did not know the meaning of the words; the Koran was not translated into Malay except some parts of it. He was having a translation made, they were all very ignorant. The young Sheykh el Bekri hardly knew, I think, what to make of it all.[62]

Indeed, according to Blunt, Abu Bakar was very nearly not given an audience by Abdülhamid, who dismissed him as yet another minor Indian prince; the Johor delegation was allegedly surprised and delighted when an intermediary finally secured them a reception.

Blunt's depiction is supported in some measure by both Ottoman and Malay sources, where the idea of any kind of political or even religious relationship is

[60] E.g. Abdullah 2010:12.
[61] Hussin 2013:270.
[62] Blunt 1921:97–98.

conspicuously absent. In the Ottoman archives, there is little mention of the Johor visit apart from a handful of telegrams from the Ottoman embassy in Vienna, confirming the heartfelt thanks of the Johor sultan and his retinue after the visit.[63] This supports Blunt's suggestion that the audience was ad hoc; the absence of any discussion of the sultan and the potential political implications of his visit is also suggestive. Normally one would expect some trace of reports and recommendations in advance from the Foreign Ministry to the Ottoman sultan on how to handle his guest. Finally, we may note the striking contrast between the treatment of the Johor and Siamese delegations; on each visit, the Siamese were lavishly showered with medals, while no honors are mentioned as bestowed upon the Johor delegation in the Ottoman sources.

Most probably, Abu Bakar did acquire a medal of some sort, for this features in the Malay accounts, in particular the verse history of his reign, the *Syair Raja Johor* composed shortly after Abu Bakar's death.[64] Yet this text makes it clear that a pan-Islamic plot was hardly top of the agenda:

> When he [Abu Bakar] sat before the Caliph, people brought cakes and sweetmeats—Various yummy delights, delicious to the tongue.

After the welcome, Sultan Abu Bakar extended his thanks, and then set off sightseeing:

> Then his Majesty [Abu Bakar] took his leave. In that country, there was to be seen a fortified palace, very impressive, and its streets were level as described. His Majesty saw many markets and shops, and was distracted by visiting every village.

The award of the medal is then described:

> Sultan Abu Bakar, of prefect wisdom, obtained an important symbol of distinction [*beroleh kemuliaan terlalu bena*].

> The peerless [Ottoman] sultan was friends with many ruling kings; the wise king, the sultan of Istanbul granted each of them medals equally.

> Abdul Hamid was the Sultan's name, wise noble and generous; Osmani was the medal's name, a recognised sign of friendship.[65]

It must be said that the *Syair Raja Johor*, just like the other main source for Abu Bakar's activities, the *Syair almarhum Sultan Baginda Abu Bakar*, devotes much less

---

[63] Kadı and Peacock 2020, vol. 1:364–367.
[64] See Abdullah 2010 for a survey of the various accounts.
[65] Fawzi Basri 1984:128–129.

space to the encounter in Istanbul than it does to those of Abu Bakar with Queen Victoria in England. Similarly, the *Syair Raja Johor* mentions how Abu Bakar's son Sultan Ibrahim on his accession received an Ottoman medal—but only after recounting how he was awarded a British one.[66] If a relationship with the Ottomans was a legitimatory device, it was only in a rather secondary fashion. In neither passage is there discussion of Islam, and, while the title *khalifa* does indeed appear in the Malay text, no special significance seems to be attached to it. At no point is the award of the medal depicted as bestowing any sort of vassal status or even legitimacy; rather, it is a sign of friendship from an emperor to a minor king, which is probably congruent with Abdülhamid's original intentions.

Ottoman Activities in Southeast Asia during the First World War

So far, I have argued that under sultan Abdülhamid II, his successors, and predecessors, Ottoman attempts to spread pan-Islam were negligible. What, however, of that allegedly key turning point, the First World War? Naturally, the British closed down the Ottomans' Singapore consulate in 1914. The Ottoman consulate in neutral Batavia was left as the sole Ottoman outpost in the Indian Ocean. It was hardly a hotbed of intrigue, although Refet Bey, the consul in Batavia in 1915, did write to the Foreign Ministry in Istanbul about the instructions communicated to him from the Ottoman embassy in Berlin:

> Today, great victories are being gained by the German, Austrian, and Ottoman armies, and [it is proposed that] pious Arabs or Turks acting as domestic servants or merchants in Singapore and Penang and the surrounding shores should be employed to disseminate this information. The individuals that are going to be employed for this purpose will be expected to spread and transmit this good news as far as to Calcutta, to communicate it to the patriotic Muslims in Delhi and Punjab, and, by means of these patriots, to the spies of the ruler of Afghanistan who need to be informed. The individuals that will be employed for this purpose will gather information about the revolutionary movements in India, and investigate whether it is possible to send money and weapons to the leaders of these revolutionary movements. The Consul-General is free to implement the contents of these instructions in such a suitable manner as he deems appropriate, and is authorized to spend the amount of money that is needed to carry out

---

[66] Fawzi Basri 1984:140.

this mission. The Vice-Consul asked whether any instructions on this issue had been received from the Imperial Government, and whether I am ready to help him. I have responded by saying that although I have not received any instructions, I am ready to help as it is our duty to harm our common enemy.[67]

This seems, then, to be the great pan-Islamic plot identified by both contemporaries and later scholars. However, while it is true that rabidly pro-Turkish sentiments were regularly expressed in the indigenous Malay-language press,[68] there is precious little evidence of much concrete plotting by Refet Bey. He seems to have remained in post throughout the war, until 1921, but the Ottoman archives record no instructions from Istanbul to stir up pan-Islamic mayhem. It is true that the British seem to have been remarkably effective in cutting off, or at least severely limiting, the consulate's communications with Istanbul; but there is little trace of outgoing messages that failed to get through, of which we would expect to find drafts in the Istanbul archives. Refet's main activities seem to have been of his own accord. In 1915, he sent Istanbul some excited reports indicating he believed the Singapore mutineers to be near victory. He had pamphlets made in Hindustani about the war, some of which he tried unsuccessfully to have smuggled into Singapore for the mutineers.[69] After this, he seems to have given up trying to implement the ambitious schemes described above. It would be unfair to place the blame for the lack of success exclusively on the consul, for Refet's effectiveness was limited by the complete lack of interest on the part of Istanbul. As he wrote to his superiors shortly after the outbreak of war:

I learned from the Istanbul newspapers that as a result of their aggressive actions against the holy Caliphate and the exalted [Ottoman] Government, the exalted government declared war on France, Russia and Britain to defend itself. I would like to communicate with regret that, although four months passed since then, I have not received any official information, either from the exalted [Foreign] Ministry or from the exalted Embassy [at The Hague]. I cannot understand the reason why the exalted [Ottoman] Government has left its only extant official between Aden and North and South China in complete darkness and ignorance with respect to these extraordinary developments and this present great struggle, which is an issue of life and death.[70]

---

[67] Kadı and Peacock 2020, vol. 2:634.
[68] van Dijk 2008:307–312.
[69] Kadı and Peacock 2020, vol. 2:636–638.
[70] Kadı and Peacock 2020, vol. 1:464.

After 1916, communications from Batavia seem to dry up completely. The Ottoman plot thus seems to consist largely of a few pamphlets that never reached their intended audience. The preoccupation of the Ottoman government with other affairs and the interruption of communications by the British may both have played their part, but in fact the response is consistent with Istanbul's nineteenth-century policy towards the region, in which pan-Islam played little part.

Conclusion

Was the Ottoman role in the region entirely a figment of overactive colonial imagination seeing plots everywhere? Not entirely. Refet Bey reported a failed rebellion just outside Jakarta in 1916, and describes how the rebels raised the Ottoman flag, but apparently without his foreknowledge or involvement, owing to a mix-up:

> An individual called Eutong Meliki,[71] who led those complaining about these oppressions, had his two young sons on either side of him. I relate with sorrow that he was martyred by bullets fired by the police whilst he was encouraging people by giving our Ottoman flag to his young and innocent children. This letter written by Meliki Efendi, the said martyr, to the consulate fifteen days before the regretable events, was presented to me two days after the events because of the negligence of the person who was entrusted with its delivery. As will be understood from the enclosed copy-translation, the letter contained complaints about the landowner and the officials, and requested my mediation for the resolution of the situation.[72]

This revolt, just like the Terengganu uprising of 1928, used Ottoman imagery through the Ottoman flag. Just as with the Singapore mutiny, it is clear there was no actual Ottoman involvement. Even a few miles from the Ottoman consulate, a rebellion that drew on Ottoman inspiration could not effectively draw on Ottoman support or mediation, owing to botched communications. Nonetheless, with the raising of the Ottoman flag and the attempt to contact the consulate, it is easy to see why colonial officials would have been suspicious, however unwarranted this would have been; for it is clear from Refet's account that he had in no way encouraged the revolt.

---

[71] The spelling of this name is given thus in Latin script in the Ottoman document. I have not been able to identify this individual in other sources.

[72] Kadı and Peacock 2020, vol. 2:653.

In this sense, then, the notion of a pan-Islamic plot that so worried colonial authorities may be discounted. Of course, at an unofficial level there were certainly individuals who brought influences and ideas from one part of the Islamic world to another, including, no doubt, the wild rumors of the conversion of the Kaiser that influenced the Singapore mutineers. Yet the imperial government's inaction actually reflected a relatively consistent policy that can be traced with clarity even in the reign of Abdülhamid II. Beyond encouraging the mentioning of the Caliph's name in prayers, Ottoman willingness to intervene and engage was limited to those regions and peoples to which Istanbul felt it had historically rooted obligations through prior conquest or affiliation, namely the Hadramis and Aceh. The seriousness with which Acehnese and Hadrami approaches were taken in Istanbul underlines this point, in contrast to the rebuffs experienced by others, such as the envoys of Riau and Jambi. Perhaps, then, the rather overused term 'pan-Islamic' is unhelpful in this context. As the visit of Abu Bakar of Johor to Istanbul suggests, it was perfectly possible for Muslim leaders from disparate parts of the dar al-Islam to meet and discuss little more than the cakes, however much on paper their encounter should have been of utmost importance to both parties as a means of mutually strengthening Islamic legitimacy. Abdülhamid showed little interest in his visitor, certainly not to the extent of involving him in any pan-Islamic schemes; and the Malay sources are more concerned with Abu Bakar's touristic agenda in Istanbul than any legitimatory value to be derived from the encounter. Rather, Ottoman involvement with Southeast Asia, such as it was, was influenced not by pan-Islamic fictions, but rather by older connections, determined not by new currents of Islamic reformism but by imperial histories that for both sides remained potent. It was most likely the memory of such connections commemorated in traditional Malay and archipelagic literature, rather than the sporadic and most probably limited use of the Caliph's name in the khutba, that inspired popular rebellions drawing on Ottoman imagery. That, however, awaits further research. For the moment, we may posit that the Ottoman-inspired imagery of such revolts was not the expression of a new modernity of trans-Asian networks, but rather the last reflection of traditional ways of perceiving the world, to be destroyed forever by the War.

Works Cited

Abdullah, A. 2010. "Sultan Abu Bakar's Foreign Guests and Travels Abroad, 1860s–1895: Fact and Fiction in Early Malay Historical Accounts." *Journal of the Malaysian Branch of the Royal Asiatic Society* 84:1–22.

Andaya, B. W. 2011. "Distant Drums and Thunderous Cannon: Sounding Authority in Traditional Malay Society." *International Journal of Asia Pacific Studies* 7:19–35.

Aswinna. 2018. *Suntingan teks Juragan Gulisman (KBG 339).* Jakarta.

Aydın, C. 2007. *The Politics of Anti-Westernism in Asia: Visions of World Order in Pan-Islamic and Pan-Asian Thought.* New York.

Blunt, W. S. 1921. *My Diaries: Being a Personal Narrative of Events, 1888–1914.* Vol. 1. London.

Braginsky, V. 2015. *The Turkic-Turkish Theme in Traditional Malay Literature: Imagining the Other to Empower the Self.* Leiden.

Casale, G. 2005. "'His Majesty's Servant Lutfi': The Career of a Previously Unknown Sixteenth-Century Ottoman Envoy to Sumatra Based on an Account of His Travels from the Topkapi Palace Archives." *Turcica* 37:43–81.

Crucq, K. 1941. "De geschiednis van het heilig kanon van Makassar." *Tijschrift van het Bataviaasch Genotschap* 81:74–95.

van Dijk, K. 2008. *The Netherlands Indies and the Great War, 1914–1918.* Leiden.

Falarti, M. M. 2014. *Malay Kingship in Kedah: Religion, Trade, and Society.* Petaling Jaya.

Fawzi Basri, A. 1984. *Warisan sejarah Johor.* Kuala Lumpur.

Gallop, A. T., Peacock, A. C. S., and Kadı, İ. H., 2020. "The Language of Letters: Southeast Asian Understandings of Ottoman Diplomatics." In Kadı and Peacock 2020:1–32.

Harper, T. 2013. "Singapore, 1915, and the Birth of the Asian Underground." *Modern Asian Studies* 47:1782–1811.

Ho, E. 2004. "Empire through Diasporic Eyes: The View from the Other Boat." *Comparative Studies of Society and History* 46:210–246.

Hussin, I. 2013. "Textual Trajectories: Re-reading the Constitution and Majalah in 1890s Johor." *Indonesia and the Malay World* 41:255–272.

Kadı, İ. H. 2015. "The Ottomans and Southeast Asia prior to the Hamidian Era: A Critique of Colonial Perceptions of Ottoman–Southeast Asian Interaction." In Peacock and Gallop 2015:149–174.

———. 2018. *The Ottomans and Siam through the Ages.* Bangkok.

———. 2021. "An Old Ally Revisited: Diplomatic Interactions between the Ottoman Empire and the Sultanate of Aceh in the Face of Dutch Colonial Expansion." *International History Review* 43.5:1080–1097.

Kadı, İ. H., and A. C. S. Peacock. 2020. *Ottoman–Southeast Asian Relations: Sources from the Ottoman Archives.* Leiden.

Kadı, İ. H., A. C. S. Peacock, and A. T. Gallop. 2011. "Writing History: The Acehnese Embassy to Istanbul, 1849–1852." In *Mapping the Acehnese past*, ed. R. M. Feener, P. Daly, and A. Reid, 163–181, 259–278. Leiden.

Kathirithamby-Wells, J. 2015. "Hadhrami Mediators of Ottoman Influence in Southeast Asia." In Peacock and Gallop 2015:89–119.

Kheng, C. B. 2006. *To' Janggut: Legends, Histories, and Perceptions of the 1915 Rebellion in Kelantan.* Singapore.

Lesure, M. 1976. "Un document ottoman de 1525 sur l'Inde portugaise et les pays du Mer Rouge." *Mare Luso-Indicum* 3:137–160.

Malhi, A. 2015. "'We Hope to Raise the Bendera Stambul': British Forward Movement and the Caliphate on the Malay Peninsula." In Peacock and Gallop 2015:221–239.

Peacock, A. C. S., and A. T. Gallop, eds. 2015. *From Anatolia to Aceh: Ottomans, Turks, and Southeast Asia.* London.

Reid, A. 1967. "Nineteenth-Century Pan-Islam in Indonesia and Malaysia." *Journal of Asian Studies* 26:267–283.

———. 2014. "Turkey as Aceh's Alternative Imperium." *Archipel* 87:81–102

Ricklefs, M. C. 1974. "Dipanagara's Early Inspirational Experience." *Bijdragen tot de Taal-, Land- en Volkenkunde* 130:227–258.

Ricklefs, M. C., P. Voorhoeve, and A. T. Gallop. 2014. *Indonesian Manuscripts in Great Britain: A Catalogue of Manuscripts in Indonesian Languages in British Public Collections. New Edition with Addenda et Corrigenda.* Jakarta.

Streets-Salter, H. 2017. *World War One in Southeast Asia: Colonialism and Anti-colonialism in an Era of Global Conflict.* Cambridge.

Zahari, A. 2017. *Islam di Buton: Sejarah dan perkembangannya.* Bau-Bau.

7

Worlds in Motion

Al-Bustani's Arabic Encyclopedia (*Da'irat al-Ma'arif*) and the Global Production of Knowledge in the Late Ottoman Levant and Egypt (1870s–1900s)

Ilham Khuri-Makdisi

It is a strange omission that the last, and in some ways greatest, work associated with Butrus al-Bustani (1819–1883), the Encyclopedia *Da'irat al-Ma'arif*, has barely attracted the attention of historians of the Modern Middle East.[1] This is especially remarkable since the author was one of the most important intellectuals of the *nahda*, the so-called Arab intellectual renaissance of the late nineteenth century. Barring a short article from 1990 by the doyen of Modern Middle Eastern History Albert Hourani, and an even more succinct one by John Jandora from 1986, the *Da'ira* has not yet been studied broadly as a coherent project.[2] In fact, even its individual articles seem to have been generally sidelined as a major source for political thought, intellectual history, the history of the Arabic language, and conceptual history.[3]

And yet, Bustani's encyclopedia was remarkable on a number of levels. It was the first modern Arabic encyclopedia (in fact the first modern Middle Eastern encyclopedia, preceding its Ottoman Turkish and Persian counterparts), and

---

[1] *Da'irat al-Ma'arif*, or "Circle of Knowledge", was initially published in Beirut between 1876 and 1887; the last two volumes were published in Cairo 1898–1900.

[2] Hourani 1990; Jandora 1986. I could not find any studies solely devoted to the *Da'ira* in Arabic either, bar a recent MA thesis completed at the American University of Beirut in 2022.

[3] One of the few exceptions to this is Marilyn Booth's chapter in her recent book, in which Booth analyzes the way the Syro-Egyptian feminist writer Zaynab Fawwaz compiled her biographical dictionary of women in Cairo in the 1890s, partly by relying on Bustani's Encyclopedia, reading between the lines and reading against it. In this case, it is an inherent and unavoidable aspect of Booth's project to use Bustani's Encyclopedia. See Booth 2015. Other exceptions include Ussama Makdisi, who has a brief paragraph on the entry "America" from *Da'irat al-Ma'arif* in his book *Faith Misplaced* (Makdisi 2010:55).

although it remained incomplete, it was a lengthy production that resulted in eleven volumes, each around eight hundred pages. It was much celebrated and hailed as a landmark and proof of civilization and progress during its time. It was also a project intimately connected with tragedy: Butrus al-Bustani died in 1883 while working on the seventh volume; his eldest son and right-hand man, Salim, also an important intellectual in his own right, took over, but died the following year in 1884. Other sons and most importantly, a prominent cousin, Suleyman, stepped in, issuing a few volumes in the late 1880s, then, after a hiatus of a decade, produced volumes ten and eleven in 1898 and 1900. The last volume, published in Cairo, stopped at the letter 'ayn', the eighteenth out of twenty-eight letters of the Arabic alphabet.[4]

My chapter proposes to address this lacuna, given the *Da'ira*'s role as a major marker and maker of its times, and to approach it as an oeuvre that sheds light on the production and hierarchy of knowledge Bustani and the *nahda* were actively shaping and promoting. The *Da'ira* was a self-consciously global project: it sought to represent the world and provide information about it, both in the past and in the present; and it relied on, absorbed, synthesized, selectively included, and engaged with works, encyclopedic and otherwise, produced in different parts of the world, different periods, and different languages through a vast project of translation (including the American Cyclopedia and most likely the Encyclopédie du Dix-Neuvième Siècle, to which I will return). At the same time, the *Da'ira* was naturally heavily reliant on local Arabic (and much less so, Ottoman Turkish) sources, both contemporary and historical.

More specifically, I will initially focus on three seemingly disconnected entries in the Encyclopedia, all of which I connect to this volume's theme of *imagined geographies*. The entries for 'Asia', 'Debt', and 'Oedipus', I argue, all gesture to alternative geographies, genealogies, and conceptions of civilization that seem to defy dominant assumptions regarding history, genealogy, as well as the world order, in the late nineteenth century, and destabilize ostensibly fixed categories and value-systems. Interestingly, but in fact not unusually for encyclopedias from the late nineteenth century, the first two entries move between providing objective and descriptive information on one hand, to adopting a prescriptive tone; and in the case of the first entry, even penning something akin to a political manifesto. In the second part of this chapter, I will argue more broadly that the entire project of Bustani's encyclopedia can be cast as a call toward "imagined and imagining geographies"—in the way it allows readers to engage with its contents, as well as in the future-oriented, developmentalist mission that undergirds many of its entries.

[4] Hourani 1990; Jandora 1986; *Da'irat al-Ma'arif*, vol. 11.

Al-Bustani and the Intellectual Ecology of Beirut during the Long 1870s

Before I turn to the specific entries, a few words are in order about Butrus al-Bustani, as well as the intellectual ecology in which the *Da'ira* emerged.[5] Bustani was one of the most influential, towering figures of the *nahda*. A key member of various learned societies, he was a reformist, educator, prolific author, lexicographer, [6] and translator, a polyglot, and a Maronite Christian convert to Protestantism who had served as a dragoman at the American consulate, and had been in close contact with American missionaries, with whom he had collaborated on various projects (most importantly the translation of the Bible)[7]—before taking his distance from them some time in the 1860s. While the *Da'ira* is attributed to him—he certainly was the instigator of the project, and its editor until his death in 1883—it is not clear how many of the entries he himself penned.[8] However, it seems almost certain that Bustani had, working with him or for him, a team of writers-cum-translators-cum-editors.

Beirut, the city where the *Da'ira* was first conceived and produced, was in the mid-1870s a major center of intellectual production spearheaded by the emergence of a new, small class of intellectuals, a tightly knit group with a shared worldview, who called for total reform in political, religious, social, intellectual, and cultural matters. This reform movement was part of a larger reformist and modernizing project implemented by local rulers, administrators, bureaucrats, and intellectuals throughout the Ottoman Empire and Egypt, which had been ongoing for decades. A central aspect of this reform project was the need for intellectuals and bureaucrats to familiarize themselves and their audiences with European ideas, learn from them, and be able to engage with them. This entailed a vast project of translation and popularization of knowledge, concepts, debates, and texts that were viewed as seminal to European civilization and helped explain its strength and power, in an era of increasing European direct and indirect intervention.

The production of knowledge, and the availability of reading material that would provide the reservoir of knowledge and information required to produce an encyclopedia in 1870s Beirut, was intimately connected to other places, regionally and globally. First and foremost was Egypt, and specifically Cairo, which under Muhammad Ali had been the center of prodigious production and publication of books. Many of the first books published by the Bulaq Press of

---

5 There is a vast literature on Bustani himself, in multiple languages.
6 He had earlier produced the 2,500 page long *Muhit al-Muhit* dictionary in 1869.
7 See the recent book by Issa (2022).
8 This is impossible to determine, given the lack of private or institutional papers pertaining to Bustani and to the *Da'ira*.

Cairo (est. 1821) were translations of European works, and some Ottoman Turkish works as well, many of them scientific.[9] Many of these books were available in Beirut. We specifically know that Khedive Ismail made available to Bustani a very large number of books from Egypt for his encyclopedic project.[10] Second was Istanbul, which by the 1870s was also a very prolific publishing center for books in Ottoman Turkish as well as Arabic. Third was the American missionary community in Beirut, active there since around 1820, with whom Bustani had been deeply connected in the previous decades. They had established an Arabic press in the city, which published both original works in Arabic as well as translations, and had also founded the Syrian Protestant College, which by the 1870s held an impressive and growing collection of books. Fourth was Europe and the rest of the world.

Indeed, the story of the *Da'ira* is inextricably linked to the integration of Beirut and other port-cities of the Eastern Mediterranean into global information and communication networks (telegraph, news agencies, a reliable postal system), as well as transportation routes (steamship lines; a bit later, railways), which allowed for news, commodities (including periodicals and books), and people to circulate at unprecedented levels and speed (we should also mention the opening of the Suez Canal in 1869). It is therefore not a coincidence that the *Da'ira* saw the light in the 1870s,[11] which seems to have been the age of modern Encyclopedias and compendia in other parts of the world as well—certainly in China[12] and Japan,[13] both of which witnessed the emergence of a genre that claimed continuities with an older, local body of knowledge, but which also made claims to modernity and novelty, and tapped into sources (mostly Western) most of which had been unavailable until then.

---

[9] On Bulaq and the translation movement, see, among others, Verdery 1971; Heyworth-Dunne 1940; Schwartz 2015.

[10] Preface to the *Da'ira*, vol. 1.

[11] As Hourani pointed out, "Da'irat al-ma'arif is not much younger than the first proper Russian encyclopedia, and its first volume came out thirteen years earlier than that of the first Turkish encyclopedia, a smaller and more limited work, the *Qamus al-a'lam* of Semseddin Sami Fraseri" (Hourani 1990:112).

[12] See Li Hsiao-t'i 2014:47.

[13] D. R. Reynolds identifies 1868 as a turning point, as "the new Meiji imperial government declared in an imperial edict, 'Knowledge shall be sought throughout the world so as to strengthen the foundations of imperial rule'." There had been encyclopedias compiled earlier in Japan, but the 1870s witnessed a surge in them, and in a different, modern kind of encyclopedia. Reynolds 2014:156.

Recentering Asia and Rethinking Civilizational Categories

Let me now turn to the first entry discussed in this chapter: Asia.[14] Appearing in the Encyclopedia's very first volume, the essay on Asia is qualitatively different from most other entries. The author, most likely Salim al-Bustani, inserts himself and his authorial voice quite openly and frequently into what our contemporary sensitivities expect from encyclopedic entries: to provide objective, 'scientific' texts, which at the surface appear to be politically neutral. Bustani, on the other hand, makes overtly political and culturalist arguments in this entry on Asia. In the long opening passage, he waxes lyrical about Asia, marking his loyalties to 'his' continent and that of his readers. The opening sentence immediately refers to Yaqut ("this is how the word Asia should be pronounced, according to Yaqut"), the famous medieval author of *Mu'jam al-Buldan*, and a major reference work throughout the Encyclopedia—hence reminding his readership that knowledge about Asia and authority to write about it begins with the Arabs, or, at least, predates Europeans or Americans.[15] The continent is not only the biggest (after America), the most populous, the most fertile, whose landscapes are the most striking; it is also the cradle of humanity, since this is "where man was first created and … was dispersed through Noah and his children after the Flood." After this nod to the biblical narrative (which seems to be inserted quite often in the *Da'ira*'s entries), the author goes on to emphasize the greatness of its various kingdoms and cities (mostly the ancient Near East, followed by the Islamic/Medieval Middle East),[16] reminding his audience that this was the locus of the greatest religious diversity on earth.[17] Asia is a place of origins not just for humanity and religions, but also for fauna and flora. It is "the mother of knowledge, arts, languages and industries." Indeed, we know that in the past its inhabitants reached the highest levels of civilization: "we read [he is here inserting himself in the text] in ancient history books that many places [in Asia] were centers of civilization … knowledge and science and that the knowledge

---

14 "Asia," *Da'irat al-Ma'arif*, vol. 1:78–103.
15 The second sentence is how Asia is pronounced in French and in English.
16 "It was the seat of the kings of Ashur and Babel and Fars and Makedonia whose kingdoms were famous in ancient times for their power and greatness … and a number of [Asia's] cities are a reminder/testimony of this greatness … such as Babel and Niniveh and Seleucia and Tadmur and Sur and Sayda and others. [Regarding the] Spread of knowledge … Baghdad, Basra, Kufa, Damascus, Aleppo, Samarkand, Balkh and others [were all centers of knowledge]" ("Asia," *Da'irat al-Ma'arif*, vol. 1:78).
17 "[P]eoples (*shu'ub*) from most kinds and religions such as the Arabs from among Bedouins and settled people (*hadar*), Armenians, Syriacs (sic), Indians (*al-hunud*), Jews (*israiliyyin*), the Chinese, the Tatar and others" ("Asia," *Da'irat al-Ma'arif*, vol. 1:78).

of Indian learned men/sages (*hukama' al-hunud*) and Chinese philosophers (*falasifat al-Sin*) were the spring that the greatest ancient people drank from, from the Greeks to others. It is likely that civilization took its course from the head of the source of knowledge in Northern India or China. And since this continent is ours, it is incumbent upon us to write about it in great details beginning with the origin of its name then its size, borders and other related matters."[18] Thus, Bustani here is promoting the idea of a common origin of civilizations, and one that begins not in the Near East, but further East—but one that is nonetheless Asian.

Linked to the concept of civilization is that of a people/peoples (*sha'ab/ shu'ub*), and an investigation of its necessary characteristics. In the section entitled "[Asia's] people and states," Bustani begins with the standard information regarding the population of Asia (more than half of the world's population; the various branches/groups into which they have been divided—eight, according to the 'geographers'), only to then gently undermine the whole classification of the world's population into these eight fixed categories, and challenge the idea of separateness and homogeneity among a group of people. He points out that "some of these peoples [in Asia] have mixed with some of Europe's peoples through marriage; some Indians with the English and some Syrians with Crusaders, and others with others."[19] He then turns to analyzing the said characteristics of Asia's inhabitants or populations, taking as a starting point for the discussion the Greek physician and thinker Hippocrates (who had been known, translated and read since the early medieval period in the Arabo-Islamic world),[20] and his claim that "the people of Asia have no courage or endurance ... they are the least brave ... compared to Europeans."[21] According to Hippocrates, the people of Asia lacked courage for two reasons: first, the climate—essentially, it is very moderate and does not fluctuate; therefore Asia's inhabitants are more

---

18 "Asia," *Da'irat al-Ma'arif*, vol. 1:78.
19 Needless to say, it is not a coincidence that Bustani mentions Syria and mixing with the Crusaders. On one hand, Syria in this article is firmly and proudly placed within Asia, both geographically as well as part of a larger civilization; on the other, some of the Syrians themselves share a mixed ancestry with Europeans.
20 Certainly his medical texts were; and most probably this one too. The translation of Hippocrates' text is very faithful to the original—or rather to the English translation that I am comparing it with. But then again, the excerpt provided in the *Da'ira* might have dated from a much earlier period, and might have been translated directly from the Greek in the medieval period.
21 This is clearly from Hippocrates' *On Airs, Waters, and Places,* the passage which begins with "I wish to show, respecting Asia and Europe, how, in all respects, they differ from one another" and ends with "manly courage, endurance of suffering, laborious enterprise, and high spirit, could not be produced in such a state of things either among the native inhabitants or those of a different country, for there pleasure necessarily reigns." For the full text (translated by Francis Adams), see part 12, http://classics.mit.edu/Hippocrates/airwatpl.mb.txt.

even-keeled and less prone to violence than their European counterparts; and, second, the nature of their political laws. Since most of the provinces in Asia "are ruled by absolute oppressive monarchs (despots),"[22] Hippocrates argues (and Bustani faithfully reproduces), "most inhabitants do not want a reputation of bravery otherwise they would run into great dangers and will be forced to go to war ... thus, even when there are brave peoples, they do not wish to use their strength for this reason."[23] Of note is that the author also pointed out that Hippocrates had made exceptions for certain peoples in Asia whose courage he recognized, before adding that, in contemporary times, there were many more people in Asia who were indeed brave and courageous.[24]

What is important, for our purposes, is the manner in which Bustani links the concept of civilization to that of a people or peoples (*sha'ab/shu'ub*) (used interchangeably with *umma*, or "nation"), to the idea of a dormant courage that can be awakened under a just ruler, or a just system of governance. Thus, by transitivity, the *Da'ira* connects civilization to justice, an argument made in other entries as well. Indeed, Bustani clearly agrees with Hippocrates' argument linking lack of courage with despotic rule (probably less so with his argument regarding "climes"). He uses Hippocrates' text and argument to remind (and probably rouse) his readers that they, and Asians in general, can and ought to be brave and courageous, and that strength and bravery have been the casualty of oppressive rulers and governments. It is clearly both a response to Orientalist stereotypes regarding the lethargic East, as well as a call for, and an endorsement of political reform—this was published in 1876, the year of the Ottoman constitution. But Bustani does not stop there: he informs his readers of the Orientalist view that "Asian nations (*umam*) are generally more like women and

---

[22] *mutliqu'l tasarruf.*

[23] This section is further down in Hippocrates' text (part 16): "And with regard to the pusillanimity and cowardice of the inhabitants, the principal reason the Asiatics are more unwarlike and of gentler disposition than the Europeans is, the nature of the seasons, which do not undergo any great changes either to heat or cold, or the like [...] For these reasons, it appears to me, the Asiatic race is feeble, and further, owing to their laws; for monarchy prevails in the greater part of Asia, and where men are not their own masters nor independent, but are the slaves of others, it is not a matter of consideration with them how they may acquire military discipline, but how they may seem not to be warlike, for the dangers are not equally shared, since they must serve as soldiers, perhaps endure fatigue, and die for their masters, far from their children, their wives, and other friends [...] Thus, then, if any one be naturally warlike and courageous, his disposition will be changed by the institutions. As a strong proof of all this, such Greeks or barbarians in Asia as are not under a despotic form of government, but are independent, and enjoy the fruits of their own labors, are of all others the most warlike ..." (Hippocrates' *On Airs, Waters, and Places*, part 16).

[24] Bustani also challenges Hippocrates' classification of certain people, including a particularly valiant and courageous group Hippocrates had placed in Europe, but which Bustani argued firmly belonged in the Asiatic camp.

have an inclination for lust and guilty pleasures," before attacking and dismantling this stereotype (although he does believe that these characteristics do in fact apply to "some southern nations," which remain unnamed). To the contrary, rather than being lethargic and feminine, many nations/peoples in Asia are in fact fierce "like lions" and will not yield to any invader.[25] Just as Europeans have in recent past and in current times conquered Asian peoples, Asians had conquered Europe in the Middle Ages, and in fact most Europeans were descendants from Asiatic tribes, Bustani argued. Arabs had also ruled over Europe, and the Ottomans now ruled over some of the best European provinces. All this, for Bustani, was the ultimate proof that no continent had the monopoly over civilization or courage, and in fact, that the histories, civilizations, successes, and conquests of both "Europe" and "Asia" suggested the blurring of boundaries between the two 'civilizations' and the two continents.

Debt: An Imagined/Alternative Geography of Capital, Civilization, and Christianity

More unexpectedly, the concept of civilization also figures prominently in the entry for Debt (*dayn*). Here too, Bustani destabilizes fixed categories and associations in order to suggest an alternative understanding and geography of civilization and, in fact, of Christianity. Different temporalities are woven together in this entry as well: past and present 'objective' treatments of debt are linked together to suggest a different trajectory of debt, to be implemented in the future. Thus, once again, the historical and the descriptive turn into something prescriptive. In the 1870s, the subject of debt was particularly pressing: the Ottoman Empire and Egypt both defaulted in the middle of that decade, and many other countries were also becoming highly indebted to European states and banks. Private debt was also on the rise.[26] After describing various kinds of debt and credit, and pasting the relevant part of the Ottoman legal code on debt and the debtor's responsibilities and sanctions, Bustani discusses debt in history: "Ancient laws (*shara'i' wa qawanin*) were not merciful or sympathetic towards the debtor, unlike the laws that were introduced after the spread of civilization, the reason being that before that there were no men who were discerning/intelligent enough to be able to discern between forgery/fraud

---

[25] "It is necessary to make an exception for the Arabs and Mongols and Tatar and the Malabar people (*ummat al-malabariyya*) which are like lions, and the Turkmen and the rebellious/revolting tribes of Maharath (*al-mutamarrida*) who will not yield to anyone and other peoples/nations (*al umam*) and the inhabitants of mountains such as those of Mount Lebanon and al-Kalbiyya [in the province of Ladiqiyya] and others" ("Asia," *Da'irat al-Ma'arif*, vol. 1:91–92).

[26] See for example Owen 1993; Khater 1996 and 2000; Holt 2017.

(*tazwir*) and genuine losses which were the result of bad luck or unforeseen circumstances and emergencies. People are under the illusion that society (*al-hay'a al-ijtima'iyya*) before civilization (*fi halat al-khushuna*) was more righteous, fairer than the society that has known great degrees of civilization. But this illusion is disproven by history."[27] The article provides a long list of gruesome punishments meted out to debtors who failed to pay back their debts, in various historical contexts. Although this entry makes no mention of its sources, the section connecting civilization to a clement and fair treatment of debt and defaulting turns out to have been a faithful translation of the second edition of the [American] *Cyclopedia*'s entry on "Debtor and Creditor" (1874–1877).[28] Needless to say, it might have originated elsewhere, or might have also been reproduced in other compilation works as is, or with some slight modifications. What is telling, though, is that the *Da'ira*'s compiler has added in a couple of sentences that do not seem to have been included in the original Cyclopedia entry: essentially, that Christianity played a crucial role in easing the oppression of debtors. In the past, "the church used to condemn/prohibit (*tuharrim*) debtors, but as those became too many, men of religion stopped intervening in matters of debt." And even more powerful is the sentence that explicitly argues that "the spread of the Christian religion was one of the reasons for the lifting of oppression of debtors in most countries, and we know the degree of civilization, good manners (*tahdhib*) and knowledge in a nation (*umma*) from the way debtors are treated."[29] And in fact, nowadays, in civilized countries the debtor is not penalized nor imprisoned unless he has committed fraud. The entry then summarizes the main clauses in Ottoman law pertaining to debt, the rights and obligations of debtors who are agriculturalists and craftsmen. From private debt, the article moves on to covering public debt. Bustani presents public debt as a corollary to modernization and development projects, suggesting that it is almost a necessary consequence of civilization. With a promise that the subject of public debt will be treated within the relevant entry for individual countries, the article ends with a long list of said countries and the amount of debt incurred by each one of them. The juxtaposition of private and public debt in one entry (not present in the American Cyclopedia, which treats them separately), as well as the insertion of Bustani's argument that debt cancellation is in fact an act and a marker both of civilization and of Christianity, allows

[27] "*Dayn*," *Da'irat al-Ma'arif*, vol. 8:81 onward.
[28] "Debtor and Creditor," *The American Cyclopaedia*, 2nd ed. 1873–1877, vol. 5 (1874):745–746. The information on debt in England and the US is almost completely discarded, and kept to a bare minimum in the *Da'ira*.
[29] "wa kana intishar al-din al-masihi min asbab raf' al-dhulm 'an al-madyunin fi akthar al-bilad wa na'rif darajat al-madaniyya wa'l-tahdhib wa'l-ma'rifa fi'l-umma bi mu'amalatihim" ("Dayn," *Da'irat al-Ma'arif*, vol. 8:340).

Bustani to indirectly make a bold argument: if European lending countries were truly civilized and truly Christian, they should cancel the Ottoman Empire's and Egypt's debt—or alternatively, their failure to do so indicates that they are neither truly civilized, nor truly Christian. Thus once again, the author(s) of the encyclopedia suggest an alternative, imagined geography of what civilization—this time, coupled with *real* Christianity—truly entails.

Familiarizing the Alien: Greek Mythology— Oedipus the Egyptian

Let me turn now to my third entry, a brief, one-page entry for "Oedipus." As Hourani noted, one of the *Da'ira*'s most striking features is the many entries devoted to Ancient Greek history and philosophy,[30] and especially to mythology.[31] In fact, Bustani himself cast a spotlight on this topic by underlining the encyclopedia's entries on Greek mythology in his Preface. He felt he had to justify such inclusions, which might displease or shock some of his readers: "We have mentioned some things that we would have liked not to mention because they do not agree with our taste/sensibilities (*dhawqina*), or that we consider wrong/unhealthy (*la sihha lahu*) from Ancient Greek mythology and others."[32] Nonetheless, he continues, given that many people value this knowledge and study it, and given that "it is knowledge that is necessary in order to understand many things, we shall be forgiven for taking the liberty of mentioning it."[33] The entry for Oedipus begins by summarizing the main 'plotline' of the Oedipus story and explaining the differences between the version of Sophocles and other versions.[34] Following the summary, Bustani insists that the story itself is set in Egyptian Thebes, and not Thebes in Greece, for two reasons: first, the mention

[30] Of course, many of the most seminal classical Greek philosophers had been known, read, commented upon, engaged with for centuries, and were an organic part of the Arabo-Islamic canon.
[31] Hourani 1990:117, but he does not provide explanations for this.
[32] The term he uses for mythology is *khurafa* ("Preface," *Da'irat al-Ma'arif*, vol. 1). There is a clear interest in mythology that is apparent throughout the *Da'ira*. Ancient Greek mythology is obviously dominant, but other mythologies are also included. See for instance the entry for Edda (on Nordic mythology), and more expectedly, on Adonis, part of Phoenician mythology.
[33] "Preface," *Da'irat al-Ma'arif*, vol. 1. This is reminiscent of Ann Blair's argument regarding early modern European compendia, where compendia reproduced ancient scientific ideas or beliefs not necessarily because the authors/compilers believed in them (they had been disproven), but because the compilers felt that the readers needed to familiarize themselves with these ideas in order to understand books that were deemed to be 'classics' or canonical. See Blair 2006:208.
[34] "Oedipus," *Dai'ra*, vol. 4:600–601. I could not identify the possible source(s) for this entry. Initially I suspected the source might have been Greek, Italian, or Ottoman Turkish, since Jocasta was turned into Iocasta, for instance. But it is not that clear. Some English books from the mid-nineteenth century also translated it as Iocasta.

of the sphinx (quintessentially Egyptian, according to the entry's author); and second, the reference to epidemic (*waba'*)—here understood to refer to cholera, another quintessential Egyptian feature, which Bustani duly explains as being due to the presence of poisonous substances contained in the soil, which evaporate and turn into poisonous vapors.[35] Thus, this entry does a number of things: 1) it claims, or reclaims, Oedipus and his story as an Egyptian one, or at least one set in Egypt—which can be read within the context of Ottoman and Egyptian intellectuals reclaiming the Ancient Greek classical heritage as theirs as well, as one shared with Europeans; 2) it illustrates the growing interest in comparative mythology among *nahda* intellectuals (see the entries on Nordic myths, as well as the entry for "Earth" that mentions Indian and Greek mythology related to the creation of the Earth and the world);[36] and 3) it sheds light on the beginning of the formation of a global literary canon, or the making of what will later be referred to as "World Literature."[37] The practice of translating Ancient Greek mythology, and the experimentation with ways to translate certain unfamiliar concepts and terms (for instance, the Oracle, which gets translated in the *Da'ira* as *wahi*, or inspiration), would reach its apogee with Suleyman al-Bustani's publication of the first Arabic translation of the *Iliad* a few years later in 1904.[38] In fact, as Donald Reid noted, Butrus al-Bustani himself had "urged the translation of Homer and Virgil into Arabic as early as 1859. His encyclopedic long entry on Homer detailed the European debate on the poet's authenticity and historicity."[39] Of course, they were not alone in introducing Ancient Greek mythology and themes to their Arab readers and speakers. Among other spaces, the theater, and especially in Egypt, was a particularly important venue for the adaptation of plays with ancient Greek themes (many adapted from French classical writers such as Racine) and their performance in Arabic.[40]

Thus, one of the most noticeable features of the encyclopedia is how imbricated the various forms and sources of knowledge on its pages were, as well as the crossing of genre boundaries that occurred in at least some of its entries: from the descriptive to the prescriptive, from the objective to the outwardly political, so that some of the entries read more like OpEd pieces as compared to entries in late nineteenth century Western Encyclopedias. The *Da'ira* can thus be viewed as an archive of intellectual exchange, of interconnected and

---

[35] On the miasma theory, see Fahmy 2018, especially ch. 3.
[36] "Ard," *Da'ira*, vol. 3:109. Unusually, this entry has the author's initials included at the end: s.b., most likely Salim al-Bustani.
[37] A point I will not elaborate here, due to space constraints. See, for instance, Casanova 1999.
[38] See, among others, Hourani 1991.
[39] Reid 2002:164.
[40] See Reid 2002; Khuri-Makdisi 2010, ch. 3: "Theater and Radical Politics"; Cormack 2017 and 2019.

global intellectual history—albeit a highly asymmetrical one, and one whose authors inserted themselves into this global body of knowledge circulating during the period, and felt the authority and responsibility to intervene in it. The three entries analyzed in this paper so far shed light on alternative conceptions of civilization that the authors of the Encyclopedia sought to promote. All three offered a different, imagined geography to that which was dominant and promoted by contemporary mainstream European (and American) epistemological systems. They destabilized fixed categories and classification systems, blurred geographical and civilizational boundaries, and, in the entry for "Oedipus," created alternative genealogies linking Syria and Egypt to ancient Greece in unexpected ways.

Imagined Geographies as a Futuristic Project

More generally, and moving beyond these specific entries, I suggest viewing Bustani's *Da'ira* as a project that keenly mapped the possibilities for future imagined and imaginable geographies. Indeed, one can read the Encyclopedia as a future-oriented project of imperial development—of its territories and landscapes, as well as its natural resources. For instance, the entry on Artesian wells (*abar artwaziyya*) concludes with a paragraph pointing out that such wells could easily be built in many regions of the East in need of water.[41] The entry for "Ottoman (the Ottoman Empire)"—intriguingly, the very last entry in the eleventh and last volume—devoted a section to the Asian territories of the empire. Kurdistan is noted for its fertile land, but like Anatolia, "its unwieldy paths (*wu'urat masalikiha*) and the uncouthness of its inhabitants and their deep immersion in barbarity (*khushunat ahliha wa tawaghghulihim fi'l-hamajiyya*) prevents the land and region from being properly exploited and developed (*istithmariha wa inma'iha*)."[42] The implication was, of course, that the taming and civilizing of the local population by an enlightened and powerful Ottoman state would change the geography and the nature of the area.

Perhaps no set of entries gives a better sense of this expansive geography of possibilities as those pertaining to plants and crops. Indeed, one of the most striking aspects of the *Da'ira*'s eleven volumes is the sheer number of entries on botany: it seems that every possible plant was included. On one hand, this is not surprising, since Bustani mentions agriculture (*zira'a*) as the first subject of knowledge required by the current times. Also, botany had been a highly developed field in the Arabo-Islamic world, with many medieval specialized botanical

---

[41] "Abar artwaziyya," *Da'irat al-Ma'arif*, vol. 1:19.
[42] "'Uthmaniyya (al-Dawla al-'Uthmaniyya)," *Da'irat al-Ma'arif*, vol. 10:721.

compilations still clearly known and read.[43] Furthermore, many contemporary encyclopedias produced in Europe or North America also devoted entries of varying lengths to plants and crops. Botany and botanical knowledge evidently were, and indeed still are, at the cusp of a number of centrally important fields, disciplines and industries, such as agriculture and food production, medicine, and pharmacology. Thus, many, if not most, of the entries about plants in the *Da'ira* provided information on the kind of soil needed to grow a specific plant; whether new kinds have been discovered, and if they are domesticable and adjustable to a specific environment; the parameters of its consumption as food (when and how is it edible); the kind of medicinal use it could have, and the required method of preparation that this entailed. The encyclopedia consistently pays attention to the history of plants: how classical authors, Arab and also Greek, wrote about them; how they were used in the past, often providing the etymology for the name, and invariably including the plant's name in Latin; as well as sometimes Greek, French, and/or English, and the plant's various local names, which could differ from one Arabic dialect to another, and sometimes from one sub-region to another.

Take, for instance, the entry for Mulberry ("*Tut*")—a major crop in parts of the Ottoman Empire, and specifically in Mount Lebanon, due to its connection to silk production. [44] The *Da'ira* provides all kinds of practical information regarding optimal planting and soil conditions for different kinds of mulberry trees, as well as pruning and vaccination. It describes different cultivation and care methods between Syrian coastal peasants and mountain peasants, and also devotes a detailed section to the medicinal properties of various kinds of mulberry, as well as the kinds of food that could be prepared based on them, including mulberry species not found in Syria. The Encyclopedia thus spreads local as well as global knowledge on plants and trees to different parts of the Ottoman and Arabic-reading worlds, suggesting new crops that might take in different regions of the empire, and the realm of effective cultivation of crops already familiar in one part of the empire. This is a developmentalist project, one involving the management of nature and society, with the aim of intensifying the exploitation of resources through the improvement of land, peoples, and techniques. [45] This could best be done by a strong state, but did not exclude individuals taking the initiative at the small, local scale—landowners and developers, merchants, and artisans could gather valuable information from the pages of the Encyclopedia, and partake in the project of modernizing and optimizing province and empire.

---

[43] For knowledge and experimentation with seeds and crops in the early modern period, see the superb work of Aleksandar Shopov, especially Shopov 2020.

[44] "*Tut*" (murrier, mulberry), *Da'irat al-Ma'arif*, vol. 6:254.

[45] For a global perspective on this, see Pomeranz 2009:4.

Conclusion: The Encyclopedia as a "Dream-Machine" and a "Dreamscape"

Beyond the concrete developmentalist agenda already discussed, I would like to close with a suggestion that the *Da'ira* should be read as "a dream-machine" (to borrow Roland Barthes's beautiful characterization of the dictionary). [46] Indeed, the Da'ira sought to unleash all kinds of dreams among its readers, who meander from one entry to the other, landing on unsuspected, hitherto unknown and unimagined worlds: a river in Brazil; a random port in Wales; an unknown, foreign plant; a pantheon of Hindu or Greek gods. One can enter this world randomly, get lost in an entry that synthesized information stemming from multiple sources, and covering different time periods. From there, the reader might decide to follow the editor's suggestion, linking this entry to another one and immediately jump to the suggested entry (through the often-present "see under:" rubric), turn the page and land on a completely different topic, or randomly pick another entry point into the same Encyclopedic volume, or another one. To borrow from and adapt Giovanni Dotoli's felicitous description of the dictionary, the Encyclopedia, and Bustani's Encyclopedia par excellence, "falls between dream and classification. It classifies the dream." [47] Bustani's encyclopedia was as much about "cultivating, curating, and circulating knowledge"[48] as it was about propelling its readers onto a global stage, helping them navigate a world more vast and seemingly legible than any of their predecessors had accessed, and encouraging them to imagine new geographies.

Works Cited

Blair, A. 2006. "A Europeanist's Perspective." In *Organizing Knowledge: Encyclopaedic Activities in the Pre-Eighteenth Century Islamic World*, ed. G. Endress, 201–216. Leiden.

Booth, M. 2015. *Classes of Ladies of Cloistered Spaces: Writing Feminist History through Biography in Fin de Siècle Egypt*. Edinburgh.

Bustani, B., ed. 1876–1900. *Kitab Da'irat al-Ma'arif*–Encyclopédie arabe. Beirut.

Casanova, P. 1999. *La république mondiale des lettres*. Paris.

Cormack, R. 2017. "Oedipus on the Nile: Translations and Adaptations of Sophocles' *Oedipus Tyranno*s in Egypt, 1900–1970." PhD diss., University of Edinburgh.

---

[46] Roland Barthes, "Préface," *Dictionnaire Hachette. Langue, Encyclopédie, noms propres* (Paris, 1980), vi, quoted in Dotoli 2014:18–19.

[47] Dotoli 2014:24.

[48] I am borrowing this triadic expression from MacDonald (2017:1).

————. 2019. "Lords or Idols? Translating the Greek Gods into Arabic in Nineteenth-Century Egypt." In *Migrating Texts: Circulating Translations around the Ottoman Mediterranean*, ed. M. Booth, 211–235. Edinburgh.

Dolželová-Velingerová, M., and R. G. Wagner, eds. 2014. *Chinese Encyclopaedias of New Global Knowledge (1870–1930): Changing Ways of Thought*. Berlin.

Dotoli, D. 2014. "Le dictionnaire espace de rêve." In *L'espace du dictionnaire. Expressions—Impressions*, ed. D. Dotoli, M. Marchetti, C. Boccuzzi, and C. Rizzo, 17–40. Paris.

Fahmy, K. 2018. *In Quest of Justice: Islamic Law and Forensic Medicine in Modern Egypt*. Berkeley.

Heyworth-Dunne, J. 1940. "Printing and Translations under Muḥammad ʿAlī of Egypt: The Foundation of Modern Arabic." *Journal of the Royal Asiatic Society* 72:325–349.

Hippocrates. *On Airs, Waters, and Places*. Trans. F. Adams. http://classics.mit.edu/Hippocrates/airwatpl.mb.txt.

Holt, E. M. 2017. *Fictitious Capital: Silk, Cotton, and the Rise of the Arabic Novel*. New York.

Hourani, A. 1990. "Bustani's Encyclopaedia." *Journal of Islamic Studies* 1:111–119.

————. 1991. "Suleyman al-Bustani and the *Iliad*." In *Islam in European Thought*, 174–187. Cambridge.

Issa, R. 2022. *The Modern Arabic Bible: Translation, Dissemination, and Literary Impact*. Edinburgh.

Jandora, J. 1986. "Al Bustani's Daʾirat al-Maʿarif." *The Muslim World* 76:86–92.

Khater, A. 1996. "'House' to 'Goddess of the House': Gender, Class, and Silk in 19th-Century Mount Lebanon." *International Journal of Middle East Studies* 28:325–348.

————. 2001. *Inventing Home: Emigration, Gender, and the Middle Class in Lebanon, 1870–1920*. Berkeley.

Khuri-Makdisi, I. 2010. *The Eastern Mediterranean and the Making of Global Radicalism, 1860–1914*. Berkeley.

Li H. 2014. "Late Qing Encyclopedias: Establishing a New Enterprise." In Dolželová-Velingerová and Wagner 2014:29–53.

MacDonald, J. M. 2017. "Malthus and the Philanthropists, 1764–1859: The Cultural Circulation of Political Economy, Botany, and Natural Knowledge." *Social Sciences* 6:1–33.

Makdisi, U. 2010. *Faith Misplaced: The Broken Promise of US–Arab Relations: 1820–2001*. New York.

Owen, R. 1993. *The Middle East in the World Economy*. 2nd ed. London.

Pomeranz, K. 2009. "Introduction." In *The Environment and World History*, ed. E. Burke III and K. Pomeranz, 3–32. Berkeley.

Reid, D. 2002. *Whose Pharaohs?: Archaeology, Museums, and Egyptian National Identity from Napoleon to World War I.* Berkeley.

Reynolds, D. R. 2014. "Japanese Encyclopaedias: A Hidden Impact on Late Qing Chinese Encyclopaedias?" In Dolželová-Velingerová and Wagner 2014: 137–189.

Ripley, G., and C. A Dana, eds. 1874–1877. "Debtor and Creditor." *American Cyclopedia*, 2nd ed. New York.

Schwartz, K. 2015. "Meaningful Mediums: A Material and Intellectual History of Manuscript and Print Production in Nineteenth Century Ottoman Cairo." PhD diss., Harvard University.

Shopov, A. 2020. "Grafting in Sixteenth-Century Mamluk and Ottoman Agriculture and Literature." In *Living with Nature and Things: Contributions to a New Social History of the Middle Islamic Periods*, ed. B. J. Walker and A. al-Ghouz, 381–406. Bonn.

Verdery, R. 1971. "The Publications of the Būlāq Press under Muḥammad Alī of Egypt." *Journal of the American Oriental Society* 91:129–132.

8

Island Topophilia

Alexandros Papadiamantis's *The Murderess* (1903)

Yota Batsaki

THE IMAGINATION CAN ATTACH ITSELF TO ANY GEOGRAPHY, infusing it with the play of emotion and association. Yet few locales have invited this imaginative work as readily and repeatedly as the island. In countless incarnations, the island has served as a figure for escape and adventure, an elusive paradise, a mythical location at the edges of the inhabited world, or a prison and a place of exile. The imagined geography of the island in the Greek tradition spans the breadth of Greek literature from Homer to the present, a privileged expression of the abiding tension between the lure of departure and the nostalgia of homecoming. Why, then, focus on yet another version of the island and yet another towering figure of the Modern Greek literary tradition, Alexandros Papadiamantis? Moreover, a writer whose continuous return, in his stories, to his native island of Skiathos, is abundantly referenced in the criticism? I propose that the island in Papadiamantis's masterpiece, *The Murderess*, published in 1903, is a radical departure from the string of commonplaces that have come to encircle the literary *topos* of the island. Rather, this uncanny story of marginality and crime, cast as the title implies in the female gender, is an extraordinary expression of *topophilia*, an explanation of how imagined geographies are formed, how they are sculpted by human labor and culture, and how they in turn shape their human inhabitants.

My approach to the island is informed by the interdisciplinary field of landscape studies, which has received renewed attention thanks to the 'spatial turn' of the past few decades. Within that expansive field, I am particularly interested in a tradition of humanistic geography dating back to the 1970s that is less focused on mapping strategies and more attuned to humans' embodied and imaginative experiences of their environments. For similar reasons, I will not draw on the rich literature that takes a topographical approach to

Yota Batsaki

the Modern Greek landscape as the mapping of the homeland in response to ideologies of nationalist expansion, identity, and continuity.[1] Rather, I am interested here in Papadiamantis's ability to convey a lived experience of place infused with his own acute topophilia. The concept of topophilia was coined by the humanist geographer Yi-Fu Tuan[2] to convey our strong attachments to places that combine intense sensory experience with acute emotional engagement. Such places may enrapture the senses through their specific combination of topography, minerals, water, vegetation, and sky, but also enthrall the intellect through their associations to present and past cultures, religions, and mythologies. This attachment to place, which derives from sensory experience but is fed by aesthetic rapture and heightened by cultural associations, is what Tuan defines as *topophilia*. The feeling can modulate from the comfort of home and the pleasures of familiarity to the lure of the unfamiliar and the raptures of the sublime. The decision to locate his fiction on his native island was for Papadiamantis, a perennially ambivalent denizen of the Athenian literary démi-monde, a strategy of displacement and a crucial recourse to the geography and community with which he was most intimately familiar.

Topophilia assumes that place is not merely a setting or background for human agency or psychology, but a dynamic element that shapes both. Traditional readings of landscape in literature or art have often considered it a passive backdrop to plot or character. More recently, landscape has been treated as a privileged and lasting medium for the inscription of cultural narratives. Simon Schama has called landscape a "text on which generations write their recurring obsessions," marked by richness, antiquity, and complexity.[3] The Greek landscape too has offered particularly fertile ground for this approach because of its classical associations and the modern demands of nation building. Yet this approach still proposes landscape as a palimpsest or archive rather than an active force. Tuan's concept of topophilia opens up the further possibility of considering how the experience of place shapes its human inhabitants, even as successive generations mold space by dwelling in it and investing it with their labor and memories.

Tuan draws a distinction between space and place.[4] Space is abstract: it connotes openness and freedom of movement, opens us up to adventure and new experiences, but also to risk. Place is where we pause: it is familiar, loaded with the value derived from frequent and intimate experience, but may also incite boredom and frustration. Space is where the imagination roams, while

[1] Leontis 1995; Gourgouris 1996.
[2] Tuan 1990.
[3] Schama 1995:12.
[4] Tuan 2001.

176

place is where the body seeks shelter and fulfillment of its needs. The imagined geography of the island exemplifies the perennial tension between these two poles: a circumscribed place surrounded by seemingly endless space. The island conjures up a reassuring finitude but may also delight with its unexpected and rich variety. It is a geographical expression of the experience of place as a spot that is small enough to be taken in by the senses yet varied enough to resist the quick attenuation of our perception that inevitably results from our concentrating on a single vista for a length of time. This combination of the varied and the circumscribed is a perfect definition of the island. Yet while the island is a haven or sanctuary, its very boundedness can feel as stifling as a prison and generate a desire for escape. This is the predicament of the protagonist in Papadiamantis's *The Murderess.*

Papadiamantis's attachment to Skiathos was one of the strongest in his ascetic life. Even though he spent many years in economic exile in Athens, he returned to Skiathos to die. His extraordinarily vivid and detailed rendition of the island induces in others a similar desire and nostalgia for place. Papadiamantis's topophilia is contagious. For example, Papadiamantis's first biographer, George Valetas, opens his 1940 book with a hymn to Skiathos. He describes the island as a world unto itself, a microcosm with an extraordinary variety of forms and shapes that create the illusion of labyrinthine infinity. For Valetas, the "closed book" of Papadiamantis's life can only be opened and read in Skiathos: "a virgin place, untouched by progress and civilization. The medieval theocratic tradition endured there for many years. In the shade of the magnificent stature of Athos, beaten down by migration and isolation" the παράμερο [out of the way] island proved fertile ground for monasticism.[5] Papadiamantis was understood in similar terms, as a κοσμοκαλόγερος, or worldly monk, who flirted with joining a monastery on Mount Athos, expressed his spirituality through Byzantine chant, and disdained the Athenian literary establishment. To be steeped in his work is to come under the spell of his island, and so Valetas describes Papadiamantis's physiognomy as a Skiathos landscape: his beard like an overgrown grove, his eyes like clear springs, his eyebrows like reeds, his nose a formidable cliff, opening up onto the serene coastline of his forehead. The biographer's ekphrasis draws on geographical elements "small enough to be known personally"[6] to convey his intimate knowledge of his human subject. Indeed, Valetas employs elements of the natural environment to humanize a figure often described as filthy, clad in rags, and associating with the lowest of Athenian society. More broadly, Valetas intuits Papadiamantis's topophilia but naturalizes it into an ethnographic

---

[5] Valetas 1940:28–31.
[6] Tuan 1990:101.

localism that fits into the national literary history under construction: his book won first prize from the Academy of Athens.

To sketch why Papadiamantis's treatment of the island is so unexpected and fruitful, I will begin by contrasting it to the imagined geography of the island in a work by another writer, *The Aegean Notebooks* by Zissimos Lorentzatos (1915–2004). This travelogue, published in 1983 with the original title *Στοῦ Τιμονιοῦ τό Αὐλάκι* ('In the Wake of the Rudder'), recounts a succession of sailing trips around the southern tip of the Peloponnese and the Cyclades. The two writers are intimately connected. Lorentzatos was crucial for the recognition of Papadiamantis, through his criticism and publication of the critical edition of his works. They share an island origin: Lorentzatos hailed from Corfu and Papadiamantis from Skiathos. They both entered the Greek university but exited without the formal degree, although Lorentzatos lived comfortably as a private intellectual while Papadiamantis struggled to eke out a living as a writer for serials. They also share a notion of Greekness imbued with Orthodox spirituality and reverence for tradition, but this should not be mistaken for provincialism. Papadiamantis was steeped in European literature, which he translated from English and French after teaching himself both languages, toiling eight or ten hours per day, fueled by a steady diet of coffee, cigarettes, and alcohol. Lorentzatos translated Ezra Pound, Edgar Allan Poe, and William Blake, and his literary criticism carries on a vivid conversation with T. S. Eliot, Ezra Pound, and George Seferis.

Unlike Lorentzatos or Seferis, writers who enjoyed financial security and were connected to international literary circuits, Papadiamantis was yoked to translation as a breadwinning profession. He translated incessantly for daily newspapers and literary journals, articles on current events and works of literature, French but also English and American (including Fyodor Dostoyevsky's *Crime and Punishment* from the French). His translations often appeared anonymously, and their full scope is still under exploration, most recently in a 2011 conference that marked the centennial of the author's death, which was devoted to his translations. In the proceedings, N. D. Triantafyllopoulos writes that whereas Papadiamantis the translator was, until the 1980s, a "sunken continent," he is now "an archipelago" whose contours have risen to the surface of critical inquiry.[7] He translated theology, history, literature, scientific articles, and foreign journalism. Through his translations, Papadiamantis was steeped both in international affairs and in the literary movements and controversies of his time.

Even as Papadiamantis negotiated the frustrations and anxieties of relying on journalism and translation for a living, he clung to his topophilia. In the

---

[7]   Triantafyllopoulos 2012:21.

first year of his collaboration with the newspaper *Acropolis* he was asked to contribute some travel writing on Greek sites ("our countryside ... our islands ... vacation destinations"), in the vein of the "picturesque, of course, rather than geographical" ('Επί το γραφικώτερον ἐννοεῖται και ὄχι το γεωγραφικώτερον). Papadiamantis was also encouraged to coordinate with another contributor—his friend, relative, and compatriot Alexandros Moraitidis—so that they could avoid writing about the same place (διά νά μή συναντηθῆτε εἰς τάς Σποράδας).[8] It appears that Papadiamantis never responded to that commission. He seems to have deliberately avoided precisely the kind of travel writing—occasional, detached, uninformed by intimate experience—that Lorentzatos succumbs to in his *Notebooks*. As a result, their treatment of the island is markedly different.

Lorentzatos, in his travels around the Aegean, singles out islands such as Folegandros as loci of cultural purity. For him the ideal map of Greece is an *isolario*: the ideal Greece would be an archipelago properly distanced from a modernity that he associated with the aping of foreign political and cultural models and the triumph of venality. He is the intellectual tourist who notes the most sheltered beaches, the best weather for swimming. He interacts with each island at circumscribed points: the harbor, the picturesque chora, the taverna. His travelogue uses the islands as launching pads for reflections on literary history or contemporary politics. Despite his attempts to individualize them, his islands and promontories are indistinguishable, interchangeable. The personification of island authenticity in his writing is the figure of an old Greek woman with violet eyes and a youthful voice, surrounded by her grandchildren, whom, incredibly, he encounters more than once on different locations.

Lorentzatos is not entirely immune to Papadiamantis's topophilia, however. In his case, it provokes a rare confessional passage that interrupts his cultural commentary with a "description of the little place by the sea that I have known since childhood and where I still go when I make my pilgrimage to the island where I was born and where I belong."[9] Lorentzatos invites the reader to follow him in his imagination along a rocky and slippery path, through olive groves and along the edge of a cliff: an itinerary that, as we will see, seems lifted straight out of the pages of *The Murderess*. The track ultimately leads to an enchanting, deserted beach, with a double cave chiseled out of the rock, its loving description graced with a Homeric quotation (σπέος γλαφυρόν). This secret haunt is an untrodden "sanctuary" where man's presence is "a violation and a desecration, and it is as though everything, from the bushes and tall grasses to the ... insects and birds ... is all aquiver because someone has seen them at the wrong

---

[8] Athini 2012:36.
[9] Lorentzatos 2013:51.

moment, has surprised them, like a young virgin, at the secret moment of their nakedness."[10]

The scene hints at the crisis in a mythological narrative, wherein Lorentzatos casts himself as the transgressive onlooker, the potential "violator" of the "virgin" and "desecrator" of the "sanctuary." The experience of place is here structured as an opposition between a male, voyeuristic narrator whose presence carries the threat of violence and a feminized, passive nature embodied as the young virgin surprised at her most vulnerable. Lorentzatos projects himself onto the landscape through the violent trope of the encounter with a nymph and mediated by the use of a Homeric quotation. The first reminds us of the ideology of cultural continuity often derived from the Greek landscape due to its remembered associations with mythological or epic narratives; the second, of the continuity of the linguistic tradition, as it survives in words or quotations. Lorentzatos's attempt to share his intimate sense of place, the locus of childhood memories and personal pilgrimage, is dictated by the cultural archive or what he calls elsewhere a metaphysical or sacred geography.[11] Highly intellectualized, his approach to place privileges the sense of vision and stages a power dynamic between a masculine self and a feminine nature. Carolyn Merchant has shown how this trope of a feminized nature, which she traces back to early modern scientific practices of observation and experimentation, opens the door to the domination of nature. Merchant's argument proceeds to connect the devaluation of women, the instrumentalization of nature, and ecological crisis.[12]

The foil provided by Lorentzatos's island itineraries throws into relief the striking novelty of Papadiamantis's imagined geography, starting with his protagonist Hadoula, or Frankojannou. She is described as a γριά or old lady (although not quite sixty) but has nothing in common with the still beautiful and prosperous violet-eyed old lady of Lorentzatos's Folegandros. Well-built and of masculine temperament, she is nevertheless known as Frankojannou, the genitive indicating that she is her husband's property. As a young girl she was married off by her parents to a pitiful husband and given a cruelly mean dowry. Her many children are a curse. She employs all her ingenuity, including her knowledge of the island's herbal remedies, to support the family, only to be set back by the serial and irrevocable departures of her sons (some to prison, others to America). Her heaviest burdens are her daughters, who either remain single for lack of a dowry or bring more hapless baby girls into the world. The novella portrays Frankojannou's descent into crime fueled by her despair over

[10] Lorentzatos 2013:52.
[11] Lorentzatos 2013.
[12] Merchant 1980. See also Plumwood 1993.

the burden of women and a pathological conviction that her calling is to redress this plight by helping girls along to an early death. She begins by smothering her sick infant granddaughter, whom she had cared for to the point of exhaustion. She proceeds to drown two young girls in a well, and to let another drown accidentally in her presence, before smothering a fifth while ostensibly nursing her and her mother back to health.

It is this older woman with a past full of hardship and trauma and a present mired in misery and resentment that Papadiamantis uses as the vehicle for his topophilia. But although Frankojannou is shaped by her relationship to the natural environment, the novella does not begin with Frankojannou in the landscape. Rather, we find her almost delirious from sleeplessness and exhaustion, caring for her sick daughter and the daughter's newborn in a miserable hovel, and reminiscing about a lifetime of sacrifice and service, first as the servant of her parents, then as the slave of her husband and children. She traces the root of her troubles to her cruel treatment by her family and especially her mother, who arranged to marry her to a weak and unpromising suitor and to deprive her of a viable dowry. Our first encounter with the geography of the island is through this dowry and it sets the stage for the novella's substantive approach to the landscape. I borrow the term *substantive* from Kenneth Olwig, a student of Tuan and a geographer and landscape theorist whose approach is inspired by the humanistic disciplines of philology and anthropology, but also deeply informed by environmental and legal history.[13] Substantive in Olwig's definition means both "real" as opposed to apparent, and also "creating and defining rights and duties" (Olwig 2019:20). He is interested in landscape as "a place of human habitation and environmental interaction" (Olwig 2019:22) that is shaped by social institutions and thus gives rise to issues of community, law, and justice. All these crystallize in *The Murderess* around the institution of the dowry, which determines what portion of the family's land will be transferred to Frankojannou upon her marriage, and how valuable (economically productive) this land will be.

Frankojannou's attempts to communicate to her suitor that he is accepting a bad deal are foiled by her mother, who arranges for her only daughter to receive a ruined house and abandoned land at the windswept northern Castle, the former village where the community resided while the fear of pirates and Ottoman invasion was imminent. The mother kept for herself, her husband, and her son the desirable houses, vineyards, and olive groves close to the new village where the family resides. The dowry understood as transfer of land (the author comments late in the novel that monetary dowries are a new and unwelcome

---

[13]   Olwig 2019.

phenomenon) exemplifies the link between self and environment as a relationship of sustenance and, indeed, survival. The dowry can be seen in two ways: as a payment or bribe to the groom to take an unproductive daughter off the family's hands, or as a form of insurance that the daughter will have a reasonably comfortable existence, or at least a viable economic start to her new life. Frankojannou is painfully aware that the latter was denied her by her family. Decades later, when she experiences the challenge of marrying off her daughters without capital or a husband (now dead) to help share the burden, she begins to view the institution of the dowry as an obligation impossible to fulfill, a burden that renders female children unwanted and dispensable.

Frankojannou is a liminal figure. She is a healer and killer, using her medicinal skills to help women through the perils of childbirth but also abortion. She traces her own misfortunes to the cruelty and selfishness of her mother, "the witch," but it is the mother who taught her every secret spring and valley of the island that she traverses barefoot and more swiftly and securely than anybody. The island's environment, its geological indentations, plant matter, birdsong, and arid cliff-sides are, respectively, her refuge, her livelihood, her solace, and her useless dowry that lies at the root of all her subsequent misfortunes and crimes.

In *Demons and the Devil*, his cultural geography of Naxos, the anthropologist Charles Stewart describes the ways in which traditions going back to antiquity have merged with Christian beliefs to produce the island's metaphysical geography. At the center is the village with its church circumscribing the safest space for human habitation. Civilization then radiates outward into the wilderness, which is dotted with apotropaic chapels and monasteries that afford some protection, and also haunted by the *exotika* (from ἔξω, outside: Latin *exotica*), supernatural beings lurking outside the 'marked' spaces of culture. These *exotika* embody the survival and assimilation of older beliefs (including those about nymphs, naiads, and gorgons) into the Christian moral and geographic imagination. Dictated by this metaphysical geography, the movement of the villagers is centripetal, for venturing out beyond the village boundaries at the wrong time of day or season of the year may entail risky encounters with these *exotika* that can steal one's speech, health, affections, or even life.

Papadiamantis's Frankojannou *is* the *exotiko*, the liminal being unexpectedly encountered along the paths of the island where she collects herbs and preys on young girls. But with her as its unlikely *genius loci*, the novella presents a richer metaphysical or sacred geography, one that, like Stewart's, is marked by chapels and ruined hermitages, but also (and unlike Stewart's) by ancient trees, springs, and caves. Instead of a center radiating outward, the island has many spots of sanctuary, danger, wonder, and pulsating energy. Papadiamantis entices us to visit those spaces, not in the character of Lorentzatos, surprising a feminized nature in all its vulnerable nakedness, but through the perspective of the persecuted nymph, fleeing violence. This change of perspective offers very different aesthetic and ethical layers to the reader. I will give two examples: one from the beginning of the novella where Frankojannou's mother is hunted by bandits on whom she had cast her evil spells; and another from the end, when the daughter is pursued by agents of the law. In both cases, the woman's vulnerability is described in environmental terms, through an analogy with the island's non-human creatures.

In the first example, which occurs only a couple of pages into the novella, Frankojannou's mother Delcharo (the unkind "witch" who taught her all the nooks and crannies of the island), is being pursued by two brigands. The term Papadiamantis uses for Delcharo is στρίγγλα (Italian *strega*, witch), a creature of island folklore that is knowledgeable about wicked herbs and concoctions. The folklorist Nikolaos Politis associates the στρίγγλα with the Sicilian *pagana*, who enters the rooms of unguarded mothers who have recently given birth and strangles them and their newborns.[14] This is why a woman stays with new mothers and their infants for the first few days after labor. In the novella's opening, Frankojannou performs both roles of guardian and malefactor to her infant granddaughter. In another version of the folktales, which reverberates with all the narrative's perverse bathings of children, a στρίγγλα is made when a child dies without being baptized, or when the ritual of baptism goes wrong.

Yet, if in the cultural geography of the island the protagonist and her mother are from the very beginning described as marginal, transgressive, and dangerous, in the symbolic geography of the island they are also endowed with mythological attributes that ennoble them and solicit the reader's sympathy. This is partly because they are framed within scenes of pursuit that present them as seeking refuge in the natural world of the island, whose ecology and topography they know so well. Frankojannou's mother, pursued by brigands who suspect her of foiling their illicit activities with her spells, is likened to a nymph or follower of Artemis, who "leaps like a deer from bush to bush, barefooted" and, "in her despair," seeks refuge in the hollow of an ancient pine. The narrator calls her move "a desperate, almost a childish expedient. She was hidden there only in her own imagination, like a child playing hide and seek."[15] Yet, miraculously, the brigands pass by and, although one of them turns around, he does not see the woman hiding in plain view. The passage activates our imagination and disturbs our easy identification with the woman's pursuers, enveloping her in

---

[14]   Politis 1904.
[15]   Papadiamantis 2010:3.

the magical thinking of childhood and myth simultaneously: "The dryads, the forest nymphs whom she perhaps invoked in her magic, were protecting her, they were blinding her pursuers, they were laying a leaf-colored mist, a green darkness over their eyes—and they failed to see her" (Papadiamantis 2010:3).

This early scene of pursuit does more than conflate the wicked witch and the nymph into a single figure of ambivalent femininity. It also draws a deep connection between the threat of violence to woman and harm to the island's nature, here in the shape of the magnificent pine. "It was a thousand years old, and at the foot of its gigantic trunk, which five men's arms could not encompass, it was hollowed out." The tree has been eviscerated over many years for kindling, its wound personified as a human sacrifice: "The shepherds and fishermen had dug into it, they had cut away its heart and hollowed out its inside to take fuel, and it had yielded plenty." The description also emphasizes the tree's resilience vis-à-vis this extraction of its resources, its generosity to the economic community around it, and presents its eventual demise as a portentous event for the island: "With this terrible wound in its guts, the pine tree lived on for another three-quarters of a century, until 1871. In July of that year, people who lived miles away down by the sea felt a severe local earthquake. That night the giant tree had crashed" (Papadiamantis 2010:3).

The pursuit of Delcharo rewrites the story of Daphne in Ovid's *Metamorphoses* and prefigures the pursuit of the daughter at the end of the novella. As her crimes catch up with her, Frankojannou flees centrifugally away from the village and culture/agriculture, following a path that takes her through vegetable gardens, orchards, then olive groves, on to the remoter hillsides where shepherds graze their flocks, and finally the inhospitable steep cliffs of the coast. Although by this point in the narrative she hopes to confess her sins and find salvation, the narrator renders this hope in ironic terms: "καιρός μετανοίας πλέον" ('it's high time for repentance'), in the words of his protagonist. And although her spiritual journey includes monasteries and chapels, the plot adds natural landmarks that are equally or more important to her itinerary, especially sources of water. Frankojannou first seeks refuge by "a deep pool of clear water that few people knew. It was a secret, untrodden place. It formed a kind of cavern of grass and tree-trunks and ivy. The cave of a Nymph, or a Dryad of ancient times, or a Naiad who perhaps found refuge here" (Papadiamantis 2010:86). There she finds brief solace but is soon tormented by terrible dreams of the children she has killed and is driven to climb further up, to "Birdspring ... a spring pouring out of high rocks ... From that spring only the birds of heaven could drink. Hadoula bent and drank" (124). After drinking from their spring, Frankojannou makes a half-biblical, half-jocular appeal to the birds to grant her the power of flight. Her wish unfulfilled, she moves again, this time to a sea cave with a twin entrance.

The water of this cave is "brackish" and Frankojannou is tormented by thirst, the sea chill, and her terrible dreams. Like the first pool, the cave is of "untrodden depth," a place where "mystery and darkness danced together," and sometimes "a groan of pain and longing rose from the sea-swell." There is a story of harm associated with this cave as well; once a boat floated in searching for crayfish and sea-turtles and became grounded on a live seal that lay across the cave's entrance. "The dark creature was disturbed, it heaved. The little boat shook, it trembled, it could go neither back nor forward. The sailor left in the boat struck out at the seal with an axe, he drew blood from it, and the wave crimsoned a little. The seal was shaken with agony. The young sailor managed to get a noose around its head ... and in great danger of the dinghy foundering, he did succeed in pulling out the seal" (118). How can a human narrative speak the suffering of the non-human? Papadiamantis's narrative finds solutions for nature's lack of voice through the protagonist's own suffering. The noose alludes to the punishment that Frankojannou fears, the blood in the water prefigures the loss of her life in the sea. She spends a few days in the cave vainly signaling for a passing sailboat to take her away from the island; but when a boat appears, it carries the agents of the law in hot pursuit.

Water, the ruling element in the definition of an island, plays a central role throughout the narrative. Papadiamantis dwells on its importance for physical survival, an aspect that makes its presence in a landscape so crucial to our embodied topophilia. Frankojannou seeks out springs to survive, unaided, in the wilderness, and the narrative conveys vividly the torment of thirst and the pleasure of its satiation. Indeed, the novella best expresses the intimate, embodied experience of place when Frankojannou is avoiding pursuit. In this sense, the hidden springs and their surrounding vegetation, which envelops and hides her from her pursuers, convey her intimate knowledge of the island, her sense of place as "a pause in movement" and "a concretion of value," where biological needs but also the need for shelter and comfort are satisfied.[16] Those scenes are replete with sensory details: the warmth of a rising sunbeam, the soothing sound of birdsong, the soaked rusks that disintegrate on the stone where she leaves them too long, ruminating on her crimes. The narrative describes how Frankojannou gathers the moist crumbs and eats one of her last meals out of the palm of her hand, surrounded by this exquisite natural beauty of wood and pond. But the significance of water in the narrative is also spiritual. Frankojannou's drownings of the young girls are a grotesque perversion of a baptism, and her saltwater drowning at the end, while seeking salvation and deliverance, upends rituals of purification. There is highly conscious artifice in

[16] Tuan 2001:138, 12.

Papadiamantis's plotting of this spiritual water journey along the natural land-marks. It is an uncanny version of the experience of highly designed gardens from the sixteenth century onward where "a procession along fountains and bodies of water [toward a primal Source or Spring of Initiation, concealed in a cave or grotto] is conceived as stations en route to illumination ... along a strictly predetermined and allegorically saturated path."[17]

The cave on the cliffside that constitutes the final station of Frankojannou's itinerary moves her from an intimate and life-sustaining place to an abstract space: from the interior of the island with its microecosystems and rich topog-raphy, its orchards and chapels, to the boundary where life can barely be sustained. At its ultimate edge, the island becomes space rather than place, a demarcated area that opens up into the abstract expanse of the map and poten-tial freedom. For the theorist, this point on the limit between land and sea where Frankojannou is stranded, where place opens into space, is where "opportuni-ties for movement are enormous."[18] That this is not the case for the old, female, criminal protagonist discloses the blind spot in the theory, the way in which the substantive landscape may weigh down, encircle, and imprison its inhabitants. In its capacity to convey complexity and stoke our empathy for these marginal experiences that are nevertheless exemplary of the way in which places shape our being, literary narrative may enrich "an understanding of landscape that has become increasingly enclosed by the visual and the spatial."[19] No matter how longingly Frankojannou stares and waves at the white sails crisscrossing the Aegean, her movement is restricted by the idyllic island turned prison. That her predicament reverberates so strongly with the experience of migrants in the Mediterranean today speaks to Papadiamantis's deep humanism and his insight that borders and boundaries are designed as much to keep people in, as to bar those outside from entering.

Frankojannou's final and desperate expedient is to flee to a hermit known for reading a sinner's most intimate secrets. His hermitage, Ay Sostis, is connected to the island by a sandbar, but half-way across Frankojannou is caught by the rising tide and drowns: "Old Hadoula met her death at the passage of the Holy Savior on the neck of sand that links the Hermitage rock with dry land, half-way across, midway between divine and human justice" (127). In one stroke, which distills the island's metaphysical geography into the moment of crisis unfolding on the precarious sandbar, Papadiamantis translates geographical indetermi-nacy into spiritual ambivalence and, ultimately, a suspension of judgment. The novella's conclusion holds Frankojannou and the reader in suspense between

---

[17] Schama 1995:275.
[18] Olwig 2019:95.
[19] Olwig 2019:86.

land and sea, crime and absolution, human and divine, nihilism and illumination. As she drowns, Frankojannou catches a glimpse of the fateful piece of land on the deserted northwestern shore of the island with which her family had endowed her. Her last words, "Oh, there's my dowry," return us to the substantive geography of the island. Through this closing shot that collapses landscape and dowry, Papadiamantis drives home the human entanglement with place and the fundamental questions of belonging, rights, and justice that it generates.

Papadiamantis had read deeply in European literature and may well have been familiar with the work of William Blake. In "There is No Natural Religion," Blake sums up the experience of living in a circumscribed universe: "The bounded is loathed by its possessor. The same dull round even of a universe would soon become a mill with complicated wheels."[20] Papadiamantis's biography suggests a profoundly spiritual person with a deep attachment to the teachings and rituals of Greek Orthodoxy. Yet his most emblematic work is not a religious, or, for that matter, a sociological or economic fable. The island is woven into every fiber of his memory—its topography intimately inscribed into his experience of the world and structuring it. His Skiathos resists allegorization. There is no true or immanent version of the island that dominates all others: its landscape features are still marked by pagan associations and by the spiritual markers of Christianity; the land is both the bountiful space of human cultivation (of orchards and cisterns) and a near-inaccessible wilderness. The island's metaphysical geography cannot be contained within the boundaries of any orthodoxy.

For Lorentzatos, the imagined geography of the island, however earnestly conveyed, remains nevertheless a construct serving a prescribed cultural and national identity, with its narratives of origin and continuity, its inescapable exclusions. Papadiamantis's imagination, on the other hand, imbues the geography of the island with inexhaustible intellectual and experiential layers. His imagined geography is born out of lived experience, the perspective of those inhabiting the place and engaging with it in multiple ways as a challenging source of dwelling and sustenance, as sensory pleasure or pain, and spiritual longing. His topophilia reframes the island and its inhabitants through the perspectives of gender and human geography and environmental history. His moral imagination is capacious enough to portray criminality born of inequality and despair; to convey the solace and perils of home and belonging; to question the foundational myth of benign maternity; and to imbue the natural formations and beings of the island with as much pathos as its human inhabitants.

---

[20] Blake 1988:2.

Landscape is the material embodiment of constraint but also a space of possibility and ultimately the stage for the negotiation of freedom and agency.

Frankojannou's centrifugal urge to escape the limits of the island speaks to much that is currently urgent and important to our understanding of belonging. We are all too familiar with the appeal of boundaries and walls that finds an outlet in nostalgic nationalism. Many towering literary figures of twentieth-century Greece engaged in the construction of what Leontis has called "topographies of Hellenism," landscapes studded with ruins and imbued with nostalgia for a lost past. Their function is to make up for the shortcomings of national belonging. Tuan emphasizes that the "modern nation as a large bounded space is difficult to experience in any direct way; its reality for the individual depends on the ingestion of certain kinds of knowledge."[21] The necessity of internalizing an imagined national landscape as a familiar, exclusive, and threatened home is not particular to Greece. Tuan quotes from Shakespeare's Richard II, the description of England as "This happy breed of men, this little world, / This precious stone set in the silver sea, / Which serves it in the office of a wall / Or a moat defensive to a house."[22] The nation is an island, a precious jewel, a home surrounded by a wall.

To this constructed notion of national space, replete with insular essentialism, Papadiamantis offers the antidote of his nuanced and authentic presentation of the island. His topophilia has the capacity to inspire empathy for the local but also convey the human desire to escape into the widest possible world, beyond the limits of the island where one happens to be born. Tuan alludes to this dual possibility when he writes: "If both empire and state are too large for the exercise of genuine topophilia, it is paradoxical to reflect that the earth itself may eventually command such attachment ... Possibly, in some ideal future, our loyalty will be given only to the home region of intimate memories and, at the other end of the scale, to the whole earth."[23] This essay was begun during a time when the desperate crossings of the Mediterranean by migrants trying to reach safety and opportunity were yielding an inhuman toll. For those lucky enough to survive the journey, the island idyll turned into a hopeless limbo, a prison built on financial austerity and political expediency. Refugees found themselves stranded on Greek islands with no possibility of advance and no desire for return; left to fester long enough, the situation corroded the initial outpouring of human feeling and empathy and fed ugly outbursts of xenophobia. The essay was finished during a different experience of confinement, dictated by a global pandemic that reinforced already deployed strategies of exclusion in the form

---

[21] Tuan 1990:100.
[22] Shakespeare 1991:454. The lines are from *Richard II*, Act 2, scene 1, lines 45–48.
[23] Tuan 2001:102.

of travel bans, immigration restrictions, and demonization of outsiders. In a turn of events that may well exert its own lasting toll of misery and inhumanity, the second confinement has drawn attention away from the ongoing predicament of those who are shut out, or are shut in, because of famine, violence, war, or political oppression. More than ever, we need Papadiamantis's humanist geography to remind us that place becomes a perversion of home when one cannot leave, and space a travesty of freedom when one is barred from entering.

Works Cited

Primary Sources

Blake, W. 1988. "There Is No Natural Religion [b]." In *The Complete Poetry and Prose of William Blake*, ed. D. V. Erdman, 2–3. New York.
Lorentzatos, Z. 1994. "Το χαμένο κέντρο (Για τον Σεφέρη)." In *Μελέτες*. Athens.
———. 2013. *Aegean Notebooks: Reflections by Sea and Land in the Archipelago*. Trans. L. Sherrard. Evia, Greece.
Papadiamantis, A. 2010. *The Murderess*. Trans. P. Levi. New York.
Shakespeare, W. 1991. *The Complete Works*, ed. P. Alexander. New York.

Secondary Sources

Appleton, J. 1996. *The Experience of Landscape*. New York. Orig. pub. 1975.
Athini, S. 2012. "Ο Παπαδιαμάντης Μεταφραστής στα Έντυπα του Βλάση Γαβριηλίδη." In *Πρακτικά Γ´ Διεθνούς Συνεδρίου για τον Αλέξανδρο Παπαδιαμάντη*, τόμος δεύτερος, 29–53. Athens.
Connelly, J. 2014. *The Parthenon Enigma*. New York.
Cosgrove, D. 1998. *Social Formation and Symbolic Landscape*. Madison.
Farinou-Malamatari G. 1987. *Αφηγηματικές τεχνικές στον Παπαδιαμάντη, 1887–1910*. Athens.
———. 2014. "Η ειδυλλιακή διάσταση της διηγηματογραφίας του Παπαδιαμάντη." In *Το σχοίνισμα της γραφής. Παπαδιαμαντ(ολογ)ικές Μελέτες*, 15–52. Athens.
Foucault, M. 1986. "Of Other Spaces." *Diacritics* 16:22–27.
Gourgouris, S. 1996. *Dream Nation: Enlightenment, Colonization, and the Institution of Modern Greece*. Stanford.
Haraway, D. 2016. *Staying with the Trouble: Making Kin in the Chthulucene*. Durham.
Jackson, J. 1984. *Discovering the Vernacular Landscape*. New Haven.
Latour, B. 1993. *We Have Never Been Modern*. Cambridge, MA.
Leontis, A. 1995. *Topographies of Hellenism: Mapping the Homeland*. Ithaca.
Merchant, C. 1980. *The Death of Nature: Women, Ecology, and the Scientific Revolution*. San Francisco.

Mitchell, W. J. T., ed. 2002. *Landscape and Power*. Chicago.

Olwig, K. 1996. "Recovering the Substantive Nature of Landscape." *Annals of the Association of American Geographers* 86:630–653.

———. 2019. *The Meanings of Landscape: Essays on Place, Space, Environment, and Justice*. London.

Plumwood, V. 1993. *Feminism and the Mastery of Nature*. New York.

Politis, N. 1904. *Paradoseis B'*. Athens.

Rigatos, G. 1996. *Τα Ιατρικά στη "Φόνισσα" του Παπαδιαμάντη*. Athens.

Schama, S. 1995. *Landscape and Memory*. New York.

Triantafyllopoulos, N. D. 2012. "Μεταφραστικός Βίος ή Χαμένος στη Μετάφραση." In *Πρακτικά Γ' Διεθνούς Συνεδρίου για τον Αλέξανδρο Παπαδιαμάντη, τόμος δεύτερος*, 17–27. Athens.

Tuan, Y. 1990. *Topophilia: A Study of Environmental Perception, Attitudes, and Values*. New York. Orig. pub. 1974.

———. 2001. *Space and Place: The Perspective of Experience*. Minneapolis. Orig. pub. 1977.

Stewart, C. 1991. *Demons and the Devil. Moral Imagination in Modern Greek Culture*. Princeton.

Valetas, G. 1940. *Παπαδιαμάντης: Ἡ ζωή, τὸ ἔργο, ἡ ἐποχή του*. Mytilene.

9

'Ten Feet by Ten Feet by Ten Feet'
Endgame's Confinement and Devastation on the Greek Stage (2009–2017)[1]

ANNA STAVRAKOPOULOU

IN THE *INTERNATIONAL RECEPTION OF SAMUEL BECKETT*,[2] which focuses mainly on his theatrical oeuvre, the geographical area covered, within Europe, goes as south and east as Italy; although Eastern Europe, including some Balkan countries, like Bulgaria, Romania, Northern Macedonia, and Albania are included, any mention of how Beckett fared in Greece is missing. In this article, we will focus on the reception of one play, *Fin de partie* (*Endgame*), in Greece, between 2009 and 2017, when the country was hit by a relentless financial crisis, with devastating side-effects for the most of its inhabitants, citizens, and migrant workers. More specifically, our exploration will revolve around the more or less empty and confined space in which Beckett sets *Endgame*'s action, thus enabling his audiences to make all kinds of projections. We will examine how Greek directors comprehended the emptiness of the space and we will explore why the Greek audiences thirsted for continuous exposure to its post-apocalyptic landscape and narrative. I will begin with some relevant information on Beckett and his play, before I proceed with presenting its multiple stagings. I will conclude with a hypothesis on space and content-related reasons

---

[1] I started working on the stagings of *Endgame* in Greece, in the context of a conference that I co-organized with Panayiota Mini, Constantina Georgiadi, and Ioulia Pipinia at the University of Crete (Rethymno) in December 2016. The focus of this conference was on servants as historical subjects and their artistic representations, and the article I contributed for a co-edited volume that we produced was entitled "Servants in Difficult Times: Greek Stagings of Samuel Beckett's *Endgame* during the Financial Crisis (2010–2017)" (Stavrakopoulou 2020); I am grateful to the co-editors and dear friends for their precious feedback on my exploration of *Endgame*. In this volume, I am expanding my argumentation from the characters to the set of the play, along with the theatrical spaces that hosted it.

[2] Nixon and Feldman 2009.

that might have impacted on its steady presence on the Greek stage, during the second decade of the twenty-first century.

Samuel Beckett was born in Dublin in 1906 and died in 1989 in Paris. His family was Protestant; that is, he belonged to a religious minority in Catholic Ireland.[3] He was a poet, prose writer, playwright, essayist, theater director, and translator, who spent the biggest part of his life "abroad"—although "home" and "abroad" are very particular categories in the case of Beckett.[4] He chose the expatriate condition for its fertilizing aspects, as he decided to write his great plays in French, so that he could focus on the essential. He thereby became "the premier bilingual writer of the 20th century."[5] His bilocality has definitely had an impact on the way he created his plays; but more on that later. He was very fortunate in his studies of English, French, and Italian literature, and in encountering in Paris the other colossus of Irish literature, James Joyce (1882–1941), who helped him in his first steps and whose influence was decisive in the intellectual and artistic development of Beckett. In his voluminous work, human existence is depicted in an allegorical tragicomic light and he leaned towards more minimal forms as years went by. He received the Nobel Prize for Literature in 1969.

According to many scholars and critics, Beckett's *Fin de partie*, in the original French title, is his masterpiece.[6] It follows *Waiting for Godot* (1953), in which the playwright had created a similar tragicomic canvas, on a backdrop of semi-dead nature. In *Endgame* (as it was rendered in English by the author), we have four characters on stage. The master Hamm, who is both blind and in a wheelchair, the servant-son Clov, who is unable to sit and is constantly in motion, and the two "progenitors," Nagg and Nell, who are half-buried in two garbage bins (or as Beckett calls them, "ashbins") and are barely alive.

The specific parameters clearly outlined in the meticulous directions prepare the reader/spectator for very little, if any, action. The play starts with Clov saying "Finished, it's finished, nearly finished, it must be nearly finished" and ends with Hamm addressing a little piece of cloth "Old stauncher! / (*Pause.*) / You ... remain. / (*Pause. He covers his face with handkerchief, lowers his arms to armrests, remains motionless.*)."[7] In between these two sentences, any movement on stage either belongs solely to, or is generated, by Clov, who runs around like an automaton following Hamm's orders or his own instinct, in order to

---

[3] For a comprehensive biography of Beckett, see Knowlson 2004.
[4] Nixon and Feldman 2009:3, where the editors point out that post-*Godot* plays were premiered in six different countries (France, US, Ireland, UK, Austria, and Germany) with Beckett himself directing several performances.
[5] Nixon and Feldman 2009:2.
[6] See especially Bloom 2011:8.
[7] Beckett 1958:1 and 84, respectively; all the quotes are from this edition.

describe for us the wasteland that surrounds the enclosure the characters live in. Nothing has survived on the planet as we know it, no nature, no natural phenomena ("the light is sunk"), no animals ("no gulls"),[8] no other human beings; the landscape of doom exists only through the descriptions of Clov, who is the only one who can look outside the right and left window with a glass. He also has visions, while Hamm tells stories. The world as we know it comes up in the reminiscences of the older characters in the bins, who remember a boat ride on Lake Como, the day after their engagement, where "the water was deep. And you could see down to the bottom. So white. So clean."[9] These words pronounced by somebody half-buried in a bin have an even stronger impact. It also appears in the dreamy suggestions of Hamm "Let's go from here, the two of us! South. You can make a raft and the currents will carry us away, far away, to other mammals!"[10] The only surviving organisms, apart from the humans on stage, are a flea in Clov's underpants (exterminated diligently with insecticide upon discovery), a rat in the kitchen, and a child spotted by Clov, somewhere out there. The lap dog that Hamm plays with is a stuffed animal, and even it is missing a leg.

The play is highly allegorical. The tone is definitely more tragic than comic, the end never comes, the lights go out at the end of the performance and things have, one could argue, not changed much. Nonetheless, the dialogue is dense with meaning. The power-dynamics between the characters are carved masterfully, their dire premise becomes our own, and their endurance while waiting for an end in this ultra-confined space makes us think twice as hard about our own life and destiny.

Let's turn now to how empty space has been used in the theater, especially among the authors and traditions that Beckett was familiar with. One can discern two main influences. The first is the Shakespearean opus, where there was no realistic representation of settings and locales, but instead places were indicated by simple objects (thrones, trees, bars, ruins, etc.). These helped the audience imagine a broader context (a palace, forest, prison, castle, etc.).[11] The impact of Shakespeare on Beckett is omnipresent and has been amply documented.[12] Among the several plays whose traces have been detected in *Endgame* is *The Tempest* (1611), in the characters, power dynamic, and spatial constraints, as both plays have been read as metaphors of colonial projects and their after-

---

[8] Beckett 1958:30.
[9] Beckett 1958:21.
[10] Beckett 1958:34. The South is the only geographical orientation mentioned in the play, while Hamm is obsessed with being at the center, of the stage, that is to say, of their known universe.
[11] Habermann and Witen 2016.
[12] See indicatively Tassi 1997 and Ackerley and Gontarski 2004, lemma on Shakespeare.

math.[13] Moreover, it should not go unnoticed that Beckett has created a new lens through which Shakespeare was staged in the twentieth century; Peter Brook, the "prophet" *par excellence* of empty space, created Beckettian stagings of Shakespeare that brought a massive reappreciation of empty space for artists and audiences alike.[14] Beyond Shakespeare, Beckett's other major influence when it comes to space is popular comedy. The playwright steeped himself in the comic tradition, erudite and popular, where empty space has had a liberating effect from the Commedia dell'Arte all the way to variety shows and vaudeville performances; his loans from comedy have also been discussed at length.

As to why Beckett turned to empty confined sets with invisible offstage space, starting with *Waiting for Godot*, the short answer is to reach wider and more varied audiences, around the globe.[15] Beckett (and the entire Theatre of the Absurd movement) was trying to cope with the very real devastation of Europe after World War II. He had experienced the horrors of the war, working as an ambulance courier, after he joined the French Resistance.[16] His landscapes of devastation have been perceived as a reflection of the ravaged post–World War II world, but they also suited him very well for a number of reasons. I mentioned earlier his bilocality. The fact that he was "steeped in European traditions, fluent in several languages,"[17] and wrote for significantly different audiences, beginning with the Anglo-Irish and the French, obliged him to give width and depth to his plots and characters. He achieved this by paring back to the absolute essence of every category (characters, sets, costumes, etc.), which as a result facilitated audience reception. In any case, theatrical productions are always geared towards their specific audiences, where live actors breathe life into characters, by absorbing the vibrations created by actual people watching what is being enacted, unlike films which are immutable and are often addressed to the anonymous viewer anywhere, anytime. Hence, we will investigate what the post-World War II Beckettian landscape of devastation was like in five recent Greek productions of *Endgame*. We will explore how the directors staged it, in what kinds of theatrical spaces, how the audience reacted, why Beckett is highly appreciated in Greece, and what is the connection to the political and social reality. And finally, why the unique Beckettian dystopias are more appealing in certain countries than in others.

---

[13] Pearson 2001:217–219.
[14] Brook 1996.
[15] Little 2020, especially ch. 5, "Political Pentimenti: *Waiting for Godot*, *Endgame*," 89–113.
[16] Knowlson 2004, ch. 14, "Aftermath of War 1945–6."
[17] Nixon and Feldman 2009:3.

Recent Greek Stagings

At first, it seems highly puzzling that this hard-to-grasp, minimal, and allegorical, semi-tragic play, about which Theodor Adorno (1903–1969) wrote an essay entitled "Trying to Understand *Endgame*,"[18] was staged so many times in Athens, in the last decade alone. For the record, the play was first performed in Greece in 1960 (directed by Dimitris Kollatos) and it has been staged numerous times ever since. Memorable performances include the 1967 staging by the National Theatre of Northern Greece, directed and translated by Christina Tsingou (who was Nell in the 1957 world premiere of the play at the Royal Court Theatre in London, directed by Roger Blin); the 1970 staging by Karolos Koun at Theatro Technis; and the 1987 staging by Alexis Minotis at the National Theatre. So, while the play had been staged at least twelve times between 1960 and 2009 (roughly in fifty years), in the span of eight years it became a staple of almost every theatrical season. Below I list the performances by chronological order and by type of production:

1. December 2009: Not-for-profit theater (ninety seats, experimental with artistic mission): directed by Nikos Kamtsis at Topos Allou, with Nikos Alexiou (Clov), Polykarpos Polykarpou (Hamm), Panos Rokidis (Nagg) and Natalia Stylianou (Nell). Duration: 80 mins. The performance was repeated in the fall of 2010.

2. April 2013: Off-Broadway type of theater (roughly the same category as the previous one, with 140 seats): directed by Dimitris Lignadis at Apo Michanis Theatro, with Dimitris Lignadis (Clov), Akis Vloutis (Hamm), Grigoris Pimenidis (Nagg), and Aphroditi Kleovoulou (Nell). Duration: 100 mins. The performance was repeated in the fall of 2013.

3. October 2014: Mainstream commercial theater (four hundred seats, owned by well-known actor): directed by Leonidas Papadopoulos at Theatro Tzeni Karezi, with Konstantinos Kazakos (Clov), Kostas Kazakos (Hamm), Yiorgos Morogiannis (Nagg), and Nina Giannidi (Nell). Duration: 95 mins. The play was performed uninterruptedly until May 2015.

4. December 2015: Art theater (the new stage, two hundred and fifty seats, of the oldest and most influential art theatre in Greece, established in 1942, by Karolos Koun): directed by Constantinos Chatzis, at Theatro Technis-Frynichou with Elena Topalidou (Clov), Lydia

---

[18] Adorno and Jones 1982.

Koniordou (Hamm), Tzina Thliveri (Nagg), Georgia Tsangaraki (Nell).
Duration: 100 mins.

5. May 2017: Black Box type theater (seventy seats): directed by Glykeria
    Kalaitzi at T Theater, production of the Peiramataki Skini Technis (the
    experimental/artistic theater group of Thessaloniki, established in
    1979) with Efi Stamouli (Clov), Dimitris Naziris (Hamm), Sofia Voul-
    gari (Nell), and Yiorgos Frangoglou (Nagg). Duration: 75 minutes. The
    performance was repeated in the fall of 2017.[19]

Regarding the size and shape of the theaters, four out of five are repur-
posed ex-warehouses, factories, or bistros, following the trend of the 1980s and
1990s that saw the flourishing of scenes beyond the traditional theatrical hubs,
whose owners and/or artistic directors focused more on the content than on
dazzling effects.[20] As for the sets of the performances, in three out of five cases
(Apo Michanis, Tzeni Karezi, and T Theater) the directors recruited seasoned
scenographers (Pezanou, Patrikalakis, and Kirkine) to create the sets, using
their imagination and following inventively Beckett's instructions; for a playwright for whom less was more, smaller spaces intensified the sense of confinement. In the Apo Michanis production, the sets were quite far from what the
play requires: Lignadis (b. 1964) and Pezanou moved the progenitors out of their
bins and into circus or amusement park ticket booths, which did not go unnoticed by the critics,[21] thus emphasizing the clownish qualities of the play and
Beckett's debts to past forms of popular entertainment. In the other two cases
(Topos Allou and Technis) the directors came up with resourceful solutions of
their own for the minimal sets, assuming the role of the scenographer for an
even less costly production.

With respect to the directorial approach, as is evident from the new translations undertaken, the lengthy playbills issued (Kamtsis, Kazakos), and the
opinions expressed in interviews, all the directors were fully aware of the diffi-
culty of their endeavor and the actors involved did their best to bring out both
Beckett's message and their own interpretation of it. Koniordou (b. 1953) used

---

[19] I am grateful to the directors, actors, and staff of the theaters for their help with material about
the stagings I am discussing; more specifically, I thank Nikos Kamtsis, Akis Vloutis, Constantinos
Chatzis, and Glykeria Kalaitzi. One more staging of the play by an internationally known
Greek director, Thodoros Terzopoulos (b. 1947), is not discussed, because it was staged at the
Alexandrinsky Theatre, in Saint Petersburg in 2014 (for more, see the website of Attis theatre
http://attistheatre.com/en/show/endgame-2014-2/).

[20] Martinidis 2003. I thank Lila Karakosta for her help with this and for our very fruitful discussions
on space.

[21] Karaoglou 2013; the critic comments on the altered sets, which deprived the play of its inten-
tional claustrophobic effect.

an all-female cast,[22] as a follow-up to a 2012 all-female production of *Waiting for Godot* by the Theatro Technis, where women replaced the male protagonists, because of their improved societal status by the twenty-first century. The parts were played in all the productions with a more or less clown-like manner in the movement and speech of Clov, and with a lot of demanding dynastic attitude for Hamm. The actors varied in their interpretations, but in all cases, they played with an awareness that Clov is not a common servant, but the epitome of all servants, exactly as Hamm is the epitome of all masters; and the way Beckett has composed his play, these two, along with the master's progenitors, are the only two societal and relational structures that have survived. Thus, in all the recent performances the characters are stereotyped, in a manner that includes a palimpsest of servants, masters, and decrepit old people, from the Commedia dell'Arte, to Goldoni, all the way to Charlie Chaplin, whose Tramp has influenced Beckett himself.[23] Similarly, the confined empty space acts as the epitome of enclosed spaces, including the prison, home, city, country, all the way to existential impasses and dead ends. As for the props, the wheelchair, ladder, and bins, they all act as defining space, because they create constraints.

As a Beckett scholar has pointed out, "for spectators unfamiliar with poetic drama the abstract, stylized quality of the characterization and acting must create certain problems and a feeling of alienation."[24] And in fact, Kenneth Tynan (1927–1980), one of the most influential theater critics of his generation, wrote about the first production that Beckett is "stamping on the face of mankind" and the performance "piled on the agony until I thought my skull would split."[25]

These observations come from seasoned theatergoers who did not see the performance in rough times. One might wonder whether the crisis factor has an impact on the reception of the play. According to a comparative volume on the international reception of Beckett, the appreciation for this play is in indirect correlation with the living conditions of the audiences. Thus in Australia, *Endgame* has not resonated at all with audiences; in the Netherlands, the work was staged as a children's play;[26] while in Poland the play has been a huge success. One of the most influential articles was written by Jan Kott (1914–2001),[27] a leading Polish intellectual who considered *Endgame* the *King Lear* of our times, and it seems that in Poland "the political situation made people

[22] Nixon and Feldman 2009:236, for an all-female cast in Finland, in 1992.
[23] Kennedy 1991:5 and 45.
[24] Campbell 2007:262.
[25] As quoted in Campbell 2007:254 and 262, respectively.
[26] Nixon and Feldman 2009:195–196.
[27] Kott 1963.

dramatically aware of the down-to-earth universality of Beckett's message."[28] Lastly, on multiple occasions it has been staged successfully in prisons.[29]

An excerpt of a 2017 article by Dimitris Kargiotis entitled "Crisis of representation, crisis of delegation" might help us understand the parameters of the Greek crisis:

> The crisis is a condition: a condition in which we live (we are born, age, and die in it), a condition that determines our existence, our being in the world. Given that the crisis is not a simple fact but a condition, it cannot be represented and understood beyond our subjectivity, but is an *a priori* category: it does not just reflect, but it also defines our condition. In other words, we are not objects of the crisis less than we are its subjects.
>
> Kargiotis 2017:78

While it is very difficult to assess the reactions of the audience in Greece, judging by how frequently the play is staged, including re-runs, it is obvious that the demanding and often obscure works of Beckett fascinate Greek thespians and the audiences alike. Why is this, one may wonder? I will attempt to provide a tentative answer.

For theater companies the small cast of four characters and ultra-spare set (designed, in some productions, by the directors or protagonists due to budgetary reasons) are probably decisive factors. The echoes of popular shows, both in Beckett's plays and in the audience's collective memory, make his allegories not only familiar, but also soothing. Like the revival of the shadow theater in Greece during the years of the crisis, Beckett's mediated truth is easier to swallow than pure realist theater and the play offers a bigger release.

The last question I'll tackle has to do with the connection of the play to political and social reality. Koniordou, after the turbulent summer of 2015, which included the Greek referendum on the country's economic bailout and the third bailout package imposing further cuts, dedicated her December 2015 performance to Wolfgang Schäuble, the German Minister of Finance between 2009 and 2017, making him a target of her frustration.[30] Furthermore, she explained in

---

[28] Nixon and Feldman 2009:176.

[29] Tworek 2006.

[30] Lambridi 2015. Koniordou in the interview says that the source of inspiration for her interpretation of the invalid Hamm had been "the German minister of Finance Schäuble," as shocking as this statement is, given that Wolfgang Schäuble (b. 1942) has been in a wheelchair since October 1990, following an assassination attempt that left him paralyzed. This attitude towards the German Minister might be connected to the fact that by December 2015, when the play was staged, the government, with Koniordou serving as Minister of Culture, had capitulated to all

the playbill that "all those arrogant managers of human fate, who think that they have the power to intervene in life and nature, have been an inspiration for my part. Until the moment comes, when 'nature forgets them' before the end." In 2014, Kostas Kazakos (1935–2022), an actor with a long-standing political agenda, who was twice a parliamentarian elected with the Communist Party, wrote in the program that "within the dire reality that our country is experiencing, we believe that theater artists have a duty to show proof on a daily basis that they are standing next to our people and that they understand their problems. With their relevant art, with complete and clear images, they can contribute in the boosting of the morale of our people and their coming to terms with this inhuman reality." In the last line of his essay, the actor claims that had *Endgame* been written by Brecht, he would have named it *The End of Capitalism*. Kazakos, apart from being an ardent Brecht lover, has been a politically engaged and vocal actor, for the longest time in the group of five that we are examining. The others did not perceive their mission in such clear-cut didactic and political terms. Lignadis (b. 1964) and Vloutis, according to their interviews, presented what they were doing in a more personal, existential, and artistic way. For Kamtsis (b. 1953), staging Beckett's plays was part of a larger project to familiarize the audience with Beckett, since the staging of *Waiting for Godot* preceded the production of *Endgame*. Lastly, in the case of the Thessaloniki performance, Glykeria Kalaitzi (b. 1960) and the protagonists have claimed that they selected it for its special weight in the theatrical canon, for the big existential questions it poses, which invite the spectator to ponder over "the big issues in life, the anxieties, paradox and quests of human existence, which hide in simple words, sarcasm and humor" (to use the words of the director).[31]

In conclusion, it may be worthwhile to share some thoughts pertaining to the spatial parameters of the play, now that the bare stage where the 'action' takes place is no longer shocking to audiences, as it was sixty-five years ago. Since the Greek landscape is very different from the iconic Irish ones Beckett carried with him all his life, one wonders whether the Greek audiences may have felt soothed by the fact that as destitute as the financial crisis has made them, they still have their landscape to hold onto. Apart from the landscape, there is no doubt that during the crisis, artistic spaces of all kinds (cinemas, theatres, museums, galleries, etc.) became a refuge from brutal reality and Beckett's non-realistic loci were twice as effective.

Beyond the spatial restraints, for the artists and audiences of the last years of the crisis, what is insinuated by the master-servant tandem is the relationship

---

the onerous terms imposed by the German government, in order to rescue Greece from its debt crisis.
[31] Mavridou 2017.

of an invalid European Union, which although weakened, is still powerful, and of a "subaltern" Greece (to use Spivak's term) which is never equal, which always tries to belong but keeps lagging behind, which runs like an automaton following orders without meaning—orders that cannot offer solutions, given that the crisis keeps going strong and the end never comes. We could say that *Endgame* epitomizes masterfully the twilight glowing on the Greek economic horizon, which continues endlessly, "until our skulls split," in the words of Tynan. Now that political, economic, and social circumstances have surpassed the imagination, especially during the ongoing pandemic, with a some-time US president showing indifference about global warming and the ensuing ecological disaster, with the 2016 temperature at the North Pole never falling below freezing in November,[32] the Spartan, poetic, philosophical, and, above all, prophetic Beckett has found a niche in the Greek stages. While ecological and environmental calamities have yet to be the subject of performances in Greece, plays of this genre, which used to be called Theater of the Absurd, have become a nostalgic narrative of another time, despite the stifling existential impasses that we find at their epicenter. In the post-Enlightenment period we are going through, with major climactic catastrophes marking the global landscape, the Spartan set of *Endgame* offered Greek audiences consolation from their financial constraints, so that despite their dire situation they needed a dose of *Endgame* year in and year out. As it has been noted, "Beckett's plays reveal more about the psyches of the people [...] than about the work itself or the psyche of its author."[33]

Works Cited

Ackerley, C. J., and S. E. Gontarski, eds. 2004. *The Grove Companion to Samuel Beckett: A Reader's Guide to His Works, Life, and Thought*. New York.

Adorno, T. W., and M. T. Jones. 1982. "Trying to Understand *Endgame*." *New German Critique*, 26:119–150. Orig. pub. as "Versuch, das *Endspiel* zu verstehen" in *Note Literatur II*, Frankfurt am Main, 1961.

Beckett, S. 1958. *Endgame: A Play in One Act*, followed by *Act without Words: A Mime for One Player*. New York.

———. 1986. *The Complete Dramatic Works of Samuel Beckett*. London.

Bloom, H. 2011. *Bloom's Modern Critical Views: Samuel Beckett. New Edition*. New York.

Brook, P. 1996. *The Empty Space*. New York. Orig. pub. 1968.

Byron, M. S., ed. 2007. *Samuel Beckett's* Endgame. New York.

---

32 Vidal 2016; Sampathkumar 2018.
33 Nixon and Feldman 2009:1.

Campbell, J. 2007. "*Endgame* and Performance." In Byron 2007:253–274.

Carpenter, C. A. 2011. *The Dramatic Works of Samuel Beckett: A Selective Bibliography of Publications about His Plays and Their Conceptual Foundations.* London.

Davies, P. 2006. "Strange Weather: Beckett from the Perspective of Ecocriticism." In Gontarski and Uhlmann 2006:66–78.

Gontarski, S. E., and A. Uhlmann. 2006. *Beckett after Beckett.* Gainsville.

Habermann, I., and M. Witen. 2016. *Shakespeare and Space: Theatrical Explorations of the Spatial Paradigm.* Syracuse.

Karaoglou, T. 2013. "Η τραγικωμωδία της ανθρώπινης ύπαρξης—Το 'Τέλος του παιχνιδιού' του Σάμουελ Μπέκετ ανεβαίνει στο Από Μηχανής Θέατρο" [The tragicomedy of human existence—*Endgame* by Samuel Beckett at Apo Michanis Theatro]. In *El Culture.* https://www.elculture.gr/blog/article/telos-paixnidiou-apo-mixanis/ (accessed April 25, 2016).

Kargiotis, D. 2017. *Γεωγραφίες της μετάφρασης* [*Geographies of Translation*]. Athens.

Kennedy, A. K. 1991. *Samuel Beckett.* Cambridge.

Knowlson, J. R. 2004. *Damned to Fame: The Life of Samuel Beckett.* London.

Kott, J. 1963. *Shakespeare, Our Contemporary.* Garden City, NY.

Lambridi, F. 2015. "Λυδία Κονιόρδου: Ο Σόιμπλε με ενέπνευσε για το ρόλο του εξουσιαστή Χαμ" [Schäuble inspired me for the role of the master Hamm]. https://tvxs.gr/news/theatro/lydia-koniordoy-o-soimple-me-enepneyse-gia-rolo-toy-eksoysiasti-xam (accessed May 5, 2016).

Little, J. 2020. *Samuel Beckett in Confinement: The Politics of Closed Space.* London.

Martinidis, P. 2003. "Small Stages in the Long Tradition of Greek Theatres." In *Six Greek Stage Designers in Prague—Prague Quadrennial 2003.* Athens.

Mavridou, M. 2017. "Γλυκερία Καλαϊτζή, Δημήτρης Ναζίρης, Έφη Σταμούλη συζητούν για το "παιχνίδι" του Μπέκετ – Θέατρο Τ." [Glykeria Kalaitzi, Dimitris Naziris, Efi Stamouli are discussing Beckett's "game"–T Theater]. http://www.piramatikiskini.gr/index.php/press/details/sizitisi-me-tois-protagonistes-kai-ti-skinothetida-toi-telois-toi-paixnidio/ (accessed November 1, 2020).

Nixon, M., and M. Feldman, eds. 2009. *The International Reception of Samuel Beckett.* London.

Pearson, N. C. 2001. "'Outside of Here It's Death': Codependency and the Ghosts of Decolonization in Beckett's *Endgame*." *ELH* 68:215–239.

Sampathkumar, M. 2018. "Temperatures Soar above Zero as Arctic Experiences One of Its Warmest Winters Ever." *The Independent* (accessed February 27, 2018).

Stavrakopoulou, A. 2020. "Υπηρέτες σε δύσκολους καιρούς: πρόσφατα ανεβάσματα του *Τέλους του παιχνιδιού* του Μπέκετ" [Servants in difficult times: Greek stagings of Samuel Beckett's *Endgame* during the financial crisis (2010–2017)]. In *Υπηρέτριες και υπηρέτες: Ιστορικά υποκείμενα και καλλιτεχνικές αναπαραστάσεις στον ελληνόφωνο χώρο (19ος-21ος αιώνας)* [Female and male servants: Historical subjects and artistic representations in the Greek-speaking world (19th–20th century)], ed. P. Mini, K. Georgiadi, I. Pipinia, and A. Stavrakopoulou, 313–328. Athens.

Tassi, M. 1997. "Shakespeare and Beckett Revisited: A Phenomenology of Theater." *Comparative Drama* 31:248–276.

Tworek, A. 2006. "*Endgame* Incarcerated: Prison Structures in Beckett's Play." *Journal of Beckett Studies* 16:247–258.

Ververopoulou, Z. 2020. "Μιλώντας για το θέατρο και την κρίση: Ο εξωσκηνικός δημόσιος λόγος των δημιουργών" [Speaking of Theater and the Crisis: the Extrascenical Public Pronouncements of the Creators]. *Proceedings of 6th European Congress of Modern Greek Studies of the European Society of Modern Greek Studies, Lund, 4-7 October 2018, The Greek World in Periods of Crisis and Recovery, 1204-2018*, vol. 5, 125–145.

Vidal, J. 2016. "'Extraordinarily Hot' Arctic Temperatures Alarm Scientists." *The Guardian* (accessed November 22, 2016).

Index

Index

Index

Index